SOCIAL POLICY F

Analysis and (
in social policy, ~~ ~ ~

Edited by Elke Heins, Catherine Needham
and James Rees

P

First published in Great Britain in 2019 by

Policy Press
University of Bristol
1-9 Old Park Hill
Bristol
BS2 8BB
UK
t: +44 (0)117 954 5940
pp-info@bristol.ac.uk
www.policypress.co.uk

North America office:
Policy Press
c/o The University of Chicago Press
1427 East 60th Street
Chicago, IL 60637, USA
t: +1 773 702 7700
f: +1 773 702 9756
sales@press.uchicago.edu
www.press.uchicago.edu

© Policy Press/Social Policy Association 2019

British Library Cataloguing in Publication Data
A catalogue record for this book is available from the British Library.

Library of Congress Cataloging-in-Publication Data
A catalog record for this book has been requested.

ISBN 978-1-4473-4398-1 hardback
ISBN 978-1-4473-4399-8 paperback SPA members' edition (not on general release)
ISBN 978-1-4473-4400-1 ePdf

Cover design by Policy Press
Front cover: photograph kindly supplied by istock
Printed and bound in Great Britain
by CPI Group (UK) Ltd, Croydon, CR0 4YY
Policy Press uses environmentally responsible print partners

Contents

List of figures and tables

Figures

Tables

Notes on contributors

Paul Bridgen is Associate Professor of Social Policy in the School of Economic, Political and Social Sciences at the University of Southampton. He has written extensively (often in collaboration with Traute Meyer) on the politics and the social impact of public–private pension mixes, both in the UK and comparatively. He is also interested in the social policy implications of migration.

Babs Broekema is Doctoral Researcher at the Department of Public Administration and Sociology at Erasmus University Rotterdam. Her research focuses on processes of institutional change in the Dutch welfare state after the 2015 decentralisation of social policies from the national government to local governments. Her research interests lie in the implications of social welfare decentralisations for local policies, local politics and local citizens.

Kevin Farnsworth is Reader in International and Comparative Social Policy at the University of York, UK. He has published widely on the political economy of welfare, welfare states and economic crisis, and corporate welfare. He is co-editor with Zoë Irving of *Social policy in times of austerity* (Policy Press, 2015) and the *Journal of International and Comparative Social Policy*. He also runs the website www.corporate-welfare-watch.org.uk.

Menno Fenger is Endowed Professor of Governance of Modern Welfare States at the Department of Public Administration and Sociology at Erasmus University Rotterdam and Co-Dean of the Netherlands School for Public Administration. His research is focused on analysing and explaining changes in the policies, governance, administration and implementation of European welfare states.

Elke Heins is Senior Lecturer in Social Policy at the School of Social and Political Science, University of Edinburgh. Her research interests mainly focus on comparative and European social policy, as well as the politics of welfare in the UK. She has most recently co-edited (with Catherine Needham and James Rees) *Social policy review 30* (Policy Press, 2018).

Rebecca Ince is Research Fellow at the Open University. Her research covers health and environmental policy, combining perspectives from both geography and social policy. Becky's projects illuminate how networks of people and organisations provide services in different and unique contexts, and how relational dynamics between actors in those networks impact the nature of service provision and equality of access.

Andy Jolly is Research Associate at the Institute for Community Research and Development at the University of Wolverhampton. His research interests are in migration, food poverty and child welfare. He previously worked as a social worker and managed a project working with undocumented migrant children and families who were at risk of destitution.

John David Jordan is a sociologist and Lecturer in Social Policy at Liverpool Hope University. His research interests include welfare, unemployment and inequality. His most recent publications explore the use and importance of ethnography in social policy research and the outcomes of the UK government's Work Programme, published in *Work, Employment and Society* and the *Journal of Social Policy*, respectively.

Jeremy Kendall is Reader in Social Policy at the School of Social Policy, Sociology and Social Research, University of Kent. He has published widely on civil society, voluntary associations and social policy, with an emphasis on comparison across countries and between sectors, policy processes, and theory building. He conducts research and teaches on these and other aspects of social policy.

Julia Lux is Lecturer in Social Policy at Liverpool Hope University. Her research interests include critical political economy and discourse analysis. Her most recent publication is entitled 'Understanding the crisis symptoms of representative democracy: the new European economic governance and France's "political crisis"', which appeared in *Social Policy and Society* (January 2019).

Rob Macmillan is a Principal Research Fellow at the Centre for Regional Economic and Social Research (CRESR), Sheffield Hallam University, and previously at the Third Sector Research Centre, University of Birmingham. His main research interests are around the long-term qualitative dynamics of voluntary action, the relationships between markets and the third sector, and capacity building and third sector infrastructure.

John Macnicol is Visiting Professor of Social Policy at the London School of Economics. He has published extensively on the history of social policy, and his most recent book is *Neoliberalising old age* (Cambridge University Press, 2016). He is currently researching the history of the 'underclass' concept in the US.

Catherine Needham is Professor of Public Policy and Public Management in the Health Services Management Centre, University of Birmingham. Her research focuses on new approaches to public service workforce development, as well as social care and policy innovation.

Theodoros Papadopoulos is a Lecturer in Social Policy in the Department of Social and Policy Sciences, University of Bath. His research interests include the transformation of European Union socio-economic governance, the political economy of familistic welfare regimes and social policy in Southern Europe and Latin America.

Martin Powell is Professor of Health and Social Policy at the Health Services Management Centre, University of Birmingham. He has published widely on UK social policy, including on Labour and Conservative governments, and on the UK National Health Service. His most recent book on the NHS is *Dismantling the NHS?* (edited with Mark Exworthy and Russell Mannion) (Policy Press, 2016).

James Rees is Senior Research Fellow and Director of the Centre for Voluntary Sector Leadership at the Open University Business School. His research focuses on the third sector, public service delivery and reform, as well as leadership, governance and citizen involvement.

Antonios Roumpakis is Lecturer in Comparative Social Policy at the Department of Social Policy & Social Work, University of York. His research interests include the political economy of familistic welfare capitalism, the transformation of European Union socio-economic governance and social policy in Southern Europe and East Asia.

Kirstein Rummery is Professor of Social Policy and Co-director of the Centre on Gender and Feminist Studies at the University of

Stirling, and a senior fellow of the Centre on Constitutional Change. She has recently completed a programme of work on comparative care policy, gender and social justice funded by the ESRC and is currently carrying out research on the costs and benefits of social care for disability and gender equality.

Jacques Wels is a sociologist of employment specialising in longitudinal data, ageing, life-course transitions and the welfare state. He is currently an affiliated lecturer at the University of Cambridge and FNRS (Fonds de la Recherche Scientifique) postdoctoral fellow at the Université libre de Bruxelles. He has been a short-term consultant for the World Bank and has held different visiting positions at King's College London and Waseda University.

Part I
A decade of social policy since the crisis – looking back and forward

Elke Heins

The UK political debate in 2018 was dominated by one single topic – Brexit. This often overshadowed other important socio-political developments, such as the funding crisis of the National Health Service (NHS), the failing social care system or the mounting problems in relation to the roll-out of Universal Credit. When the draft European Union (EU) Withdrawal Agreement was finally presented in November, a number of cabinet members instantly resigned in opposition to the deal negotiated by the Prime Minister. Among them was Esther McVey, the Secretary of State for Work and Pensions. Her resignation was met with little sympathy on social media, to put it mildly; a frequent comment on Twitter was that she should have resigned much earlier, namely, when it transpired that she misled Parliament over Universal Credit mistakes. Other social media commentators remarked that the timing of her resignation might not be coincidental given the imminent publication of a condemning report by the United Nations (UN) special rapporteur on extreme poverty and human rights, Philip Alston, on the state of poverty in the UK. His fact-finding mission collected a vast array of evidence on the misery caused by the controversial Universal Credit roll-out that McVey had defended staunchly during her time as Work and Pensions Secretary.

The scorching review published on 16 November 2018 criticised the immense growth in foodbanks, the number of people being homeless and rough sleeping, a sense of deep despair, and unheard levels of loneliness and isolation. In his accompanying statement, the special rapporteur criticised the UK government in Westminster for being in 'a state of denial' over the dire consequences of its austerity-framed welfare reform. The government was furthermore accused by Alston of overturning the post-war welfare state consensus under the guise of economic necessity, while pursuing an ideological commitment to 'achieving radical social re-engineering'. As a consequence, great misery has been inflicted unnecessarily, especially on the working poor, single mothers, people with disabilities and millions of children (United Nations Human Rights Office of the High Commissioner, 2018).

It is worth repeating the devastating verdict that was reached by Alston as it sums up overall developments in social policy over the past decade. The year 2018, of course, also marked the 10-year anniversary of the collapse of Lehman Brothers, which became the catalyst of the global financial and economic crisis that has had such a long-lasting impact on social policy in the UK and elsewhere. The first part of the book therefore invited previous editors of *Social policy review* as key experts to analyse the developments in their respective areas of social policy research over this past decade, while also looking ahead to what the near future may bring in these turbulent times of Brexit and continued austerity.

In the first chapter of this volume, Martin Powell examines the NHS in a 'cold climate' of a decade of austerity. This period has, first, seen a broad move from the optimism of the NHS's 60th anniversary to the greater pessimism of its 70th anniversary. Second, it has seen 'a game of two halves', from a preoccupation with the reorganisation of the Health and Social Care Act 2012 towards ways of working around or undoing that reorganisation. One sad constant in the period is the continuation of inquiries into failings in the NHS. The chapter concludes with an assessment of the 'birthday present' of increased funding associated with the NHS's 70th anniversary, and some thoughts on the outlook of things to come. While the increased funding is welcome, it is unlikely to have the promised transformative effect because: it does not match the NHS's historical rate of funding increase; it includes promises that have been made in the past but have not been delivered; and it excludes wider elements of health-related activity and social care. Powell argues that if life is to begin at 70 for the NHS, future birthday presents must include greater integration with social care, perhaps even a transformation into a National Health and Social Care Service.

Kirstein Rummery, in her chapter 'Disability and austerity: the perfect storm of attacks on social rights', paints a similarly gloomy picture when focusing on the impact that the post-2008 austerity regime has had on the lives of disabled people in the UK. She traces the way in which previous hard-fought-for rights in social care and welfare that had been developing since 1997 have been stripped back under austerity. The chapter describes, in particular, the stigmatisation of disabled people as 'shirkers', increased welfare conditionality and budget cuts. Looking at social care, direct payments and self-directed support, the move from Disability Living Allowance (DLA) to Personal Independence Payments, and the impact of other changes in the benefits system, she argues that these changes have created a 'perfect storm' of welfare cutbacks. Rummery also looks at how disability intersects with gender and age to further reduce rights and support, particularly with the reduction of support available to informal carers. Looking forward, the chapter examines the impact of the devolution of Universal Credit and DLA in Scotland to see whether there is likely to be some divergence in disability rights within the UK. It concludes by speculating about the possible outcomes of Brexit and the UK's withdrawal from the EU.

As academic colleagues will certainly remember, 2018 saw a long period of industrial action over a dispute about university staff pensions. Pensions are a very complex policy area that many of us tend to avoid thinking about. It is surely not a particularly popular topic with the majority of our students. Nevertheless, as the debates during the strike made clear, it is a vital policy field with huge implications for our future well-being, and is influenced by important dimensions of inequality, thus deserving much more attention in both public and scholarly debate. Paul Bridgen, in his chapter 'Financialisation *and* social protection? The UK's path towards a socially protective public–private pension system', provides a much-needed analysis in this respect. Rather than seeing the increased financialisation of pensions in the UK as driven by a neoliberal agenda deeply embedded within an Anglo-liberal growth model, Bridgen argues in his chapter that UK pension financialisation has been a much less straightforward process of negotiation, involving a diversity of agendas and actors. It has not been solely driven by the state or left neoliberalism unchallenged as an ideological policy guide. Instead, this negotiation has been balancing financialising rationales with those of social protection. It has resulted in a system that has changed the nature of public responsibility rather than removed it entirely. Bridgen discusses how a public policy of pensions has developed that has resulted in a hybrid system of public and private sector regulation. He continues by outlining two reform suggestions that would not automatically assume a one-way track to further financialisation of the UK pension system and risk-shifting at the expense of employees. One suggestion is the improvement of pension adequacy by phased rises in the employer contribution; another one is a new approach to risk-sharing by creating 'a halfway house' pension form between defined benefit and defined contribution based on pooling, similar to occupational pension reforms in the Netherlands or Denmark. He concludes on a more positive outlook that sees scope for a potentially transformative incremental reform agenda by which the current system could be made both more generous and more predictable. Proponents of neoliberal financialisation, including private pension providers, will oppose this but, as his analysis of the past decade has shown, there is no reason to believe that they will inevitably be successful in preventing a more progressive agenda.

The role of private providers in the delivery of welfare is also examined in the following chapter by Kevin Farnsworth, titled 'Towards a whole-economy approach to the welfare state: citizens, corporations and the state within the broad welfare mix'. The chapter places the activities of businesses at the centre of the analysis and argues for a broadening of social policy focus, beyond the mixed-economy approach (which incorporates social, private, informal/familial, voluntary, fiscal and occupational welfare) towards a whole-economy approach that 'brings in' corporate welfare and a broader focus on taxation, public policies that overlap with social policy objectives, power and the economy. It maps the multiple and complex threads between social, public and economic policies and examines state support for businesses and other elite groups, thereby revealing connections between a range of state and non-state actors that are hugely important to the study of welfare systems. His comparative analysis shows, for example, that the UK, which introduced deep cuts to unemployment benefits and embraces austerity, still provides relatively generous business subsidies. Farnsworth demonstrates how power influences the distribution of resources, and how the decisions of actors or policy measures in one area can influence the actions or decisions of other actors and other policy measures and thus presents a convincing case for broadening the focus of social policy analysis in the future.

We conclude this first part of *Social policy review 31* by extending our analysis beyond the UK. Menno Fenger and Babs Broekema provide an instructive international perspective on key developments in welfare state reform over the past decade by critically discussing recent developments in the Dutch welfare state. Their chapter, 'From welfare state to participation society: austerity, ideology or rhetoric?', shows how, in contrast to the UK, ideas akin to the 'Big Society' gained significant traction in a number of social policy areas in the Netherlands. Emerging from the social investment paradigm that dominated European welfare state reform since the late 1990s, the introduction of the so-called Participation Society in 2013 heavily borrowed from Big Society ideas. In the view of Fenger and Broekema, the introduction of the Participation Society demarcates a step further on the road from collective to individual responsibility. In contrast to the social investment paradigm, which focuses on individual responsibility for individual welfare, the Participation Society paradigm highlights individual responsibility for collective welfare. They consider the shift towards the Participation Society as a newly emerging era in the development of the Dutch welfare state, with important lessons to learn for other welfare states, including the British one.

Taken together, these diverse contributions highlight the manifold implications of austerity and a broader neoliberal ideology on welfare in the UK and beyond over the past decade. The announcement by the new Secretary of State for Work and Pensions, Amber Rudd, to end the benefit freeze in 2020 and introduce changes to the much-criticised Universal Credit system is thus welcome news. However, as many authors in this book highlight, the challenges ahead are multidimensional, complex and entrenched. Brexit – with the caveat that, at the time of writing, there is still much uncertainty over which form it will take, and indeed if it happens at all – will clearly add to the woes of the UK welfare state. Even if a decade of austerity might come to an end, another decade of upheaval may lie ahead for UK social policy.

Reference

United Nations Human Rights Office of the High Commissioner (2018) Statement on visit to the United Kingdom, by Professor Philip Alston, United Nations special rapporteur on extreme poverty and human rights, www.ohchr.org/Documents/Issues/Poverty/EOM_GB_16Nov2018.pdf

1

The English National Health Service in a cold climate: a decade of austerity

Martin Powell

Introduction

It has been claimed that the first half of the 2010–15 Coalition government was taken up with debate on the Health and Social Care Bill 2012 (HSCB), which was introduced by Conservative Health Secretary Andrew Lansley, while the second half was devoted to limiting the damage caused by the Bill and dealing with the effects of growing financial and service pressures in the National Health Service (NHS) (Ham et al, 2015: 1; Powell, 2016). This chapter examines the longer period of the cold climate of a decade of austerity in the English NHS, focusing on two broad moves. First, there was a broad move from the optimism of the NHS's 60th anniversary to the greater pessimism of its 70th anniversary. Second, there was a similar game of two halves based on the argument of Timmins (2018) of the rise and fall of marketisation and privatisation, with the Health and Social Care Act 2013 (HSCA) perhaps being the high-water mark of faith in 'competition and choice' as the key drivers of NHS reform, and the period since then seeing efforts to 'work around' the Act. However, in addition to the 'constant' of austerity, some things stayed the same, such as the continuation of inquiries into failings in the NHS, continuing inaction on social care and 'policy retreads' on issues such as prevention and integration.

A tale of two birthdays

This section focuses on the move from the optimism of the NHS's 60th anniversary in 2008 (under the Labour government of 1997–2010) to the greater pessimism of its 70th anniversary in 2018. In 2008, some 'official' accounts entered the celebratory birthday spirit, for example, according to then NHS Chief Executive David Nicholson: 'the NHS is performing extremely well'. He continued that the NHS was on course to achieve the historic 18-week maximum waiting time by the end of 2008, and to meet challenging targets for reducing rates of health-care-associated infection. Mortality rates for cancer and cardiovascular disease had been substantially reduced, while access to GP and other primary care services was quickly improving. In its 60th anniversary year, public confidence in the NHS and patient satisfaction with the quality of NHS care were both at their highest level for years (DH, 2008a: 3). According to Delamothe (2008), the NHS's 60th birthday should be its most benign anniversary in recent memory. Timmins (2013) noted that back in 2008, the Nuffield Trust produced a publication for the NHS's 60th birthday (Timmins, 2008), in which the service felt tolerably comfortable in its own skin. Looking back, Timmins (2013) pointed out that spending had doubled in real terms during the decade, waiting times were at record lows and performance on a whole range of key measures was rising. Generally, the service felt better than it had done in decades.

The party spirit continued into a White Paper of December 2009 (SSH, 2009), which began in celebratory mode. It stated that 15 years ago, 'the NHS had sunk to such a low ebb that many voiced doubts over its long-term survival' (SSH, 2009: 3). It was a 'huge turnaround in fortunes and a great success story' (SSH, 2009: 3). It had gone 'from struggling to generally good', but a new ambition would take it 'from good to great', implementing the government's vision of a preventive, people-centred, productive NHS (SSH, 2009: 3). The document pointed to a decade of record, sustained investment, which meant that funding had doubled in real terms over the previous 12 years and was almost exactly the average among the Organisation for Economic Co-operation and Development (OECD) countries (SSH, 2009: 8). It stated that the following year, the NHS would receive a substantial increase in funding and that the Pre-Budget Report confirmed that this uplift would be locked into front-line budgets for the following two years (SSH, 2009: 10). All this meant that the NHS had made 'huge progress over the last decade' (SSH, 2009: 7).

Almost as an afterthought, the elephant in the room was mentioned: there would be a 'new financial era' and 'the greatest challenge the NHS has taken on in its history' (SSH, 2009: 7), which involved finding some £15–20 billion in 'efficiency savings' over the three-year period from April 2011 (SSH, 2009: 10). Moreover, in the section 'Strengthening regulation, dealing with failure' (SSH, 2009: 54), there was no mention of the other elephant in the room of 'Mid Staffordshire', the subject of a damning Healthcare Commission report in March 2009 and an apology by the Secretary of State in April 2009 (Klein, 2013: 266–7). However, a change in government in the 2010 election led to a very different vision of the 2010 White Paper *Equity and excellence'* (SSH, 2010).

At least with hindsight, the NHS at 60 can be seen as the 'calm before the storm' (Timmins, 2008). Timmins (2013) reflected on what a difference three months, let alone five years, can make. He noted that the Nuffield Trust's 60th-anniversary publication (Timmins, 2008) was largely positive, with no hint in that July publication of the storm about to break, with the credit crunch becoming a global financial crisis. As Timmins (2013) pointed out, five years later for its 65th birthday, the words used by key contributors included: 'tender', 'fragile', 'fragmented', 'strained', 'vulnerable', 'challenged' and 'in disarray'.

The 70th anniversary of the NHS in 2018 was set within the longest financial squeeze in the history of the NHS, and widespread concerns of 'crisis'. The years leading to the 70th anniversary had seen widespread discussions of the crisis in the NHS. For example, a Google search on (*Guardian* newspaper journalist) 'Toynbee+NHS+crisis' brings up at least ten articles in 2017.

As we shall see later, there is a spectrum of views on the situation of the NHS, which vary in tone, with 'official' publications such as those from NHS England stressing a more nuanced or mixed position, accentuating the positive, while parliamentary committees and 'unofficial' commentators, including stocktakes on the NHS's 70th anniversary, use more critical terms, such as 'crisis'. Reports from bodies such as NHS England (2018), Monitor (2018), the NHS Trust Development Authority (2018) and the National Audit Office (2018) tend not to use the term 'crisis', but rather terms such as 'challenging' and 'struggling'. However, the House of Lords Select Committee on the Long-term Sustainability of the NHS and Adult Social Care (2017) stated that our NHS was in crisis (with the term used many times by different commentators in the oral and written evidence) and that the adult social care system was on the brink of collapse. It noted that the NHS had survived a long series of crises since its foundation. Accusations of underfunding, back-door privatisation and unnecessary reorganisations have plagued successive secretaries of state for health. Many witnesses portrayed an NHS at breaking point. However, 'this crisis is different from the other crises' (House of

Lords Select Committee on the Long-term Sustainability of the NHS and Adult Social Care, 2017: 10). Similarly, according to the House of Commons Committee of Public Accounts (2018), the financial position of the NHS remains in a perilous state, with the service still very much in survival mode. A number of commissions set up for the NHS 70th anniversary (eg Darzi, 2018a, 2018b; Dayan et al, 2018) all broadly pointed to declining performance in terms of access measures and targets, such as waiting times. For example, Darzi (2018a) pointed to 'a decade of disruption' that had been the most austere decade in the NHS's history, which has led to reaching a tipping point in the health and social care system. Although disagreeing on the precise figures, they all agreed that the NHS required significantly more resources (see later).

A game of two halves

The longer game of two halves may involve the continuing rise and perhaps partial fall of marketisation and privatisation (Timmins, 2018). Many commentators regarded the reorganisation of the White Paper *Equity and excellence: Liberating the NHS* (SSH, 2010) and the subsequent HSCA as the biggest change in the history of the NHS. Timmins (2013) pointed out that the vast HSCB, with more than 280 clauses and some 550 pages in all, was three times the size of the 1946 Act that founded the service. In response to sustained opposition, the government set up an unprecedented 'pause' and 'listening' exercise through the independent 'Future Forum'. The government accepted most of its recommendations, but critics argue that this did not change the fundamental direction of travel. Some 2,000 amendments had been made, although the overwhelming majority were technical, such as name changes. The HSCA passed into law in 2012, which some commentators saw as the end of the NHS (see Powell, 2015).

Timmins (2018) presented a broad argument of the retreat from Lansley's 2013 Act under Health Secretary Jeremy Hunt and Chief Executive of the NHS Simon Stevens. When Hunt was appointed Health Secretary in 2012, few would have predicted that he would become the longest-serving Health Secretary in the history of the NHS, with some six years in the post. In 2014, Stevens, a former Blair advisor and private-sector health lobbyist in the US, was appointed as the new Chief Executive of NHS England. The NHS *Five year forward view* (FYFV) is a joint vision by the Care Quality Commission, Health Education England, Monitor, NHS England, the NHS Trust

Development Authority and Public Health England (NHS England, 2014), although it is generally associated with Stevens. The FYFV is a plan to bring about patient-centred, coordinated, integrated care. It focuses on prevention, out-of-hospital care and the integration of primary, secondary and community care. It argues for a radical upgrade with regards to prevention and public health, and radical health-care delivery options such as new care models. Ham et al (2015) state that taking the longer-term view, the FYFV may well be seen by historians as one of the most important events in health policy under the Coalition government.

Timmins (2018) points out that the FYFV said little that could not have been said, and, indeed, had often been said, over the previous decade or more. However, he argues that it differed from what went before in five crucial ways. First, almost uniquely for an NHS document, there was no national 'one size fits all' approach, but local variation with a range of 'new models of care'. Second, it signalled a distinct break with the 'choice and competition' model that lay behind Lansley's Act and the Blairite reforms. Third, it made an open and public bid for money. Fourth, the HSCA had turned the chief executive of the NHS into a public official with their own voice, which gave Stevens the authority to publish a document that no previous chief executive could have produced, let alone have named a sum of money. Fifth, in publishing the document, it was Stevens who was acting more as the Health Secretary, setting out the long-term vision for the NHS, while Hunt was acting more like a chief operating officer.

Timmins (2018) goes on to discuss the steps to bypass Lansley's legislation in a series of 'workarounds'. In December 2015, local 'sustainability and transformation plans' (STPs) were created that divided the country up into 44 areas. Timmins claims that as STPs evolved, more elements of the market-like mechanisms were being unpacked. For example, in September 2016, Stevens was 'entirely open' to the idea that the NHS could locally stop using the NHS price list, otherwise known as payment by results or the NHS tariff, to pay for each 'click of the turnstile' in hospitals. Five months later, Stevens went much further, telling the Public Accounts Committee that between six and ten of the STPs would be set up as 'accountable care organisations or systems, which will for the first time since 1990 effectively end the purchaser/provider split, bringing about integrated funding and delivery for a given geographical population' (quoted in Timmins, 2018: 76). As Timmins (2018) comments, given that the original legislation on the purchaser–provider split, Labour's consolidation of it through the creation of foundation trusts in 2000 and Lansley's reinforcement of it in the HSCA had produced three of the biggest parliamentary rows over the NHS in the previous 30 years, it was, indeed, utterly remarkable that its demise – or partial demise – was being announced not by the Health Secretary in Parliament, but by the chief executive of the commissioning board to a bunch of MPs.

Timmins (2018) considers that the HSCA proved, ironically, to be the high-water mark of faith in 'competition and choice' in the NHS. Faith in the 'purchaser–provider split' and in 'choice and competition' as key drivers of NHS reform has been dissolving since the day the Act became law, with the language now being all about 'integration'. He points out that *Equity and excellence* (SSH, 2010) referred to 'competition' a dozen times and 'choice' more than 70 times, but FYFV (NHS England, 2014) did not contain the word 'competition' at all and referred to 'choice' only half-a-dozen times. Moreover, Timmins admits that while it is true that – partly as a result of the Act – the private provision of NHS services has increased, from around 8 per cent of all clinical activity when Labour left office in 2010 to perhaps 12 per cent, or from 4.4 per cent to 7.7 per cent of expenditure over eight years, and has occurred much more visibly in community services than in hospital ones, this has only happened at a slow rate: 'So if this is "creeping privatisation", it is still pretty creeping' (Timmins, 2018: 102).

Similarly, Darzi (2018a: 41) argues that one of the central charges levelled at the 2012 Act was that its hidden agenda was to 'privatise the NHS'. In a striking failure of democratic scrutiny, this became the near-exclusive focus of the parliamentary process, rather than the fragmentation and complexity that it was creating. Since then, health campaigners have focused obsessively on the privatisation dimension. However, 'there is scant evidence to support the charge of widespread privatisation' (Darzi, 2018a: 41). The rate of growth in expenditure on the private sector has slowed and the vast majority of health-care provision remains in the public sector. That is why privatisation is neither the problem – it pales in comparison to the funding and workforce crises – nor the solution to the NHS's problems as more than 90 per cent of provision is public.

While these views are a welcome corrective to those that appear to see privatisation as the main or only problem of the NHS, or that that NHS has ceased to exist (see Powell, 2015), they perhaps understate the significant problems associated with private providers such as

Carillion (which entered compulsory liquidation in January 2018) and the large 'credit card bills' of paying the debt to private companies (some based outside the UK and not paying UK taxation) through the Private Finance Initiative (PFI). Moreover, different variants of the 'internal market' have become deeply ingrained in the NHS over the last 30 years or so, and have been increasingly entrenched within both general European Union (EU) and UK competition law and sector-specific competition regulation (eg Allen et al, 2017; Sanderson et al, 2017). Some commentators (eg Benbow, 2018) point to a process of 'juridification', whereby laws, such as contract law and EU public procurement and competition laws, have increasingly come to regulate the NHS. Transactions such as mergers, acquisitions, joint ventures and commissioning have been subject to a range of changing regulatory bodies, such as Monitor, the Competition Commission, the Office of Fair Trading and the Competition and Markets Authority (eg Sanderson et al, 2017). Against this background, it is difficult to predict how 'formal policy' such as the HSCA and the FYFV might change policy direction. For example, under the HSCA, Monitor was empowered as a sector regulator to prevent anti-competitive behaviour, which was regarded as being contrary to service users' interests (Sanderson et al, 2017). Allen et al (2017) point out that Monitor has argued that competition still has an important role in the NHS. Similarly, despite the notable lack of any mention of competition or the market in the vision of the FYFV, the regime introduced by the HSCA cannot easily be reversed (Sanderson et al, 2017). Finally, while Brexit may allow the NHS to escape from any Transatlantic Trade and Investment Partnership (TTIP) deal, there are concerns that post-Brexit trade deals might include health care (eg Benbow, 2018).

But some things stay the same

However, some things stay the same, with 'Groundhog Day' in terms of inquiries, discussions about long-term care and policy retreads.

Inquiries

There have been many inquiries into failings in care since the NHS was created in 1948, but the continuation of inquiries into all types of care is one sad constant in the period under review. The government set up an independent inquiry into standards of care at Mid Staffordshire NHS Hospital Trust (Francis, 2010), which concluded that the failings in care between 2005 and 2009 brought suffering to a large number of patients and may have been responsible for an unknown number of premature deaths. However, the report also flagged up failings that went beyond the trust, involving regulatory bodies, commissioners and the wider management system. A second inquiry that included the wider health-care system ('Francis II') in 2013 contained 290 recommendations, with an 'executive summary' of 125 pages and the full report being over 1,700 pages in length (Francis, 2013). It called for a 'fundamental culture change' across the health and social care system to put patients first at all times, with action across six core themes: culture; compassionate care; leadership; standards; information; and openness, transparency and candour. The Francis Report was so good (or bad) that the government responded thrice: *Patients first and foremost* (SSH, 2013a); *Hard truths* (SSH, 2013b); and *Culture change in the NHS: Applying the lessons of the Francis inquiries* (SSH, 2015).

The Winterbourne View Inquiry (DH, 2012) focused on a private hospital where staff were convicted of the abuse of patients with learning disabilities. In the Foreword, Minister of State for Care and Support Norman Lamb wrote that management allowed a culture of abuse to flourish. Warning signs were not picked up or acted on by health or local authorities, and concerns raised by a whistleblower went unheeded. He called for a 'fundamental culture change'.

A report following the death of 18-year-old Connor Sparrowhawk, who drowned in a bath in 2013 following an epileptic seizure while a patient at Oxford's Slade House, stated that the deaths of hundreds of mental health and learning-disability patients over four years were not properly examined, and blamed a 'failure of leadership' at Southern Health NHS Foundation Trust (Mazars, 2015; see also Ryan, 2018).

Following concerns over serious incidents in Furness General Hospital's maternity department covering January 2004 to June 2013, the report of the investigation into University Hospitals of Morecambe Bay NHS Foundation Trust (Kirkup, 2015) concluded that the maternity unit was dysfunctional and that serious failures of clinical care led to the avoidable and tragic deaths of mothers and babies.

The Liverpool Community Health NHS Trust Inquiry (Kirkup, 2018) regarded the trust as a dysfunctional organisation from the outset, with serious shortcomings in organisational leadership and culture, and where external oversight failed to identify the service problems for at least four years. This resulted in unnecessary harm to patients over a period of several years and unnecessary stress for staff, who were, in some cases, bullied and harassed when they tried to raise concerns about deterioration in patient services.

The Gosport Inquiry (Jones, 2018) was established some 22 years after the first concerns were raised. It is a 'story of missed opportunity and unheeded warnings' (p 7), where the lives of over 450 people were shortened as a direct result of the pattern of prescribing and administering opioids that had become the norm at the hospital, with at least another 200 patients probably similarly affected. It stated that when relatives complained about the safety of patients and the appropriateness of their care, they were consistently let down by those in authority – both individuals and institutions.

An inquiry into the activities of breast surgeon Ian Paterson, who was jailed for 15 years (increased to 20 years on Appeal) for carrying out 'extensive, life changing operations for no medically justifiable reason', was set up in December 2017, chaired by Graham James, the Bishop of Norwich.[1] Concerns about him were first raised in 2002, but despite three reports into his actions, he carried on working until 2011. The current inquiry follows inquiries into Paterson's NHS activities by Professor Sir Ian Kennedy, as well as into his activities at the private Spire Hospital.

Finally, at the time of writing, the independent Infected Blood Inquiry, chaired by Sir Brian Langstaff, has started preliminary hearings, although the full inquiry will start in April 2019 and is expected to last a minimum of 15 months. It will investigate how up to 25,000 people became infected with, and up to nearly 3,000 people came to die from, HIV and hepatitis from contaminated blood products and transfusions. The inquiry is the biggest of its kind to be held in the UK, with more than 1,270 infected victims and their family members taking part and more than 100,000 documents already submitted (Taylor and Donnelly, 2018).

Long-term care

Tackling funding shortages for long-term care has been ducked for a while. Labour set up a Royal Commission, only to dismiss its recommendations, which were partially introduced in Scotland. In 2008, Prime Minister Gordon Brown talked of a 'National Care Service', which had little in common with the 'National Health Service' (Powell, 2014a). The Coalition appointed Sir Andrew Dilnot to review the long-term care funding issue, who proposed a cap on the maximum that individuals could be asked to pay towards the cost of their care of about £35,000 (Dilnot Commission, 2011). The Care Act 2014 set the cap at £72,000. This was due to come into force in 2016 but after the 2015 election, the Conservatives postponed this to 2020, effectively kicking the matter into the (by now very) long grass once again (Glasby, 2016; Jarrett, 2017, 2018). One of the main elements in the bid of the Conservatives' 2017 election manifesto to become 'the longest suicide note in history' (a contemporary reference to the 1983 Labour election manifesto, which was regarded by many as its most left-wing, and led to one of the largest election defeats in the party's history) was long-term care. In an object lesson in how to alienate your core supporters, Prime Minister Theresa May shot herself in the foot with a perceived shooting of older voters through their wallets with announcements seemingly abandoning the 'cap' of the Dilnot Report, which led to critics terming the proposal a 'dementia tax' (see Jarrett, 2017, 2018).

According to Thorlby et al (2018), despite 12 Green and White Papers and five independent commissions over the last 20 years, successive governments have ducked the challenge of social care reform. As Darzi (2018a) puts it, if the NHS has suffered from ill-conceived reforms, social care has been challenged by an unwillingness on the part of politicians to follow through with the funding reforms it so desperately needs. The time for reform is now, as it has been for at least 20 years (see later). At the time of writing, the promised Green Paper on social care had been postponed to 2019.

Policy retreads

The period has also seen the continuation of the NHS 'talking a good game', with a number of policy retreads. The FYFV (NHS England, 2014) stresses integration, prevention and public health. However, these solutions have been discussed over many years. A document termed *Prevention and health* (DHSS, 1976) appeared under a Labour government nearly 45 years ago. It stated that 'much of the responsibility for ensuring his own good health lies with the individual' and that 'much ill-health in Britain today arises from over-indulgence and unwise behaviour' (quoted in Powell, 2014b: 188). Similar arguments emerged under subsequent Conservative (DH, 1992) and Labour (DH, 1998, 1999) governments. For example, in 2006, Tony Blair considered that 'our public health problems are not, strictly speaking, public health questions at all. They are questions of individual lifestyles' (quoted in Powell, 2014b: 189). As Wanless

(2004: 23) pointed out, numerous policy statements and initiatives in the field of public health have not resulted in a rebalancing of policy away from health care ('a national sickness service') to health ('a national health service'). The de jure ('paper' or 'discourse') health service has always been a de facto sickness service. The Darzi Report (DH, 2008b) echoed a long line of claims that we need to create an NHS that helps people to stay healthy, arguing that the NHS needs to focus on improving health as well as treating sickness (Powell, 2009). Similarly, there has been a series of initiatives over the last 50 years that have attempted to bring health and social care services more closely together, though with limited success (Exworthy et al, 2018).

However, while the NHS has seen much radical reform, it is less clear if this has been associated with radical change. New Labour's *NHS plan* (SSH, 2000) set out a ten-year plan that had to deliver reform in return for investment. At least in hindsight, Lord Darzi, the former Labour Health Minister, argued that while the extra spending in the 2000s brought big benefits, 'we missed the best opportunity in the history of the NHS to actually reform it ... we just threw money at it' (quoted in Timmins, 2013: 13). Similarly, Sir David Nicholson, Chief Executive of NHS England, concedes that the extra money 'allowed us to subsidise poor care when we shouldn't have done' (quoted in Timmins, 2013: 13).

The HCSA has given reform a bad name, with an anonymous Conservative cabinet minister declaring in 2014 that it was 'our biggest mistake in government' (quoted in Timmins, 2018: 2). There is little appetite in government or NHS circles for organisational change (Timmins, 2018). However, Darzi (2018a: 48) argued that 'pouring more money' into health and social care will not be enough: 'the health and care system will need bold reform ... to be fit for the future'. He continued that:

> the traumatic nature of the 2012 healthcare reforms – both in their conception and execution – has induced a collective state of post-traumatic stress disorder. The term 'reform' has become a trigger-word for the NHS that understandably provokes alarm and distress, yet the current situation is simply not sustainable: reform needs to be back on the table. (Darzi, 2018a: 50)

This 'reform' seems to refer to 'service' or 'delivery' change rather than organisational change. The House of Lords Select Committee on the

Long-term Sustainability of the NHS and Adult Social Care (2017: 7) stated that 'Our conclusion could not be clearer. Is the NHS and adult social care system sustainable? Yes, it is. Is it sustainable as it is today? No, it is not. Things need to change'. It concluded that 'whatever short-term measures may be implemented to muddle through today, a better tomorrow is going to require a more radical change' (House of Lords Select Committee on the Long-term Sustainability of the NHS and Adult Social Care, 2017: 10). The House of Commons Committee of Public Accounts (2018) criticised short-term thinking, arguing that the Department of Health and Social Care, NHS England and NHS Improvement are too focused on propping up the system and balancing the books in the short term and have not paid enough attention on transforming and improving patient services in the long term. The committee was disappointed that the department's lack of action means that they had to repeat some of the same messages as their previous reports on the dangers of short-term measures used to balance the NHS budget and the risks of raiding investment funds to meet day-to-day spending. It concluded that the department's system for funding and financially supporting the NHS focuses too much on short-term survival and limits the NHS's ability to transform services to achieve sustainability in the long term.

However, 'transforming' services may be a code for changes that have traditionally been unpopular with the public, such as closing small hospitals and accident and emergency (A&E) departments in order to both centralise specialist care and decentralise 'care closer to home'. The perception of closing local services has often been the reef on which bold plans have foundered. The public really have had enough of experts − if these experts are trying to close 'their' local facilities. Put another way, not only is the devil in the detail, but the inexactitudes are in the implementation.

Happy birthday and many happy returns?

This section provides a brief 'stocktake' of the NHS to determine how happy the NHS's 70th birthday is, and looks forwards to consider whether it is likely to see many happy returns.

Happy birthday?

There are many conflicting official and unofficial evaluations, based on a bewildering variety of criteria, both over time and cross-nationally (eg Powell, 2016). First, trends in the NHS can be examined over time. The NHS England annual report for 2017/18 (NHS England, 2018) perhaps provides the most optimistic account. Stevens suggested that the past year has again been one of both progress and pressure, with genuine and measurable advances secured in many critical services. The document points out that NHS England has balanced its books and met or exceeded all financial goals set by the government for the fifth year in a row. However, there has also been intensifying and inescapable pressure in other important areas. The document's Appendix, 'How we have delivered against the Government's mandate to the NHS', states that the NHS has continued to respond to rising levels of demand for its services during 2017/18. The recent winter period has been one of the most demanding on record for the NHS, and standards such as 'referral to treatment' and 'four-hour A&E waits' continue to face significant pressure. However, the NHS has managed to deliver the overwhelming majority of what it was mandated by government to achieve in 2017/18. Of the 71 deliverables set out in the mandate, 68 (96 per cent) are assessed as on track, which represents real progress, with tangible benefits to patients. It sums up that while the NHS is by no means perfect, for most people, most of the time, it provides high-quality and steadily improving care.

The 'state of care' report for 2017/18 (CQC, 2018) points to a story of contrasts. On the one hand, despite continuing challenges around demand and funding, overall quality has been largely maintained, and in some cases improved, from last year. On the other hand, while most people receive good care, access to this care increasingly depends on where in the country you live and the type of support you need.

The Monitor (2018) annual report noted that 2017/18 was a challenging year for the NHS. While, overall, the NHS did not meet the A&E and referral to treatment standards, and the financial deficit grew, providers made progress on efficiency and quality. The NHS Trust Development Authority (2018: 4) annual report points to 'continued pressure' in a 'challenging year', including 'undoubtedly one of the most high pressure winters in the NHS' history'. However, rises in demand meant that although trusts treated 160,000 more A&E patients within four hours compared to the previous winter, the percentage of patients seen within the four-hour target slipped and, at about 81 per cent, was well short of the 95 per cent target.

In its sixth report on the financial sustainability of the NHS, the National Audit Office (2018) stated that its past two reports in December 2015 and November 2016 concluded that financial problems in the NHS were endemic and that this situation is not sustainable. Later, it pointed out that in 2016/17, demand for health services continued to increase and performance against key access targets had declined further.

Regular monitoring by bodies such as the Kings Fund[2] and Quality Watch[3] stress broadly declining access measures and missed performance targets. For example, Appleby (2017) concludes that the broad picture of NHS performance over the last seven years or so does not look encouraging. Of the trends across ten measures of service quality (including what other sources refer to as access measures), seven have deteriorated and are currently on trend for even poorer performance; two (MRSA and C. difficile) have plateaued, following improvement in previous years; and one (diagnostic waiting times), while now on a downward trend, remains above target and similar to levels in 2011. Moreover, performance across a majority of the quality metrics analysed began to deteriorate three or four years into the period of much slower funding growth for the NHS.

Many commissions set up for the 70th anniversary provide a stocktake of the NHS. Darzi (2018a) declared that despite a decade of austerity, quality across most areas of the service has been maintained or improved. However, if quality has been maintained or improved, the same is not true for access to services. Moreover, the picture on population health over the last decade has been mixed. Darzi (2018b) argued that in many ways, the NHS indicated a story of success: despite a decade of austerity, the quality of care provided by the health and social care system has been maintained or improved. Yet, it is plain that the health and care system is under serious strain. They point to issues such as large and growing inequalities, quality of care being 'at a tipping point', the return of rationing, and reaching the limits of productivity growth.

According to Charlesworth and Johnson (2018), although waiting times have crept up again, and targets have been missed in recent years, this remains a far better performance than was achieved in the 1990s and, in general, the NHS continues to perform far better on most measures than it did 20 years ago. Similarly, although public satisfaction levels are beginning to fall, they remain at historically high levels, far above where they were before the funding increases of the 2000s. Finally, Dayan et al (2018) suggest that, overall, the NHS performs neither as well as its supporters sometimes claim nor as badly as its critics often allege.

Second, the English NHS can be compared to health systems outside the UK. There are many different studies, but international comparisons are problematic, with different studies at different times stressing different measures and producing rather different results (see Powell, 2016). The Commonwealth Fund (2017) study of 11 countries, the NHS's comparative study of choice, ranked the UK best overall, best on the criteria of care process and equity, and third on access and administrative efficiency, but tenth (and kept off bottom place by the US) on health-care outcomes, despite experiencing the fastest reduction in deaths amenable to health care in the past decade.

Other studies that focus more on outcomes show that the NHS performs less well. For example, although cancer survival rates have increased, this has tended to be slower than in some other countries, and they still lag the best nations. Similarly, life expectancy has continued to rise over the past decade but at a much slower rate than in other countries (Charlesworth and Johnson, 2018). Dayan et al (2018) suggested that compared with health systems in similar countries, the UK's has some significant strengths but also some notable weaknesses. Health-care spending in the UK is slightly lower than the average in comparable countries, both in terms of the proportion of national income spent on health care and in terms of spending per person. The UK has markedly fewer doctors and nurses than similar countries, relative to the size of its population, and fewer CT scanners and MRI machines. However, its main weakness is health-care outcomes. The UK appears to perform less well than similar countries on the overall rate at which people die when successful medical care could have saved their lives.

More recent data suggested an even more pessimistic verdict. According to the BBC (2018), data from the Office of National Statistics (ONS) show that increases in life expectancy in the UK have stalled and the slowdown is one of the biggest among 20 of the world's leading economies. Rises in life expectancy dropped from 12.9 weeks per year for women from 2006 to 2011, to 1.2 weeks per year from 2011 to 2016. This increase in life expectancy for women was the lowest of the 20 nations, while for men, only the US was worse. Analysis of mortality rates found a similar slowdown in improvement between 2011 and 2016. For men, the improvement slowed most in England and Wales, and for women, mortality rates increased slightly in Wales and showed no improvement in Northern Ireland. It should be noted that factors explaining life expectancy are complex and disputed, but it is generally considered that 'internal' health-care factors are less important than those associated with the wider 'external' economic and social environment.

Many happy returns?

Prime Minister's Theresa May's (2018) speech on the NHS looked forward to the 100th birthday on the NHS in 2048, while Secretary of State for Health and Social Care Jeremy Hunt (2018) looked forward even further to its next 70 years. However, will the birthday present of more funding allow it to survive even until its 80th birthday?

As with previous views on the NHS, there are glass half-full and half-empty versions. One obvious glass half-full view is to raise a birthday toast to the NHS simply because it is still here. Over the years, but especially since the 1980s, many commentators have pronounced the end of the NHS. However, like Mark Twain, announcements of its death have been premature (Powell, 2015).

The glass half-empty version suggests that the promised funding will be insufficient to improve the NHS. The birthday present of an additional £20.5 billion in real terms by 2023/24 represents an average growth rate of 3.4 per cent each year. However, Charlesworth and Johnson (2018) suggest that UK spending on health care will have to rise by an average 3.3 per cent a year over the next 15 years just to maintain NHS provision at current levels, and by at least 4 per cent a year if services are to be improved. Social care funding will need to increase by 3.9 per cent a year to meet the needs of an ageing population and an increasing number of younger adults living with disabilities. Similarly, Darzi (2018a) suggests that by 2030, demand pressures – without changes to the way the NHS works – will rise to £200 billion in today's prices. Pressures on social care are, if anything, even greater. As a minimum, adult social care will require an extra £10 billion by 2030 – and that is just to maintain the existing provision of the system (which we know is inadequate and needs reform, and therefore likely even more resources).

The long-delayed *NHS long term plan* (DHSC, 2019: 11–12) was eventually published in January 2019. It promises 'a new service model for the 21st century', with 'five major, practical, changes' over the next five years: boosting 'out-of-hospital' care and finally dissolving the historic divide between primary and community health services; reducing pressure on emergency hospital services; more control over people's own health and more personalised care; digitally enabled primary and outpatient care going mainstream across the NHS; and an increasing focus on population health and local partnerships with local authority-funded services through new Integrated Care Systems (ICSs) everywhere. However, some of the chapter titles continued the 'Groundhog Day' and 'policy retread' themes (see earlier), such as 'More NHS action on prevention and health inequalities' and 'Further progress on care quality and outcomes'. To its credit, the document sets out a series of timed 'milestones' up to 2028. However, given the financial and workforce pressures on the NHS, commentators broadly consider that the strategy would at best stabilise the service rather than leading to major improvements, and cast some doubt on the promise that 'looking forward to the NHS' 80th Birthday ... we have a service that is fit for the future' (DHSC, 2019: 10).

In short, the 70th birthday present is unlikely, as claimed by May, to lead to a 'profound transformation to the foundation of the NHS'. (Hunt mentioned the 't' word five times in his speech, while May mentioned it seven times.) First, the promised growth rate is less than the historical growth rate in funding since 1948. Second, this relative feast follows the worst famine in the history of the NHS. Much of this funding will go to repairing the roof rather than to ambitious new building plans. Third, the money may be both too little and too much at the same time. A below historical average growth rate will hardly transform the NHS, especially at a time with a rapidly ageing population. However, in the short term, it is not fully clear how the NHS will use the money to best effect. We have fewer hospital beds, doctors and nurses compared with most other economically developed nations. It takes time to build new facilities and to train new staff. Fourth, similar promises have been made in the past and have rarely been delivered in full. To some extent, this is copying the homework of the last Labour government. The current promised ten-year plan that provides investment in return for reform sounds very similar to the *NHS plan* (SSH, 2000) of Tony Blair's Secretary of State for Health, Alan Milburn. Claims such as 'it must be a plan that tackles wastes, reduces bureaucracy, and eliminates unacceptable variation, with all these efficiency savings reinvested back into patient care' (May, 2018) are almost identical words to the earlier ten-year plan. Similar words to 'it must be a plan that enjoys the support of NHS staff across the country – not something dreamt up in Whitehall and centrally imposed' – could have been said about the plan of clinician and Labour minister Lord Darzi in 2008, and even about Conservative Andrew Lansley's HSCA of 2012 (though he was about the only person who thought so). May's five priorities – 'putting the patient at the heart of how we organise care; a workforce empowered to deliver the NHS of the future; harnessing the power of innovation; a focus on prevention, not just cure; and true parity of care between mental and physical health' – have all been said many times before in an NHS version of 'Groundhog Day'. Fifth, at present (pending a Green Paper on social care), the grand vision does not include social care, which is like buying an expensive designer bucket to catch a leak without calling a plumber to fix it. At the time of writing, the Green Paper has been postponed to sometime in 2019.

Conclusions

This chapter has shown that ten years is a long time in the history of the NHS. It has suggested two broad moves: from optimism to pessimism; and, more arguably, the rise and fall of markets. As is often the case, it may be wise to steer a course between the over-pessimism of the end of the NHS and the over-optimism of transformation. A great deal of hope appears to be placed on 'Groundhog Day' policies, such as prevention, integration and care closer to home, which have largely failed to deliver in the past. It is possible that 'necessity is the mother of invention' and that NHS leaders are really serious about them this time, but to adapt the words of Aneurin Bevan, 'gazing into the crystal ball' may be more optimistic than 'reading the bloody book'. Put another way, it is said that Einstein's definition of madness was doing the same thing but expecting different results. While the 70th birthday present of increased funding is welcome, it is unlikely to have the promised 'transformatory' effect because it is less than the NHS's historical rate of funding increase, it includes promises that have been made in the past but have not been delivered, and it excludes wider elements of health-related activity and social care. However, a transformation will be required in order for the NHS to escape from a Narnia-like land of 'always winter, never Christmas' – as 'winter pressures' continue throughout the year, not just over the winter (Timmins, 2018). If life is to begin at 70 for the NHS, in addition to its 70th birthday cash present, futures birthday presents for its 75th or 80th birthday must include greater *real* integration, perhaps including a phoenix-like transformation into (to match the name of the newly established Department of Health and Social Care) a National Health *and* Social Care Service.

Notes

1 See: www.patersoninquiry.org.uk/
2 See: www.kingsfund.org.uk
3 See: www.qualitywatch.org.uk

References

Allen, P., Osipovič, D., Shepherd, E., Coleman, A., Perkins, N., Garnett, E. and Williams, L. (2017) Commissioning through competition and co-operation in the English NHS under the Health and Social Care Act 2012: evidence from a qualitative study of four clinical commissioning groups, *BMJ Open*, 7: e017745.

Appleby, J. (2017) 10 crucial trends: quality in the NHS 2009 to 2017, www.qualitywatch.org.uk/blog/10-crucial-trends-quality-nhs-2009-2017

BBC (2018) UK among worst for life expectancy rises, 7 August, www.bbc.co.uk/news/health-45096074

Benbow, D. (2018) Juridification, new constitutionalism and market reforms to the English NHS, *Capital & Class* (Early View).

Charlesworth, A. and Johnson, P. (eds) (2018) *Securing the future: Funding health and social care to the 2030s*, London: IFS/THF.

Commonwealth Fund (2017) *Mirror, mirror 2017: International comparison reflects flaws and opportunities for better US health care*, New York, NY: The Commonwealth Fund, www.commonwealthfund. org/interactives/2017/july/mirror-mirror/

CQC (Care Quality Commission) (2018) *The state of health care and adult social care in England 2017/18*, HC 1600, Newcastle: CQC.

Darzi, A. (2018a) *The Lord Darzi review of health and care: Interim report*, London: IPPR, www.ippr.org/research/publications/darzi-review-interim-report

Darzi, A. (2018b) *The Lord Darzi review of health and care. Better health and care for all. Final report*, London: IPPR, www.ippr.org/research/publications/better-health-and-care-for-all

Dayan, M., Ward, W., Gardner, T. and Kelly, E. (2018) *How good is the NHS?*, London: the Health Foundation, the Institute for Fiscal Studies, The King's Fund and the Nuffield Trust.

Delamothe, T. (2008) NHS at 60: A fairly happy birthday, *British Medical Journal*, 337(5 July): 25–29.

DH (Department of Health) (1992) *The health of the nation*, London: HMSO.

DH (1998) *Our healthier nation*, London: TSO.

DH (1999) *Saving lives*, London: TSO.

DH (2008a) *Developing the NHS performance regime*, London: DH.

DH (2008b) *High quality care for all, next stage review final report (Darzi review)*, Cm 7432, London: TSO.

DH (2012) *Transforming care: A national response to Winterbourne View hospital – Final report*, London: DH.

DHSC (Department of Health and Social Care) (2019) *The NHS long term plan*, London: DHSC.

DHSS (Department for Health and Social Security) (1976) *Prevention and health*, London: HMSO.

Dilnot Commission (2011) *Fairer care funding: The report of the Commission on Funding of Care and Support*, London: Dilnot Commission.

Exworthy, M., Powell, M. and Glasby, J. (2018) The governance of integrated health and social care in England since 2010: great expectations not met once again?, *Health Policy*, 121(11): 1124–30.

Francis, R. (2010) *Independent inquiry into care provided by Mid Staffordshire NHS Foundation Trust January 2005–March 2009*, London: TSO.

Francis, R. (2013) *The Mid Staffordshire NHS Foundation Trust public inquiry – Final report*, London: TSO.

Glasby, J. (2016) 'It ain't what you do, it's the way that you do it' – adult social care under the Coalition, in H. Bochel and M. Powell (eds) *The Coalition government and social policy*, Bristol: Policy Press, pp 221–41.

Ham, C., Baird, B., Gregory, S., Jabbal, J. and Alderwick, H. (2015) *The NHS under the Coalition government: Part one: NHS reform*, London: King's Fund.

House of Commons Committee of Public Accounts (2018) *Sustainability and transformation in the NHS*, HC 793, London: TSO.

House of Lords Select Committee on the Long-term Sustainability of the NHS and Adult Social Care (2017) The long-term sustainability of the NHS and adult social care, HL Paper No. 151, London.

Hunt, J. (2018) Secretary of State's oral statement on the NHS funding plan, 18 June, www.gov.uk/government/speeches/secretary-of-states-oral-statement-on-the-nhs-funding-plan

Jarrett, T. (2017) Social care: government reviews and policy proposals for paying for care since 1997 (England), House of Commons Library Briefing Paper, Number 8000, 23 October.

Jarrett, T. (2018) Social care: announcements delaying the introduction of funding reforms (including the cap) (England), House of Commons Library Briefing Paper, Number 7265, 23 February.

Jones, J. (2018) *Gosport War Memorial Hospital: The report of the Gosport Independent Panel*, HC 1064, London: TSO.

Kirkup, B. (2015) *Morecambe Bay Inquiry investigation report*, London: The Stationery Office.

Kirkup, B. (2018) Report of the Liverpool Community Health Independent Review, https://improvement.nhs.uk/news-alerts/independent-review-liverpool-community-health-nhs-trust-published/

Klein, R. (2013) *The new politics of the NHS* (7th edn), Abingdon: Radcliffe Medical.

May, T. (2018) PM speech on the NHS, 18 June, www.gov.uk/government/speeches/pm-speech-on-the-nhs-18-june-2018

Mazars (2015) *Independent review of deaths of people with a learning disability or mental health problem in contact with Southern Health NHS Foundation Trust April 2011 to March 2015*, London: Mazars.

Monitor (2018) *Annual report and accounts 1 April 2017 to 31 March 2018*, HC 1347, London: NHS Improvement.

National Audit Office (2018) *Sustainability and transformation in the NHS*, London: NAO, www.nao.org.uk/wp-content/uploads/2018/01/Sustainability-and-transformation-in-the-NHS.pdf

NHS England (2014) *Five year forward view*, Leeds: NHS England.

NHS England (2018) *Our 2017/18 annual report*, HC 1328, Leeds: NHS England.

NHS Trust Development Authority (2018) *Annual report and accounts 2017/18*, HC 1348, London: NHS Improvement.

Powell, M. (2009) Beveridge's giant of disease, in K. Rummery, I. Greener and C. Holden (eds) *Social policy review 21*, Bristol: Policy Press, pp 67–86.

Powell, M. (2014a) Health policy, in H. Bochel and G. Daly (eds) *Social policy*, London: Routledge, pp 349–70.

Powell, M. (2014b) Neo-republican citizenship and the British National Health Service since 1979, in F. Huisman and H. Oosterhuis (eds) *Health and citizenship: Political cultures in modern Europe*, London: Pickering and Chatto, pp 177–90.

Powell, M. (2015) Who killed the English National Health Service?, *International Journal of Health Policy and Management*, 4: 267–9.

Powell, M. (2016) Coalition health policy: a game of two halves or the final whistle for the NHS?, in M. Fenger, J. Hudson and C. Needham (eds) *Social policy review 28*, Bristol: Policy Press, pp 23–40.

Ryan, S. (2018) *Justice for laughing boy: Connor Sparrowhawk – A death by indifference*, London: Jessica Kingsley.

Sanderson, M., Allen, P. and Osipovic, D. (2017) The regulation of competition in the National Health Service (NHS): what difference has the Health and Social Care Act 2012 made?, *Health Economics, Policy, and Law*, 12(1): 1–19.

SSH (Secretary of State for Health) (2000) *The NHS plan*, London: TSO.

SSH (2009) *NHS 2010–2015: From good to great. Preventative, people-centred, productive*, Cm 7775, London: TSO.

SSH (2010) *Equity and excellence: Liberating the NHS*, London: TSO.

SSH (2013a) *Patients first and foremost: The initial government response to the report of the Mid Staffordshire NHS Foundation Trust public inquiry*, London: TSO.

SSH (2013b) *Hard truths: The journey to putting patients first*, London: TSO.

SSH (2015) *Culture change in the NHS: Applying the lessons of the Francis inquiries*, Cm 9009, London: TSO.

Taylor, R. and Donnelly, L. (2018) Tainted blood scandal: at least 25,000 victims could be infected, *Daily Telegraph*, 24 September, www.telegraph.co.uk/news/2018/09/24/tainted-blood-25000-victims-could-infected/

Thorlby, R., Starling, A., Broadbent, C. and Watt, T. (2018) *What's the problem with social care, and why do we need to do better?*, London: the Health Foundation, the Institute for Fiscal Studies, the Kings Fund and the Nuffield Trust.

Timmins, N. (ed) (2008) *Rejuvenate or retire? Views of the NHS at 60*, London: Nuffield Trust.

Timmins, N. (ed) (2013) *The wisdom of the crowd: 65 views of the NHS at 65*, London: Nuffield Trust.

Timmins, N. (2018) *'The world's biggest quango': The first five years of NHS England*, London: Institute for Government.

Wanless, D. (2004) *Securing good health for the whole population*, London: HM Treasury.

2

Disability and austerity: the perfect storm of attacks on social rights

Kirstein Rummery

Introduction

Social rights can be conceptualised as the enforceable choice to access resources to meet your needs. Marshall maintained that social rights distributed through the welfare state were an important measure of a mature citizenship-based society, after political and civil rights (Marshall, 1950). Since its inception, disabled people have had an uneasy relationship with the welfare state as the means of distributing these resources. On the one hand, the foundations of the post-war UK welfare state gave disabled people important rights to access state welfare, health and education, as well as sheltered employment and accessible housing. On the other hand, the paternalism associated with the rise of the power of the welfare professional meant that disability is, as Stone (1986) argues, an administrative category that requires access to be decided not on the basis of enforceable choices decided by individual citizens, but on the basis of need defined by professionals. Over 70 per cent of welfare costs go towards the salaries of welfare professionals rather than directly meeting needs.

Prior to 1997, two developments in post-1980s' disability policy had a particularly significant impact on disabled people. The first was the NHS and Community Care Act 1990. Prior to this, low-income disabled people had the right to use their income support payments to access residential care, without any assessment of their needs. Although this was arguably a limited 'right' (in that it was to a segregated form of living that would not necessarily be the first choice for most disabled people), it was not contingent on the gatekeeping or assessment of welfare professionals. This led to a growth in demand, so the 1990 Act introduced care management, whereby services were shifted to the community wherever possible but access was gatekept by welfare professionals (local authority care managers, usually social workers), who ensured that only those 'in need' of services were given them. This did not place disabled people in control of their care or support, despite the fact that they were usually asked to pay service charges as a contribution (Rummery and Glendinning, 1999).

Further developments in the provision of community care services followed. A neoliberal commitment to individualisation over state support, coupled with demands from service users for more control over their care services, led to the development of direct payments, whereby disabled people were granted money to purchase their own support rather than it being directly provided by the state. In 1996, with the Community Care (Direct Payments) Act, direct payments were legalised, enabling disabled people to control their own social care budget, for example, to directly employ their own personal assistant. This has since developed into Self Directed Support (in Scotland) and Personal Budgets/Direct Payments (in England and Wales) but the principle in both cases is essentially the same: disabled people who are eligible for social care are able to take that care in the form of a personalised budget to use on services, rather than have those services commissioned for them by a care manager (they can still opt for the local authority to commission or purchase services on their behalf). Crucially, this is not an 'on demand' right in the sense of an enforceable choice: disabled people must be assessed as *needing the service* by welfare professionals (usually assessment or care managers employed by local authorities). However, even prior to 2008, legal challenges made it clear that the 'right' to access social care support was contingent on there being a budget to meet those needs: local authorities' overriding legal obligation was to stay within their resources, not to provide services. In other words, as resources tightened, so did the criteria to access support, with the result that only disabled people who are considered to be 'at risk' are now eligible in most local authorities to receive social care.

The second significant policy change to affect disabled people was the shift away from social security benefits towards employment programmes and welfare to work. While the social right to be excused from the obligation to work was useful in terms of allowing disabled people to access an income (albeit a very low one) without having to engage with the labour market, it was not without problems. It gave no structural or individual incentive for disabled people to engage in paid work, which was often the most effective route out of poverty and social isolation. Moreover, it reinforced an idea of 'welfare dependency' among disabled people, which was at odds with their abilities and aspirations. Most working-age disabled people want to work but face significant barriers in terms of inflexible workplaces, skills, transport, education, support and so on.

The New Deal for Disabled People therefore sought to reduce welfare use while, at the same time, removing barriers to work (Roulstone, 2000). Schemes were introduced to provide tailored employment support and advice for disabled people, as well as grants to help overcome initial barriers to work. Funding was also earmarked to help overcome the 'benefits trap' (whereby starting work and losing benefits leaves the worker financially worse off because of the additional costs of accessing work) and to ensure that disabled people who engaged in paid work but had to leave within a year did not have to be reassessed for benefits.

However, the 2010 Coalition government (after the 2008 banking crisis) chose to adopt a policy of welfare reform and austerity, attempting to cut public spending rather than stimulate the economy. This effectively meant that many of the social rights won by disabled people through the community care and disability benefits reforms came to an abrupt halt, as will be discussed in more detail in the following section.

Post-2008 social care policy for disabled people

Under welfare reforms after 2008, we have seen a further move away from universal, social-rights-based welfare towards austerity-driven cuts to provision in the area of social care. Although the 1990 community care reforms were explicitly intended to curb demands for services (Lewis and Glennerster, 1996), they did give disabled people and carers the right to be assessed for services, and placed a duty on local authorities to register unmet need. However, the largest austerity-driven cuts in funding that have directly affected disabled people have been to the funding available to local authorities.

Overall, English local authorities have seen a 42 per cent cut in real terms to their funding over the last decade. Between 2010 and 2012, funding for adult social care in England was cut by around £1.9 billion (ADSS, 2012). This not only means a sharp cut in directly provided services, but also cuts to grants to the voluntary sector, who provide specialist and advocacy services totalling around 17 per cent of overall social care provision (CQCRI, 2010), and who rely on local government for 47 per cent of their funding (House of Commons

Library, 2017). As part of the introduction of markets into the community care reforms, both the private (for-profit) sector and third (not-for-profit) sector have seen significant rises in their involvement in the provision of social care, but it is difficult to disaggregate English data into services for older and younger disabled people; certainly, residential and nursing-home provision are dominated by the private sector but these tend to be overwhelmingly services for the over 65s. Crucially, for younger disabled people, the real-term cuts mean cuts to the funding of personalised schemes such as direct payments and self-directed support, largely through the tightening of eligibility criteria so that only those considered to be at high risk are eligible for support, and the amount of funding available to them has declined significantly in real terms. The September 2018 budget submission estimated that adult social care services face a funding gap of £1.5 billion in 2019, which is estimated to rise to £3.5 billion in 2024 – but, again, these figures are based on projections of an ageing population and not on the needs of working-age disabled people.

As children's services are effectively ring-fenced due to statutory safeguarding obligations, this has further reduced the funding available for adult social care, leaving mental health services, services for carers and services for those with non-life-threatening illnesses particularly vulnerable. Moreover, both Wales and Scotland have opted to ring-fence part of their block grants for the National Health Service (NHS), which further reduces the funding available for social care. In addition, the option to mitigate cuts in funding by raising local taxes has proved politically untenable. Around 400,000 fewer adults received social care in England in 2013/14 compared to 2009/10 (Thorlby et al, 2018). Informal carers are bearing the brunt of the cuts, with 75 per cent of them saying that they have not received a break in the past 12 months (Care and Support Alliance, 2018).

These cutbacks have happened at a time of rising demand. Accurate figures for the whole of the UK are difficult to ascertain, but the Institute for Fiscal Studies has estimated that to maintain publicly funded social care at 2009/10 levels per head, the government would have to spend between £2.8 billion and £4 billion more than it is forecast to in 2019/20. Local authorities do not publish accurate data on social care expenditure in England and Wales, and so it is difficult to ascertain UK-wide figures; however, the need index in Scotland for social care services is roughly the same as the rest of the UK and local authorities there do provide the Scottish government with annual figures on social care spending. Scottish figures show a decline in the rate of home-care service use per 1,000 population, while the rate of disability (using government definitions and figures) among this population rose from 25 per cent to 35 per cent over the same period (see Figure 2.1).

Moreover, most working-age home-care clients are receiving either very low or very high numbers of hours of support, and the numbers have dropped dramatically between 2014 and 2017 (compare Figures 2.2 and 2.3).

Figure 2.1: Home-care clients in Scotland aged 18–64

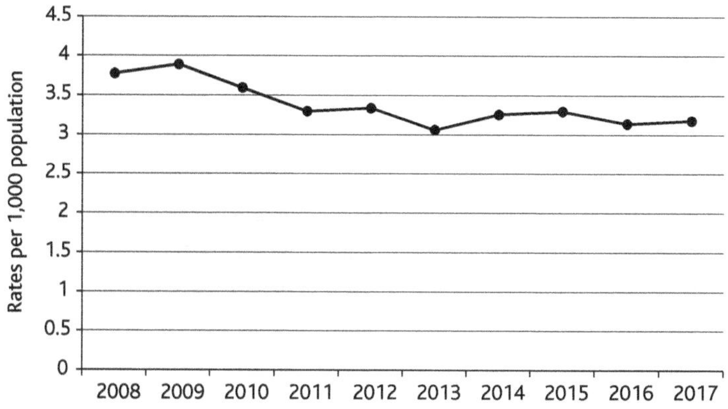

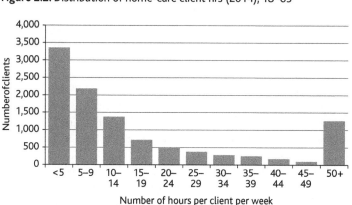

Source: Scottish Government Social Care Survey 2013–17 and Home Care Census 2007–12

Figure 2.2: Distribution of home-care client hrs (2014), 18–65

Source: Social Care Survey 2014

Figure 2.3: Distribution of home-care client hrs (2017)

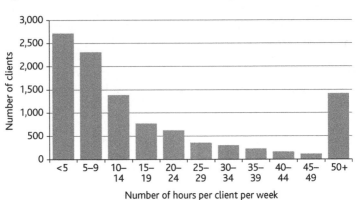

Source: Scottish Government Social Care Survey 2017

This pattern of distribution can be explained by the fact that those receiving 50+ hours are likely to be long-standing recipients of Independent Living Fund grants, which, in theory, allow those with very high levels of need to live in the community rather than in residential care; those under this threshold will be likely to be subject to the changes in access criteria limiting access to hours of care that have been implemented particularly since 2010, although accurate figures are only available post-2014. These cutbacks come at the same time as the rise of personalisation. Schemes such as direct payments, personal budgets and self-directed support ostensibly give disabled people much more choice and control over the support they receive from local authorities. They arose, in part, from bottom-up pressure from disabled people themselves, who wanted to challenge dependency on local authority-provided services, which were inflexible and not tailored to needs, as well as insufficiently under disabled people's control to provide support in an empowering way. However, they also arose from top-down pressures to curtail rising costs resulting from rising demand. When austerity hit the public purse in 2008, they were then services that were subject to rationing in two ways. First, the criteria to access services were made more stringent. These are set by local authorities individually, and they have an obligation to not allow any more people to access services than they have funding available; if this appears to be becoming the case, local authorities are under an obligation to tighten the criteria for accessing services in order to reduce access to within fundable demand. As funding has become reduced, criteria are now set so tightly that only those disabled people who are at significant risk, and do not have informal care support, are likely to be able to access services. Second, the amount of funding available to those who are eligible for services has reduced, with the result that hourly payments to carers are capped (reducing the ability to recruit highly skilled carers) and the flexibility that makes personalised services empowering for disabled people is reduced. As, in many cases, local authorities have delegated responsibility for managing budgets and services to disabled people, they are placed in the position of having to deal with reduced budgets and services rather than the local authority absorbing the cuts. Personalisation effectively means the delegation of austerity onto service users.

Post-2008 welfare reform and its impact on disabled people

At the same time as radical cuts to funding and the provision of social care services have been introduced, disabled people have also been subject to radical changes to the benefits system under the guise of welfare reform. New Labour's policy of workfare – encouraging people off benefits and into work – continued to drive the normative framework of social security policy. However, the mechanism by which this was to be achieved changed from the New Deal approach predicated on supporting disabled people into work to a more punitive, sanctions-based regime. Moreover, both social security and other welfare reforms were explicitly designed to reduced expenditure: the move from Disability Living Allowance (DLA) to Personal Independence Payments (PIPs) was designed to save £1.2 billion, and time-limiting Employment Support Allowance (ESA) was intended to save another £1.2 billion. Cuts to tax credits, housing benefit and other welfare reductions mean that austerity is costing the average disabled person £4,410 a year, with severely disabled people being £8,832 a year worse off, 19 times the national average (Duffy, 2015).

Workfare in the social security system was brought about by the introduction of ESA to replace Incapacity Benefit, and the introduction of a stringent Work Capability Assessment (WCA) at three months after the beginning of benefit payments. WCA assesses a claimant's ability to undertake work on a points-based system, and the expectation is that most of those on ESA will be place in a Work-Related Activity Group and undertake training courses to improve their readiness for work. Those who do not comply are subject to sanctions (the removal of benefits), and these are applied strictly, with no right of appeal. Those who are assessed as unable to work are placed in the Support Group and are exempt from undertaking the work-related activities, and also receive an additional payment to relieve poverty.

The changes to both DLA and ESA are intended to reflect the idea that the nature of physical illness and impairment itself does not necessarily produce the same limitations in functioning for everyone. Instead, the assessments are designed to be functional, to ascertain how a claimant's ability to function is affected rather than the condition itself. The aim is to limit 'dependency' on social security by encouraging a 'psychosocial' self-reliance (Litchfield, 2013). In the case of PIPs, this model is based on a 'bio-psychosocial' model of illness, whereby individuals are perceived as needing to change their psychological approach to their illness to reduce its incapacitating effects. The flaw in this approach is that while the evidence is clear that it can be helpful in some cases (eg for people living with mild mental health conditions or chronic pain), it does not work in others. One cannot alter the impact of serious mental or physical illness, particularly that which is substantial and permanent, by adjusting one's psychological approach: you cannot *think* your eyes into working if you are blind, or use meditation to repair a severed spinal column or a schizophrenic mind (Shakespeare et al, 2017). Even where such approaches can support people to live better with illness and incapacity, they do not necessarily improve their ability to engage in paid work.

Prior to the introduction of ESA, functional assessments focused on whether a claimant had a practical chance of being able to find a job that they could do. The new assessments now investigate whether the claimant has the ability to, in theory, do some form of work. This is a considerable tightening of eligibility as it takes no account of the claimant's skills or the local job market. The 13-week assessment period takes into account a person's ability to perform physical, mental and cognitive functions, determining whether or not they will be eligible for ESA at all. Then their capacity to undertake work-related activities is assessed, and if they are deemed capable of undertaking these activities, they are obliged to do so or risk sanctions. Those who are judged unable to take part in work-related activities are placed in the Support Group, receive a higher allowance and are not subject to any conditionality. After six months, those deemed able to undertake work-related activities are moved onto Jobseeker's Allowance (which is paid at a lower rate than ESA and is means-tested), regardless of whether their capacity to engage in work has improved or not.

A further problem with the sanctions-driven workfare system of benefits is that the responsibility for assessments has been outsourced to private sector providers who have clear targets for moving people off benefits to save money. Although the initial provider (the French firm ATOS) was replaced after criticism with the American company Maximus, this did not remove the targets or welfare sanctions. The theoretical basis for moving claimants through the system from a permanent Incapacity Benefit social security payment, to time-limited ESA and then to time-limited and means-tested Jobseeker's Allowance is predicated on the idea that the failure to secure work is down to the personal failings of chronically sick and disabled people, not an educational and work environment that is not flexible or supportive enough to enable them to gain skills and engage in work. This is in line with a more punitive approach to welfare generally: commentators have noted a sharp ideological shift away from rights-based approaches and towards residualism and welfare conditionality in the Coalition government post-2010 and in both Conservative governments in 2015 and 2017 (Dwyer, 2018).

The role that health and social care professionals, who arguably know the claimant's functional limitations best, has been much reduced in the revised workfare system. This was as a result of GPs and other health practitioners being seen as being too lenient and encouraging welfare dependency (Piggott and Grover, 2009). There may be some basis to this: medical professionals tend to work with an individual model of disability, which assumes that medical conditions and impairments cause functional limitations, not taking into account the social, cultural, physical or political environment in which these conditions are experienced (Barnes, 2000). They may be working with an approach to disability that stigmatises chronically ill and impaired people, further disabling them. However, both health and social care professionals are likely to have been working over a period of time with disabled people, and social workers in particular tend to focus on using a social and holistic approach to assessing need rather than a biomedical one. Providing information to new assessors with no previous knowledge of or connection to the claimant is, in and of itself, highly stressful and debilitating for disabled people, and there is evidence that reassessment is particularly likely to lead to a permanent decline in mental health (Marks et al, 2017).

The changes have caused much concern and hardship, particularly among the lowest-income and most vulnerable groups of claimants. They have had to endure income uncertainty caused by delays and sanctions, which are often wrongly imposed. Recent figures indicate that around 30 per cent of ESA claimants were found to be fit for work but that these decisions were overturned at appeal in 30 per cent of cases. The proportion of successful appeals is rising as more claimants undertake appeals and, in some cases, are on the second and third round. The cost of administering the appeals system is significant and, when added to human cost, means that the changes are more expensive to administer than the savings gained. Moreover, while figures indicate that the mortality rate for those on ESA is lower than it was on its predecessor, Incapacity Benefit, over 4,000 people died within six weeks of being assessed as 'fit for work' in 2014/15 (DWP, 2014).

The 'perfect storm' of welfare reform

A 'perfect storm' is a combination of events that have a significant cumulative impact far beyond what the individual events would have achieved by themselves. In the case of disabled people, the combined effect of losing ESA due to time limits and sanctions, and losing income by being moved from DLA to PIPs, is costing disabled people on average £17,000–23,000 over five years, depending on when they are reassessed for PIPs (Wood, 2013). Those who are living in social housing or are using housing benefit are also affected by changes such as the so-called 'bedroom tax' on spare bedrooms, which affects the ability of many disabled people to employ live-in or overnight carers (and also does not take into account the limited availability of accessible and affordable housing, reducing disabled people's options of moving to smaller properties). The direct changes to Incapacity Benefit, DLA, social care and housing have taken place across seemingly unconnected policy areas, being the responsibility of several different government departments, but together they have had a significant impact on disabled people's lives that individual policymakers would have found it hard to predict. Indirect impacts, adding to the cumulative effect, have also been felt by real-term cuts to NHS and continuing care funding, the reduction in public sector staffing and pay, the increase in transport prices, cuts to education support services, leisure services and other public sector provision, and the stagnation in real terms of the value of both social security benefits and wages, particularly public sector wages.

As with other areas of welfare reform, social divisions in addition to disability play a significant role in differentiating the impact experienced. Disabled women over the age of 50 are disproportionately affected by the changes due to their lower workforce participation over the life course, leading to fewer skills and savings that could mitigate the changes. The cuts to public sector jobs that were also part of the post-2008 austerity regime also disproportionately affect working-age disabled women, who would traditionally find employment in this sector. ESA is intended to address the problem that Incapacity Benefit was too easy to claim and not easy enough to leave (DWP, 2006). By making it more difficult to claim than previous social security benefits, and by ensuring that time limits and sanctions move people off the benefit whether they have found work or not, work is mandated for a large group of people with: no account of caring, childcare and other commitments; no account for skills gaps experienced, particularly by low-income and female disabled people; and certainly no additional obligations on employers to create supported, accessible and flexible jobs.

Despite public pressure from campaigners, there has been no official cumulative impact assessment of the welfare reforms and cuts to social care on disabled people. It is clear that not only the 'perfect storm' of welfare reform, but also the timing and interaction between it and changes to social care, have had a significant impact on the well-being and social participation of disabled people. Brawn et al (2013) reported that 36 per cent of their survey of working-age disabled adults in England were unable to 'eat, wash, dress or get out of the house' due to the lack of services, 47 per cent were unable to take part in community life, and 34 per cent were unable to work, volunteer or undergo training as a result of losing social care services. A total of 53 per cent reported feeling anxious or isolated, or declining mental health, and families are feeling the strain, with 38 per cent of family members seeking support due to stress, strained relationships and declining well-being.

Duffy (2015) has estimated that disabled people – 8 per cent of the population – have borne 29 per cent of the combined cuts to social care and social security benefits, with severely disabled people (2 per cent of the population) bearing 15 per cent of the cuts. Moreover, research commissioned by the Equalities and Human Rights Commission questioned whether the distributional impact of the changes to taxes and benefits had been properly assessed, particularly as they intersected across disability, age and gender. Wood et al (2011) also argues that the speed, complexity and volume of changes across the range of social security benefits will hit disabled families, particularly those with disabled children and/or non-working parents, particularly hard.

The post-2016 Conservative government has come under particular scrutiny from the United Nations (UN) for its treatment of disabled people. In 2017, the UN Convention on the Rights of Persons with Disabilities Committee concluded that the UK's welfare reform programme was in danger of breaching 30 of the convention's 33 treaty articles, and recommended 80 changes to ensure that disabled people's human rights were protected. In 2018, the UN special rapporteur on extreme poverty found that nearly half of those in the UK living in poverty were from families with a disabled member, and disabled families had lost on average more than 30 per cent of their annual income as a result of tax and social security changes (Alston, 2018).

The targeting of disabled people to pay for austerity has not gone unnoticed by the general public. Social attitudes to disabled people have shown a marked shift since 2008. Briant et al (2013), using a comprehensive content analysis of mainstream newspapers in 2004/05 and 2010/11, found that the number of articles discussing disabled people had risen by 48 per cent and that writing about disabled people was increasingly politicised, characterising disabled people as a burden on the state and disability as a benefits problem.

Devolution and the mitigation of harm: the example of Scotland

In this case, potential policy lessons can be learned from variance in social policy for disabled people due to devolution across the UK. In September 2014, Scotland rejected the option of independence and voted to remain part of the UK. However, the vote was far closer than had been predicted (45 per cent with an 85 per cent turnout) and the Smith Commission was set up to reach a consensus on whether further powers should be devolved to the Scottish Parliament, and if so, which. As well as representation from all five Scottish political parties, the commission took submissions from over 14,000 organisations and individuals. The two pro-independence parties, the Scottish National Party (SNP) and Greens, as well as many civic organisations, wanted devolution of the full range of taxation and welfare powers in order to be able to control economic growth and develop what was claimed to be a 'fairer' welfare system. However, these ambitions were blocked by the pro-unionist parties, Labour in particular, who were adamantly opposed to the development of differentiated welfare systems across the UK.

In the end, two major areas of welfare benefits that affected disabled people were devolved: DLA/PIPs (and Attendance and Carers Allowance), and Universal Credit, with additional tax-varying powers. Bearing in mind that Scotland had already been controlling social care and health funding through its block grant (which it has delegated responsibility for administering without ring-fencing), this gave the Scottish Parliament some considerable leeway to vary the administration and delivery of welfare, care and support to disabled people and their families. Although the power to substantially change benefits is limited, there are several indications that the Scottish government intends to take a different theoretical and governance approach than the UK government.

First, there is a strong commitment to the cooperative production of policy. 'Experience Panels' of users of social security benefits have recruited over 2,000 volunteers to work over a four-year period to shape the social security system (Scottish Government, 2017). New grants for young carers are being designed, and Carers Allowance has been increased to bring it in line with Jobseeker's Allowance. The use of third-party private organisations to undertake assessments for both the ESA component of Universal Credit and DLA/PIPs has been expressly ruled out following expert testimony from academics and disability organisations (Scottish Government, 2017). This reflects a 'cooperative' style of governance favoured by the Scottish government (Cairney and Rummery, 2018), whereby civic society is involved in both the formulation and the implementation of policy to a far greater extent that at Westminster. In particularly, third sector organisations of disabled people, such as Inclusion Scotland, have long played a cooperative role in designing welfare policy for disabled people in areas such as transport, housing and social care. In part, this is facilitated by the economies of scale: with a lower population (5.5 million), there are correspondingly fewer identifiable stakeholders in policy areas, and it is reasonably possible to involve most of the key third sector organisations in policy. It is also due, in part, to the electoral system used in the Scottish Parliament: a mix of 'first past the post' and proportional representation, it is designed to ensure that it is difficult for any one party to hold an electoral majority, enabling cross-party coalition and consensus building, with negotiators commonly involving third sector organisations in order to achieve consensus on issues. However, this also means that when one political party is able to secure a majority (as the SNP did in 2012), this push towards consensus building is far weaker: parties can rely on the whip to push through their policy objectives and do not need to engage in cross-party negotiation, which leads to fewer opportunities for civic society to become involved in the policy process.

Second, there is a strong political incentive for the current SNP government to demonstrate that it is capable of good governance, particularly in the light of contrasting problems in the rest of the UK, such as issues with the rollout of Universal Credit. Unlike the pro-unionist parties, who have a strong political incentive to show that Scottish social policy is the same as the rest of the UK (thus showing equity across the whole of the UK and bolstering political arguments against further devolution or independence), pro-independence parties have a strong political incentive to show that it is not only different, but better. Much of the White Paper 'Scotland's future' (Scottish Government, 2013) – essentially the SNP's manifesto for independence in the 2014 referendum – was designed to demonstrate that an independent Scotland would be 'fairer' than the rest of the UK in welfare terms. Therefore, promises like mitigating the spare-room subsidy (the so-called 'bedroom tax', whereby households on welfare benefits who had a spare bedroom were penalised), scrapping Trident and using the saved money to invest in childcare ('bairns not bombs'), and promised investment in the NHS and social care were intended to appeal to cautious voters who might not feel inclined to trust the SNP to govern an independent Scotland responsibly.

Finally, recent figures suggest that long-term care spending in Scotland is not quite feeling the calamitous freeze from austerity that the rest of the UK is experiencing. In real terms, spending on long-term care has reduced in England by 35 per cent and in Scotland by only 7 per cent. The efforts by the Scottish government to mitigate the severity of cuts, as well as its commitment to raising taxes for the wealthiest and changing the design of welfare, indicate that it is willing to make different decisions than the rest of the UK, and that this is likely to benefit disabled people.

However, there are also signs that one should be cautious about Scotland being 'fairer' to disabled people. Every government since devolution has opted to protect NHS spending at the cost of social care spending. There has been little progress made on mitigating the 'postcode lottery' of self-directed support, with the result that there are still 32 local authorities allocating funding to users in different ways (and, indeed, Scottish government figures reveal that there is no correlation between need and spending on social care across the local authorities). Local taxation rates remain capped, limiting how much local authorities can spend on social care, with the result that self-directed support is now only realistically available to those in the most 'critical' need. The rollout of PIPs has not been halted, and disabled people in Scotland are therefore still losing access to income through the reassessment of their needs using a questionable theoretical and financial model. Other areas, such as accessible transport and housing – particularly in rural areas – remain problematic for disabled people (DES, 2017).

Finally, there is no indication that there is much appetite in Scotland for radical systematic change (eg introducing a universal basic income instead of work-related benefits; providing a national rather than local authority-based system of social care and self-directed support; introducing social care insurance; or diverting funding from the NHS to long-term care). Indeed, with the uncertainty of Brexit at the time of writing, we can reasonably suppose that any economic penalty from market insecurity will likely fall on the poorest members of Scottish society, just as it will do in the rest of the UK, and that these members are disproportionately made up of families that include a disabled person.

Conclusions

If we measure the success of a civilised society by how well it treats its most vulnerable citizens, then it cannot be said that the last decade of UK social policy offers us much hope. Disabled people have disproportionately borne the brunt of welfare cuts under the guise of austerity and are likely to continue to do so. The linking of welfare to labour market participation is likely to continue even if a change of government comes about as all the major political parties still explicitly place 'working families' at the core of their welfare plans. There is little political appetite to radically restructure the world of work to accommodate disabled workers, or to improve the lives of those who cannot engage with the labour market, and this has a disproportionately damaging effect on disabled people and carers. Even if the most optimistic of economic predictions comes true under Brexit, it will be at least a decade before public finances return to pre-2008 days and the option of more generous welfare and social care benefits for disabled people becomes politically or economically feasible.

The fact that disabled people are a relatively easy target for welfare cuts is not unlinked to the fact that they are not highly visible in positions of power. Only 1 per cent of MPs (five) in the current Westminster government self-identify as disabled. The barriers to running for elected office are huge; the lack of access to elite groups that form the decision-making bodies of political parties, the lack of support for care and personal assistance, and the lack of access to mainstream political activity are just a few of them. However, in the 2017 council elections, the Scottish government ran an 'Access to Elected Office' fund designed to support disabled candidates who would not otherwise be able to run: 39 disabled politicians received funding, and 15 were eventually elected to local councils. This is a clear indication that it is not a lack of merit or talent that is preventing disabled people from running for elected offices. Local councils are the ones who make key decisions regarding funding allocations for social care, and it will be interesting to observe in the forthcoming years whether disabled councillors will be successful in challenging attitudes and funding decisions.

References

ADSS (Association of Directors of Social Services) (2012) *Budget survey 2012*, Birmingham: ADSS.

Alston, P. (2018) Statement on visit to the United Kingdom, by Professor Philip Alston, United Nations Special Rapporteur on extreme poverty and human rights, www.ohchr.org/Documents/Issues/Poverty/EOM_GB_16Nov2018.pdf (full report available at: www.ohchr.org/EN/Issues/Poverty/Pages/CountryVisits.aspx).

Barnes, C. (2000) A working social model? Disability, work and disability politics in the 21st century, *Critical Social Policy*, 20(4): 441–57.

Brawn, E., Bush, M., Hawkings, C. and Trotter, R. (2013) *The other care crisis: Making social care funding work for disabled adults in England*, London: Scope, Mencap, the National Autistic Society, Sense and Leonard Cheshire Disability.

Briant, E., Watson, N. and Philo, G. (2013) Reporting disability in the age of austerity: the changing face of media representation of disability and disabled people in the United Kingdom and the creation of new 'folk devils', *Disability & Society*, 28(6): 874–89.

Cairney, P. and Rummery, K. (2018) Feminising politics to close the evidence–policy gap: the case of social policy in Scotland, *Australian Journal of Public Administration*, 77(4): 542–53.

Care and Support Alliance (2018) Voices from the social care crisis, http://careandsupportalliance.com/wp-content/uploads/2018/05/Final-report-CSA.pdf

CQCRI (Care Quality Commission Registration and Inspection Data) (2010) GQC database, www.lse.ac.uk/LSEHealthAndSocialCare/pdf/SSCR-Scoping-Review_2_web.pdf

DES (Disability Equality Scotland) (2017) Accessible travel framework survey: baseline results, http://accessibletravel.scot/surveys/

Duffy, S. (2015) *Counting the cuts*, Sheffield: The Centre for Welfare Reform.

DWP (Department for Work and Pensions) (2006) *A new deal for welfare: Empowering people to work*, Cm 6730 https://assets.publishing.service.gov.uk/government/uploads/system/uploads/attachment_data/file/272235/6730.pdf

DWP (2014) DWP quarterly statistical summary, May, https://assets.publishing.service.gov.uk/government/uploads/system/uploads/attachment_data/file/387429/stats_summary_nov14_final_v1.pdf

Dwyer, P. (2018) Punitive and ineffective: benefit sanctions within social security, *Journal of Social Security Law*, 25(3): 142–57.

House of Commons Library (2017) Charities and the voluntary sector, briefing paper SN05428.

Lewis, J. and Glennerster, H. (1996) *Implementing the new community care*, Buckingham: Open University Press.

Litchfield, P. (2013) *An independent review of the Work Capability Assessment*, London: The Stationery Office.

Marks, A., Cowan, S. and Maclean, G. (2017) Mental health and unemployment in Scotland, www.advocard.org.uk/wp-content/uploads/2017/02/2017-02-Heriot-Watt-Mental-Health-Report-on-WCA.pdf

Marshall, T.H. (1950) *Citizenship and social class: And other essays*, Cambridge: Cambridge University Press.

Piggott, L. and Grover, C. (2009) Retrenching Incapacity Benefit: Employment Support Allowance and paid work. *Social Policy and Society*, 8(2): 159–70.

Roulstone, A. (2000) Disability, dependency and the New Deal for Disabled People, *Disability & Society*, 15(3): 427–43.

Rummery, K. and Glendinning, C. (1999) Negotiating needs, access and gatekeeping: Developments in health and community care policies in the UK and the rights of disabled and older citizens, *Critical Social Policy*, 19: 335–51.

Scottish Government (2013) *Scotland's Future: Your guide to an independent Scotland*, www2.gov.scot/resource/0043/00439021.pdf

Scottish Government (2017) Social Security Committee session 5, www.parliament.scot/parliamentarybusiness/report.aspx?r=10637 &mode=pdf

Shakespeare, T., Watson, N. and Alghaib, O.A. (2017) Blaming the victim, all over again: Waddell and Aylwards biopsychosocial (BPS) model of disability, *Critical Social Policy*, 37(1): 22–41.

Stone, D. (1986) *The disabled state*, Philadelphia, PA: Temple University Press.

Thorlby, R., Starling, A., Broadbent, C. and Watt, T. (2018) *What's the problem with social care and why do we need to do better?*, London: Kings Fund.

Wood, C (2013) *Health in austerity*, London: Demos.

Wood, C., Cheetham, P. and Gregory, T. (2011) *Coping with the cuts*, London: Demos.

3

Financialisation *and* social protection? The UK's path towards a socially protective public–private pension system

Paul Bridgen

Introduction

The concept of financialisation has been used by scholars in a range of disciplines since the turn of the century to describe structural developments in late-modern capitalism. Financialisation refers broadly to 'the increasing role of financial motives, financial markets, financial actors and financial institutions in the operation of the domestic and international economies' (Epstein, 2006: 3). A larger role for finance has been identified as a generator of growth, as a political actor and in the everyday lives of citizens (van der Zwan, 2014). Most commentators regard this process as inextricably connected to a broader neoliberal economic and social transformation (eg Langley, 2010).

Social policy scholars have been slower to enter this debate, though pension commentators have long been interested in financial markets given the greater use of private pensions, since the 1990s, to manage the fiscal demands on public provision stemming from population ageing (eg World Bank, 1994). Consideration of financialisation has focused particularly on the rise of defined contribution pensions, highlighting the greater level of individualised and personal interaction this has encouraged between citizens and the financial sector. This development has also generally been seen as unequivocally neoliberal, hand in glove with retrenching reforms designed to substitute private provision for public (eg Cutler and Waine, 2001). Thus, Berry has recently argued that the UK state has driven forward a consistent Thatcherite pension financialisation agenda since the late 1980s, under which '[f]inancial risks that might have at one time been shouldered by the state are instead individualised' (Berry, 2015: 510; see also Berry, 2016).

This chapter, in contrast, argues for a less rigid, more fluid understanding of UK pension financialisation – one that is less deterministic and more negotiated. Following van der Zwan (2014: 118), it suggests existing accounts paint too neat a picture of financialising processes that fails to fully incorporate 'the possibilities for agency by local actors'. Specifically, the chapter argues that UK pension financialisation has involved the interaction of financialising and progressive social protection agendas[1] over the last three decades. Thus, rather than constituting an inexorable and continuous path, driven by a determined neoliberal state, 'emergent forms of collectivity and solidarity within the financialized political economies' (van der Zwan, 2014: 119) are evident. These emerged as socially progressive values interacted with neoliberal ideas in a politics richer, and more diverse and negotiated, than proposed in the current literature. The result of this process is that the public–private pension mix in the UK in 2018 thus constitutes not a simple 'retreat of the state at the behest of the market', but 'the emergence of an altogether different type of state intervention' (van der Zwan, 2014: 117; see also Leisering, 2011), one in which at least some traditional social protection objectives are achieved by different means (see Hyde et al, 2003; Hyde and Dixon, 2008; Bridgen and Meyer, 2007).

The chapter makes this argument by first outlining the dimensions, objectives and generally favoured means for achieving a progressive socially protective pension policy. A more fully developed analytical framework is then established that is used to trace the interaction of the financialising and social protection agendas in the UK pension system since 1990. Finally, to emphasise the continuing space for agency in today's UK financialised pension system, the chapter finishes by proposing two ambitious, but feasible, regulatory reforms that would render the system more fully able than at present to meet progressive social protection objectives.

Social protection in retirement: the role of the public and private sector

Considerations of what constitutes a socially protective pension system in late-modern economies inevitably rest on normative judgements about the appropriate balance between individual and collective responsibility in the provision of a retirement income. Progressive judgements on this issue have traditionally been founded on conceptions of social citizenship (Marshall, 2009), which regard social rights guaranteeing individuals' protection against need as equally important as civil and political rights in upholding equality of social status between retired citizens. At the least, these rights should ensure all citizens a universal minimum level of economic, social and political inclusion. Marshall's own limited conception of where the social minimum lay was exemplified in the UK by Beveridge's 1942 pension scheme. This was universal but set the pensions at a low level (Veit-Wilson, 1994) and organised entitlement in relation to workplace contributions. Influenced by the more egalitarian approaches of Titmuss (1958) and Townsend (1979), social democrats have, since Marshall, favoured a more generous social minimum, dynamically set in relation to customary social practices. Thus, from this perspective, social rights should guarantee that all retired citizens avoid relative poverty (Townsend, 1979). They should also diminish social divisions in retirement caused by the privileged access of some workers to occupational pension provision (Titmuss, 1958; Meyer and Bridgen, 2008), and should prevent substantial falls in income on retirement (income protection).

The state has been favoured to meet these objectives, particularly the first one. Here, universal public provision without means testing has been preferred, with entitlement conditions unrelated to citizenship minimised (Esping-Andersen, 1990). Only through redistributive provision are workers with low working-life incomes and/or intermittent labour market activity guaranteed a retirement above the poverty line. Such provision is particularly important for the social protection of women, who have remained over-represented as carers and have thus generally experienced greater periods outside the labour force or on lower wages (eg Ginn, 2003; Grady, 2015; Foster and Heneghan, 2018).

Public provision has also been favoured to deliver income protection given concerns about the coverage, income-related nature and risks of private pensions – but occupational provision has sometimes been a 'second choice' option (Trampusch, 2007). Certainly, the coverage in the UK of workplace defined benefit pensions extended up to the mid-1990s, well beyond a level required simply to retain skilled workers, often as a consequence of union pressure (Mares, 2001). Moreover, by defining benefits in advance, such provision involved employers taking until recently most of the risk of delivering them

(Titmuss, 1958). Such schemes, like all private provision, entailed no redistribution and were firmly employment-based, meaning that women often missed out or had lower levels of entitlement, but where available, they provided strong pension guarantees to workers.

In the UK, the apotheosis of a progressive state-dominated approach to social protection was Labour's 1957 National Superannuation proposal (see Pemberton, 2012). This promised an earnings-related but redistributive state scheme that would provide a guaranteed overall pension of about half average earnings. It would probably also have resulted in the replacement of existing occupational provision (Pemberton, 2012: 1429). This never came to pass (see Pemberton, 2012; Oude Nijhuis, 2013), but the establishment of State Earnings Related Pensions (SERPs) in 1975, nevertheless, promised to significantly increase public provision and established a much tighter regulatory framework within which occupational provision had to operate. Women's protection improved through the dilution of work-based entitlement conditions and the introduction of Home Responsibilities Protection (Timmins, 1995).

This proved to be the zenith of social democracy in UK pension provision. Indeed, as has been mentioned, some commentators regard most steps taken since as moves away from progressive values and towards neoliberal ones. Starting with the second Thatcher government's mid-1980s' emasculation of SERPs and acceptance of private personal pensions as a means to contract out of it, the public sphere has been in decline and privatisation and individualisation has increased. It is the drivers, dimensions and consequences of this process that the recent analytical emphasis on financialisation has attempted to illuminate.

Financialisation: neoliberalism contested

The added value of financialisation as a conceptual lens through which to view changes in public–private pension mixes over recent decades is the particular attention that it directs to the changing nature of private provision and the goals and objectives underpinning these developments. Pension financialisation thus involves, it is suggested, the concerted development of an ever-closer, direct relationship between individuals and the financial sector as a means of encouraging greater individual self-reliance and risk-taking, and thus imbuing and promoting financialised identities (Langley, 2010: 34). This process also serves a macro-level agenda: it assists the development of an

Anglo-liberal growth model under which finance plays an ever-greater role and consumption is maintained by private rather than public borrowing (Berry, 2015).

Berry suggests that such motivations have underpinned UK pension reforms since the early 1990s, regardless of government coloration; they have been driven concertedly by state-directed neoliberalism (Berry, 2015: 510; see also Berry, 2016: 3). The goal has been the establishment of a new growth model through a '*re*orientation of the relationship between individuals and the state with concomitant implications for how welfare is conceived of and supported by public authorities' (Berry, 2015: 522, emphasis in original). Indeed, financialisation has sometimes been more important than retrenchment: UK governments have been 'content to commit additional public resources to welfare ... if it reinforces this agenda' (Berry, 2016: 14).

Understood on this basis, pension financialisation is a singular, immutable and deeply embedded process; it is 'something for citizens to come to terms with', not challenge (Berry, 2015: 521). Democratic oversight and/or socialisation are unlikely because regulation of this type would 'fundamentally contradict' financialising agendas (Berry, 2015: 521); it would require a transformation of the growth model within which financialisation is a central component. Financialised pension systems thus inevitably involve a diminution of socially protective functions; they inexorably and 'perniciously' drive social exclusion, with attempts to put a progressive gloss on such developments being largely rhetorical (Berry, 2015: 514–15).

However, has pension financialisation in the UK really been this neat and tidy? Have only superficial attempts been made to contest and arrest it? Is the current UK public–private mix consequently largely devoid of any substantively progressive features? This chapter argues otherwise. It suggests that UK pension financialisation has, in fact, been a negotiated process involving a diversity of agendas and actors. Specifically, this negotiation has been between financialising rationales and those associated with social protection (see also Massala, 2018). The latter have often been pursued not by traditional statist means, but through social regulation, that is, a public policy of pensions has developed that operates both through the public and private sector (Leisering, 2011). The outcome is consequently a system that has *redefined* rather than surrendered public responsibility, a 'new socially regulated hybrid', rather than 'simply [the substitution of] market welfare for state welfare' (Leisering, 2011: 271; see also Hyde and Dixon, 2008).

The next two sections develop this argument by tracing the interaction of financialising and social protection rationales in the development of UK pension financialisation since the late 1980s. The following section identifies the main continuing problems with the UK variant from a progressive perspective and proposes two feasible reforms to improve it.

Financialisation and social protection in UK pension policy since 1990

Berry is right to suggest that pension financialisation began in the UK with the second Thatcher government's promotion of personal pensions in 1986 as a means to contract out of the much-diminished SERPs (see also Davies et al, 2018). Previously, only defined benefit occupational pensions could be used for this purpose (Timmins, 1995: 402–3). The 1986 reform thus brought individualised defined contribution pensions to the heart of the UK pension system. Individuals carried all the risk under such schemes that investment of pension contributions might generate insufficient returns to provide an adequate income in retirement (Mabbett, 2011).

Yet, rather than signifying the start of an inexorable process of ever-greater state-led, neoliberal financialisation (Berry, 2015, 2016), policy development since has, in fact, been dominated by a concern to square the rise of defined contribution pensions with the goals of social protection. This imperative arose initially because of the financial impropriety of insurers, exemplified by the 'misselling' of personal pensions to people who already had better-quality occupational provision (Waine, 1995). It was strongly reinforced by the shift from defined benefit to defined contribution schemes in the occupational sphere from the mid-1990s, caused by growing insecurities among companies about the financial sustainability of their occupational pension provision (Bridgen and Meyer, 2005). This financialising process, probably the most significant of the last two decades, had very little to do with the state, which was largely taken by surprise by it (Meyer and Bridgen, 2012).

New Labour's pension policy between 1997 and 2010 is best understood as an attempt, in the face of these developments, to incrementally make more progressive the UK's public–private mix in circumstances not considered conducive to a thoroughgoing paradigm-shifting reform (Bridgen, 2010). It was initially very cautious: means-tested Pension Credit was introduced to reduce pensioner poverty

(Evandrou and Falkingham, 2005: 168); SERPs was renamed 'State Second Pension' (S2P) and made more redistributive (Agulnik, 1999); and tentative social regulatory measures were taken to address the failings of defined contribution pensions. Insurance companies were encouraged to offer 'Stakeholder' pensions, with charges pegged,[2] to meet a new requirement on companies to guarantee workers access to a personal pension (DWP, 1998). There was still a belief at this stage that regulated competition, greater transparency and more information would be enough to resolve market deficiencies, particularly the issue of high pension fund charges (Mabbett, 2011).

Progress was much more rapid and significant after the reports of the Pension Commission in 2004 and 2005. The commission was set up in the face of the evident failure of Stakeholder pensions, growing finance industry concerns about policy coherence (particularly the disincentive impact of mean-testing on private savings) and rising union pressure as the defined benefit–defined contribution shift accelerated (Meyer and Bridgen, 2012; Bridgen and Meyer, 2018; Gelepithis, 2018a, 2018b). It urged on New Labour a more ambitious reconfiguration of the public–private mix. The state, as provider, should focus its attention on a universal, basic pension that was more inclusive, particularly for women, and was targeted at poverty reduction. However, it should also take greater steps to socially regulate the private pension market. Thus, the commission proposed that:

- future entitlement to the Basic State Pension (BSP) should be based on residency, rather than contributions and credits, and entitlements to the S2P should be broadened, particularly for carers;
- BSP uprating should revert to an earnings basis from 2010;
- the shift of the S2P to a flat-rate basis should be accelerated[3]; and
- a National Pensions Savings Scheme should be introduced based on automatic enrolment and a minimum employer contribution. (Pensions Commission, 2005)

The Pension Acts of 2007 and 2008 were largely based on the Pensions Commission's recommendation, although a residency-based pension was rejected and the earnings link was delayed until 2012. These reforms certainly had financialising aspects: they extended the scope of defined contribution pensions through auto-enrolment, and did very little to reverse the shift out of defined benefit provision in the existing occupational system. However, were they unequivocally neoliberal? Watson (2009) thinks so. He regards them as unambiguously designed to facilitate privatised welfare and the generation of an 'active worker-saver-investor subject' (Watson, 2013), with provision turned away from the 'passive receipt of state-provided welfare services and towards active management of assets through which individuals become personally responsible for releasing future income streams' (Watson, 2009: 42). Likewise, for Berry (2015: 518), the agenda was 'focused not on maintaining or adapting collective forms of protection against risk, but rather displacing ultimate responsibility for welfare to the individual level': citizens were (softly) compelled 'to become financially included or more intimately financially included, whether [they liked] it or not'.

However, such arguments significantly downplay the progressive elements of the reforms. In the public sphere, the system was made more redistributive and more accessible, being designed to provide a more generous and universal minimum standard (Bridgen, 2010). In the non-state sphere, while auto-enrolment encouraged citizens to engage more with the financial sector, the regulatory direction of travel with respect to defined contribution pensions was towards social regulation. The reform's overall objective was to improve the non-state system's success in delivering pensions for those on below-average wages based on quasi-compulsory employer as well as employee contributions. From a situation where employers had the final say on occupational pension contributions, this decision was shifted to employees. The coverage of workplace pension provision in the UK consequently significantly increased after 2012. Overall, active membership of occupational schemes rose by more than 5 million to 8.8 million by 2017. This increase pushed occupational pension coverage higher than at any time since the 1990s (ONS, 2017).

Moreover, as Benish et al (2017) insightfully argue, the setting up of the National Employment Savings Trust (NEST), as the national savings scheme proposed by the Pensions Commission, involved a clear shift away from beliefs that information and transparency were sufficient to correct the failings of the pension market. Instead, it represented the establishment of a 'public option' within the market, 'a new policy tool, in which public provision is not an alternative to the market, as the welfare state was originally conceived, but a public alternative within the market' (Benish et al, 2017: 327; see also Clark, 2012). NEST was thus a non-profit, trustee-based organisation whose establishment was subsidised by the state (Clark, 2012). Its role in the marketplace was to push down on providers' fees, thus maximising individual returns. The finance industry certainly regarded

NEST as a threat (Bridgen, 2010). It tried unsuccessfully to secure a greater role in the operation of the new institution (Bridgen, 2010) and also attempted to limit its scope by means of smaller maximum yearly contributions than those initially proposed by the government (ie £5,000) (DWP, 2006: 141). This would severely curtail NEST's market penetration by ensuring that only those on below-average wages had access to it. NEST would be a backstop provider of last resort. On the latter, the government duly reduced the maximum to £3,600 (2005 prices), though, as will be seen, this success for the financial sector was to prove short-lived (Personal Accounts Delivery Authority, 2009).

Pension financialisation under the Coalition government

Many of the progressive parts of New Labour's reforms were reinforced during implementation, notwithstanding that this task mainly fell to a Conservative–Liberal Democrat government.[4] Flat-rate public provision was made more generous by the phased introduction of a single-tier pension, set above the level of means-tested provision and indexed on the basis of the 'triple lock' (see Pension Policy Institute, 2014).[5] Social regulation was also extended. This was motivated by indications that market providers were beginning to innovate to compete for auto-enrolment business. Insurance companies began repackaging Master Trusts to this end as instruments to mimic NEST. This form of provision pools workplace pensions from a number of employers under the oversight of a single trustee board (The Pension Regulator, 2018), which has responsibility for investment funds, service provision and regulatory compliance. Employers retain responsibility for benefit and contribution levels in their section of the general fund. The economies of scale released by these pooling arrangements have enabled Master Trusts to compete in the auto-enrolment market with NEST. Thus, by 2018, there were around 90 Master Trusts (including NEST), with 3.6 million members in market schemes and 6.4 million in the NEST 'public option' (Cumbo, 2018; NEST, 2018).[6]

The Coalition government welcomed these developments, but concerns also arose about the governance and regulation of these new entities. These focused particularly on the question of charges, their lack of transparency and the limited monitoring undertaken by employers and scheme trustees. This was a problem because research suggested that excessive charges in some auto-enrolment default funds were a more significant determinant of pension outcomes than their investment strategy (OFT, 2013; Harrison et al, 2014). Moreover, a series of government reports raised further doubts about whether market competition alone was capable of putting downward pressure on charges (DWP, 2014).

A two-pronged extension of social regulation followed. First, the annual contribution cap on NEST was lifted in 2017. This freed up NEST to compete openly with the new Master Trusts, extending its market penetration beyond the lowest paid; potentially, it could move from being a limited default scheme at the bottom end of the market to a 'public option' provider competing for all auto-enrolled pensions. Steve Webb, the Coalition's Liberal Democrat Pension Minister, explained the change as an attempt to extend NEST's role as 'a force for good in the marketplace, driving up standards and best practice' (quoted in Paterson, 2013; see also Cumbo, 2014a).

This significant extension of the state's 'public option' role was reinforced by direct action in 2015 to control insurance company charges (DWP, 2015a), a move strongly resisted by the financial sector (Cumbo, 2014b, 2015). Thus, all defined contribution schemes used for auto-enrolment had to abide by:

- a 0.75 per cent charge cap on default arrangements in defined contribution workplace schemes (with effect from April 2015);
- a ban on consultancy charges in defined contribution contract-based schemes (April 2015);
- a ban on Active Member Discounts in defined contribution workplace schemes (April 2016); and
- a ban on member-borne commission-related payments in defined contribution workplace schemes (April 2016).

Introducing the changes, Steve Webb warned insurance companies 'to stop trying to fight the direction of travel' on social regulation (Cumbo, 2014b) and later threatened to 'name and shame' companies who persisted in levying excessive charges outside the unregulated auto-enrolled part of the market (Cumbo, 2015).

However, there was one important exception to these social regulatory moves under the Coalition. This was the introduction of 'pension freedoms' in 2015 (DWP, 2015b). A manifestation of the ideological fissures within the Coalition government, this policy idea was strongly financialising and emanated from the Conservative Chancellor, George Osborne. It removed the requirement for pensioners to convert their pension pot into an annuity within ten years of retirement. Henceforward, they were encouraged to engage with the financial sector to manage the provision of an adequate retirement income during the rest of their lifetime.

The UK public–private pension mix in 2018

The identification of progressive features in the reform of the UK's public–private pension system since 2004 should not be taken to suggest that there are not significant continuing limitations. These are as follows:

- The public pension is still contributory, and in the long term, its generosity will diminish (Crawford et al, 2013: 9). This is a particular problem for women and other citizens more likely to be on lower incomes.
- The overall level of contributions into non-state provision is still too low to deliver, in combination with public pensions, income protection for many citizens, particularly those on medium to higher incomes.
- The employer mandate remains very low by international standards.
- The increased role of defined contribution pensions means that risk is borne almost entirely by individuals, a situation further complicated by the introduction of 'pension freedoms'. The latter means that the investment risks that individuals already carried during the accumulation stage of defined contribution provision (see earlier) are extended to the de-cumulation stage. Individuals' success or otherwise in securing an adequate income throughout their retired life will now additionally depend on their varying abilities to manage longevity risks as consumers in a complex de-cumulation market.

However, notwithstanding these limitations, downplaying the social regulatory features of reforms over the last two decades denies the agency of actors with agendas different from a neoliberal one. This, in turn, leads to an underestimation of the potential for further meaningful reforms to the system, reforms that could further incrementally shift the underpinnings of the current public–private mix in a progressive direction (see Ebbinghaus, 2005). Yet, in circumstances where few expect the overarching financialisation paradigm to be overturned (Berry, 2015: 511), the only alternative to the promotion of such an agenda is a counsel of despair.

In the final section, two such reforms will be suggested as priorities. These represent feasible ways of addressing in a significant way some of the existing system's limitations.

Enhancing the socially protective features of the UK's financialised pension system

The main focus of this chapter has been on the interaction between socially protective agendas and pension financialisation as it has transformed the non-state sphere over the last two decades. The aim has been to show the possibilities for agency in mitigating some neoliberal features of pension financialisation. It is thus on this aspect of the current UK public–private mix that this section will concentrate. Two policy proposals are outlined, designed to improve the socially protective features of non-state provision, making it more generous and more predictable. Concentration on these policy areas should not, however, be taken to suggest that no important reforms of the public system are also required. Of these, the most important is further progress towards a citizenship or residence-based minimum standard, particularly to ensure equal entitlement between men and women. This was proposed by the 2005 Pension Commission report but was not picked up by New Labour. While the triple lock, the single-tier pension and improved crediting arrangements have significantly improved the situation for citizens mainly reliant on flat-rate public provision, entitlement gaps still persist that only a non-contributory provision can fill (Pension Policy Institute, 2014; Foster and Heneghan, 2018).

Improving pension adequacy by phased rises in the employer contribution

The increased coverage of workplace pensions since auto-enrolment is an important achievement but the quality of this provision,[7] particularly the level of contributions, is also central if it is to play a significant role in the universal delivery of an adequate retirement income. In this respect, the post-2012 situation looks less positive. Average contribution levels have fallen, for two reasons. First, when replacing their defined benefit schemes, employers have set contribution levels in new schemes at a much lower level. Thus, in 2012, before the impact of auto-enrolment (see later), the weighted average total contribution to defined contribution schemes was only 9.7 per cent of earnings compared to 20.2 per cent for defined benefit schemes (ONS, 2012). The second reason has been the very low contribution level associated with auto-enrolment. Thus, on its introduction, employers were only required to contribute 1 per cent of band earnings to schemes, with employees contributing another 1 per cent. This rose to 3 per cent from both parties in April 2016 and is due to increase to 8 per cent overall in April 2019 when employee contributions rise to 5 per cent. ONS data show that many employers with new auto-enrolled employees have paid the lowest contribution to which they are mandated (ONS, 2018a). Consequently, the weighted average contribution level for defined contribution pensions has fallen from 9.7 per cent in 2012 to 3.4 per cent in 2017 (ONS, 2017). In short, occupational pension coverage has sharply increased but only quite small amounts of money are going into many citizens' pension pots.

Most commentators agree that such contribution levels are too low to secure pensions that, in combination with public provision, provide citizens with an adequate retirement income. The independent Pensions Policy Institute, using the Pension Commission's target replacement rates[8] as its indicator of adequacy, suggests that a 25-year-old median earner with a full national insurance contribution record would need to save 10 per cent throughout their working life to hit their adequacy target. A woman of the same age on the same wages who takes caring breaks would need to save 8.5 percentage points more than this (Pension Policy Institute, 2013). Similarly, research done by the International Longevity Centre in 2017, using an adequacy standard of a 70 per cent net replacement rate, found that citizens entering the workforce today would require an 18 per cent savings rate every year to achieve this target (Franklin and Hochlaf, 2017: 34–42).

The Department for Work and Pensions accepts contribution levels are too low. Its latest review of auto-enrolment concedes that '[c]urrent saving levels present a substantial risk that the retirement expectations for a significant proportion of the working-age population will not be supported' (DWP, 2017: 8). Around 12 million individuals, it suggests, are projected not to be 'saving enough' for an adequate retirement income, constituting 38 per cent of the working-age population (DWP, 2017). Its solution is more saving by individuals (Lewis, 2017). In the meantime, removing the lower earnings limit, which would increase saving levels among part-time workers, and beginning auto-enrolment from 18 rather than 21 are proposed to increase savings levels (DWP, 2017).

Yet, these proposals ignore an obvious alternative that has much more to commend it given stagnant wage levels and young citizens facing severe financial challenges in the housing market and as a consequence of student fees. This is a phased increase in the minimum employer contribution. This was the path taken by the mandated Australian occupational system after its establishment in 1992. From a starting point of 3 per cent, the employer contribution has risen incrementally since such that it now stands at 9.5 per cent with 12 per cent planned by 2025 (Gelepithis, 2018a). A similar, and perhaps quicker, increase is a reasonable expectation in the UK, particularly for large and medium-sized companies currently paying the minimum rate or who have substantially decreased their pension contributions after closing their defined benefit schemes. Employer organisations would no doubt resist such a change but they are not in a strong position to argue against it on the basis of affordability: corporate profitability has been robust since the financial crisis in 2009 (ONS, 2018b); dividend payments have remained high in 2018 (Link Assets Services, 2018) after a record year in 2017; and the mean pay ratio between FTSE 100 chief executive officers and the mean pay package of their employees was 145:1 in 2018, significantly up from 2017 (CIPD, 2018). Moreover, at least some companies have benefited financially in recent years from the closure of their defined benefit schemes, some to existing members as well as new ones (Tichá, 2018). The Trades Union Congress (TUC) favours a rise to 10 per cent of banded earnings, with employees paying 5 per cent, but even a doubling of the current lower rate by the early 2020s would make a significant difference to the projected size of workers' pension pots.

However, such a change, while welcome, would do nothing to change the risk burden that individuals face in today's more financialised system. It is to this issue that we now turn.

New approaches to risk-sharing

The great shift of risk away from collective institutions (public or work-based) and towards individualised defined contribution provision in the delivery of pensions above the minimum standard has increased uncertainty and raised the scope for arbitrary variations in pension levels between individuals, particularly between cohorts. Similar levels of lifetime contributions can deliver very different pension outcomes. This is illustrated by projections undertaken by the Pensions Policy Institute, using historic investment returns, which show the varying size of projected pension pots over time for individuals identical in terms of pay, size and years of contribution and age of retirement (Sharp, 2017). Thus, in 2000, a man on median pay who paid 8 per cent of their wages into a typical defined contribution scheme for 40 years would have accrued a pension pot of £306,272. A year later, this would have been £18,000 lower due to the collapse in shares following the bursting of the Dot.com bubble. A further fall, to £213,844, would have been experienced if the individual retired in 2003, but up to 2017, the size of pots would have risen as stock markets recovered (Sharp, 2017).

Up to 2015, these variations in the accumulation stage could be compounded by the similarly arbitrary impact in the de-cumulation stage of varying annuity rates. Post-2015 liberalisation has removed this unpredictability as an inherent feature of the system, but this means that outcomes will now mainly be a product of individuals' varying abilities to manage risk in a complex de-cumulation market. Early indications are not promising. Knowledge of the relevant financial products and their limitations is shockingly deficient (International Longevity Centre, 2016). The take-up of advice is low (Thurley, 2018: 26). Evidence of scams and 'misselling' is already strong (Maclean, 2018). Even increased financial education and advice, the current government's favoured response, would likely have a minor impact. As the Pensions Institute has concluded: 'some risks have to be experienced before they can be genuinely understood, and often it is too late by that stage to do anything about them' (Blake, 2016: 35).

It is clear there were concerns within the Coalition government about these developments and their possible consequences. Parallel to Osborne's promotion of individualisation through 'pension freedoms', the Liberal Democrat Pensions Minister, Steve Webb, was considering new strategies for sharing risk during accumulation. He particularly sought to promote a halfway house pension form between defined benefit and defined contribution. This would set a 'defined ambition' for participants' final pension but allow greater flexibility in the delivery of this target. One model for such schemes was Dutch and Danish occupational schemes, which operated on a conditional defined contribution (CDC) basis. Instead of having individual accounts, investments in these schemes are pooled and managed by trustees. Pooling means that benefits are more stable than in individual schemes, with a smoothing between generations of retirees of arbitrary variations in investment markets. Proponents of such reforms argue that as well as collectivising risk between members, collective investing also leads to superior returns as costs are lower and longer time horizons can be taken (Pitt-Watson et al, 2014), but evidence is still mixed on this (DWP, 2014).

CDC was presented in 2013/14 mainly as a means by which employers, considering further closures of their defined benefit provision, could do so without passing risk entirely onto their employees. Yet, as some commentators have more recently suggested (Parker, 2013; Bennett, 2018), it has potential beyond this rather limited objective: it could also be used to increase risk-sharing options in the defined contribution world, particularly its auto-enrolled part. Such an approach would involve the introduction of CDC options as part of NEST and, in time, the other Master Trusts. For example, new members of NEST could be given the option of placing their money in a collective fund rather than the default retirement date funds, or this decision could be made by employers in consultation with workers. Collective funds would specify a target retirement income for members, thus offering a greater degree of certainty than present schemes, and would smooth arbitrary variations in returns between generations, meaning that risk-sharing was increased.

Conclusion

In his analysis of public–private interaction in the development of US pension and health policies, Jacob Hacker (2002: 42) referred to the 'subterranean' nature of the political processes surrounding the private elements of welfare systems when compared to purely public ones. These tended to be less visible and of lower political salience, and because they were generally more complex, they were less traceable in terms of responsibility for particular outcomes (Hacker, 2002: 43). Yet, these private elements provided large amounts of benefit to a wide range of citizens and had significant distributive consequences.

This chapter has focused on the 'subterranean' politics of UK pension financialisation in the last two decades. It has argued that such an approach is essential if the nature and impact of this process is to be properly understood. By highlighting public–private interaction, the clash between financialising agendas and socially protective ones, and the importance of public (social) regulation as well as public provision, the chapter has shown UK pension financialisation to have been a negotiated process, involving a much greater diversity of agendas and actors than recently suggested. It has not solely been driven by the state and it has not left neoliberalism unchallenged as an ideological policy guide. It has resulted in a system that has changed the *nature* of public responsibility rather than removed it entirely.

There is scope for further consideration of this subterranean world by social policy scholars. Important work has been – and continues to be – done on tax relief (eg Sinfield, 2000), but, generally speaking, research has not engaged as fully as it might have done with the regulatory interface between public and private pension spheres. This is not just a problem for policy analysis; it is also problematic for those anxious to move pension policy in a more progressively socially protective direction. What scope is there for political agency if the regulatory debates and struggles outlined in this chapter are discounted, and pension financialisation is instead presented as a fully determined neoliberal process deeply entrenched for the foreseeable future? In contrast to this latter view, the chapter has thus also sought to show that continued possibilities for potentially transformative incremental reforms exist in 2019, and that a feasible reform agenda is available by which the current system could be made more progressive. Proponents of untrammelled neoliberal financialisation will oppose this agenda but, as has been shown earlier, there is no reason to believe that they will inevitably be successful.

Notes

[1] I am grateful to Thomais Massala for this valuable analytical insight.

[2] Initially to 1 per cent, and after industry pressure, to 1.5 per cent.

[3] To pay for these reforms, the state pension age would rise incrementally to 68 between 2020 and 2050, a change that could be justified given increasing longevity. The Pensions Commission (2005: 96) sought to stabilise the percentage of the adult life spent in retirement, a figure that had increased steadily since 1950.

[4] The Coalition government also introduced a Single Tier State Pension, on a phased basis, set above the previous means-tested minimum, and abolished contracting out. In the short term, this benefits more citizens than it disadvantages, but over the longer term, it means lower public pensions for most, notwithstanding that it rises in line with wages, inflation or 2.5 per cent, whichever is highest (Crawford et al, 2013).

[5] The BSP is increased in relation to wages, inflation or 2.5 per cent, whichever is larger.

[6] The Pension Regulator has been promising to publish a list of authorised Master Trust schemes, detailing which financial companies are providing them, but has not yet done so.

[7] This is not to say that more could be done to improve coverage among part-time workers, the self-employed and those working on irregular and short-term contracts.

[8] Updated to 2012 earnings, these suggested: 80 per cent replacement rates for those with annual earnings up to £12,000; 70 per cent for incomes between £12,000 and £22,100; 67 per cent for the £22,100–£31,600 band; 60 per cent for the £31,600–£50,500 band; and 50 per cent for those above this.

References

Agulnik, P. (1999) The proposed S2P, *Fiscal Studies*, 20(4): 409–21.

Benish, A., Haber, H. and Eliahou, R. (2017) The regulatory welfare state in pension markets: mitigating high charges for low-income savers in the United Kingdom and Israel, *Journal of Social Policy*, 46(2): 313–30.

Bennett, P. (2018) Written evidence from Philip Bennett to the House of Commons Work and Pensions Select Committee inquiry into collective defined contribution schemes, www.parliament.uk/ business/committees/committees-a-z/commons-select/work-and-pensions-committee/inquiries/parliament-2017/collective-pension-schemes-17-19/

Berry, C. (2015) Citizenship in a financialised society: financial inclusion and the state before and after the crash, *Policy and Politics*, 43(4): 509–25.

Berry, C. (2016) Austerity, ageing and the financialisation of pensions policy in the UK, *British Politics*, 11(1): 2–25.

Blake, D. (2016) Independent review of retirement income report: we need a national narrative: building a consensus around retirement income, www.pensions-institute.org/IRRIReport.pdf

Bridgen, P. (2010) Towards a social democratic pension system? Assessing the significance of the 2007 and 2008 Pensions Acts, in I. Greener, C. Holden and M. Kilkey (eds) *Social policy review 22: Analysis and debate in social policy 2010*, Bristol: Policy Press, pp 71–96.

Bridgen, P. and Meyer, T. (2005) When do benevolent capitalists change their mind? Explaining the retrenchment of defined benefit pensions in Britain, *Social Policy and Administration*, 39(4): 764–85.

Bridgen, P. and Meyer, T. (2007) Private pensions versus social inclusion? Three patterns of provision and their impact, in T. Meyer, P. Bridgen and B. Riedmuller (eds) *Private pensions versus social inclusion? Non-state provision for citizens at risk in Europe*, Cheltenham: Edward Elgar.

Bridgen, P. and Meyer, T. (2018) Individualisation reversed: the cross-class politics of social regulation in the UK's public/private pension mix, *Transfer: European Review of Labour and Research*, 24(1): 25–41.

CIPD (The Chartered Institute of Personnel and Development) (2018) Executive pay: review of FTSE 100 executive pay, http://highpaycentre.org/files/CEO_pay_report.pdf

Clark, G.L. (2012) From corporatism to public utilities: workplace pensions in the 21st century, *Geographical Research*, 50(1): 31–46.

Crawford, R., Keynes, S. and Tetlow, G. (2013) A single-tier pension: what does it really mean?, Institute for Fiscal Studies, www.ifs.org.uk/comms/r82.pdf

Cumbo, J. (2014a) Nest pension restrictions to be lifted in 2017, *The Financial Times*, 8 September, www.ft.com/content/23f8d51a-374f-11e4-b45c-00144feabdc0

Cumbo, J. (2014b) 'No going back on pension charges' – Webb, *The Financial Times*, 16 October, www.ft.com/content/ebe39dba-5556-11e4-89e8-00144feab7de

Cumbo, J. (2015) Webb threatens to 'name and shame' high-charging pensions, *The Financial Times*, 27 February, www.ft.com/content/4ac67706-bdaa-11e4-8cf3-00144feab7de

Cumbo, J. (2018) Popular workplace pension schemes to quit UK market, 7 August, www.ft.com/content/80bd716a-9976-11e8-9702-5946bae86e6d

Cutler, T. and Waine, B. (2001) Social insecurity and the retreat from social democracy: occupational welfare in the long boom and financialisation, *Review of International Political Economy*, 18(1): 96–118.

Davies, A., Freeman, J. and Pemberton, H. (2018) 'Everyman a capitalist?' or 'Free to choose'? Exploring the tensions within Thatcherite individualism, *Historical Journal*, 61(2): 477–501.

DWP (Department for Work and Pensions) (1998) *Partnership in pensions*, London: HMSO.

DWP (2006) *Personal accounts: A new way to save*, London: DWP.

DWP (2014) *Better workplace pensions: Further measures for savers*, London: DWP.

DWP (2015a) *The charge cap: Guidance for trustees and managers of occupational schemes*, London: DWP.

DWP (2015b) Pension freedoms protected and new breed of pension schemes become law, www.gov.uk/government/news/pension-freedoms-protected-and-new-breed-of-pension-schemes-become-law

DWP (2017) *Automatic enrolment review 2017: Maintaining the momentum*, Cm 9546, London: DWP.

Ebbinghaus, B. (2005) Can path dependence explain institutional change? Two approaches applied to welfare state reform, MPIfG Discussion Paper 05/2, www.mpifg.de/pu/mpifg_dp/dp05-2.pdf

Epstein, G.A. (2006) Introduction: financialization and the world economy, in G.A. Epstein (ed) *Financialization and the world economy*, Cheltenham and Northampton: Edward Elgar, pp 3–16.

Esping-Andersen, G. (1990) *The three worlds of welfare capitalism*, Cambridge: Polity Press.

Evandrou, M. and Falkingham, J. (2005) A secure retirement for all? Older people and New Labour, in J. Hills and K. Stewart (eds) *A more equal society? New Labour, poverty, inequality and exclusion*, Bristol: Policy Press, pp 167–88.

Foster, L. and Heneghan, M. (2018) Pensions planning in the UK: A gendered challenge, *Critical Social Policy*, 38(2): 345–66.

Franklin, B. and Hochlaf, D. (2017) The global savings gap, https://ilcuk.org.uk/the-global-savings-gap/

Gelepithis, M. (2018a) Three paths to more encompassing supplementary pensions, *Journal of Social Policy*, 39(7): 764–85.

Gelepithis, M. (2018b) Institutional mismatch, party reputation, and industry interests: Understanding the politics of private-heavy pension system. *Political Studies*, 66(3): 735–51.

Ginn, J. (2003) *Gender, pensions and the life course. How pensions need to adapt to changing family forms*, Bristol: Policy Press.

Grady, J. (2015) Gendering pensions: making women visible, *Gender, Work and Organization*, 22(5): 445–58.

Hacker, J. (2002) *The divided welfare state. The battle over public and private social benefits in the United States*, Cambridge: Cambridge University Press.

Harrison, D., Blake, D. and Dowd, K. (2014) *VfM: Assessing value for money in defined contribution default funds*, London: Cass Business School, http://openaccess.city.ac.uk/6808/1/ValueForMoney%20%282%29.pdf

Hyde, M. and Dixon, J. (2008) A comparative analysis of mandated private pension arrangements, *International Journal of Social Economics*, 35(1/2): 49–62.

Hyde, M., Dixon, J. and Drover, G. (2003) Welfare retrenchment or collective responsibility? The privatisation of public pensions in Western Europe, *Social Policy and Society*, 2(3): 189–97.

International Longevity Centre (2016) What works? A review of the evidence on financial capability interventions and older people in retirement. A report by the International Longevity Centre, https://ilcuk.org.uk/wp-content/uploads/2018/10/What-works.pdf

Langley, P. (2010) *The everyday life of global finance: Saving and borrowing in Anglo-America*, Oxford: Oxford University Press.

Leisering, L. (ed) (2011) *The new regulatory state. Regulating private pensions in Germany and the UK*, Basingstoke: Palgrave.

Lewis, P. (2017) Workplace pensions: employers need to pay more into our pensions, *The Financial Times*, 16 August, www.ft.com/content/e88d7192-790a-11e7-a3e8-60495fe6ca71

Link Assets Services (2018) UK dividend monitor Q3 2018, www.linkassetservices.com/our-thinking/uk-dividend-monitor-q3-2018

Mabbett, D. (2011) The regulatory politics of private pensions in the UK and Germany, in L. Leisering (ed) *The new regulatory state. Regulating pensions in Germany and the UK*, Basingstoke: Palgrave, pp 191–210.

Maclean, M. (2018) Pension freedoms guidance is too little too late, *Money Marketing*, 2 March, www.moneymarketing.co.uk/issues/1-march-2018/malcolm-mclean-pensions-freedoms-guidance-faff-little-late/

Mares, I. (2001) Firms and the welfare state: when, why, and how does social policy matter to employers?, in P. Hall and D. Soskice (eds) *Varieties of capitalism: The institutional foundations of comparative advantage*, Oxford: Oxford University Press, pp 184–212.

Marshall, T.H. (2009) Citizenship and social class, in I. Manza and A. Sauder (eds) *Inequality and society*, New York, NY: W.W. Norton and Co, pp 148–54.

Massala, T. (2018) Restructuring social protection: investment, regulation and the financialization of UK pensions, Thesis submitted for the degree of Doctor of Philosophy, University of Bath.

Meyer, T. and Bridgen, P. (2008) Class, gender and chance: the social division of welfare and occupational pensions in the United Kingdom, *Ageing & Society*, 28(3): 353–81.

Meyer, T. and Bridgen, P. (2012) Business, regulation and welfare politics in liberal capitalism, *Policy and Politics*, 40(3): 387–403.

NEST (National Employment Savings Trust) (2018) NEST corporation publishes its annual reports and accounts 2017/18, www.nestpensions.org.uk/schemeweb/nest/nestcorporation/news-press-and-policy/press-releases/NEST-Corporation-publishes-its-annual-reports-and-accounts-2017-18.html

OFT (Office of Fair Trading) (2013) Defined contribution workplace pension market study, OFT 1505, https://webarchive.nationalarchives.gov.uk/20131101172428/http://oft.gov.uk/shared_oft/market-studies/oft1505

ONS (Office for National Statistics) (2012) Occupational pensions schemes survey, UK: 2012, www.ons.gov.uk/peoplepopulationandcommunity/personalandhouseholdfinances/pensionssavingsandinvestments/datasets/occupationalpensionschemessurvey

ONS (2017) Occupational pensions schemes survey, UK: 2017, www.ons.gov.uk/peoplepopulationandcommunity/personalandhouseholdfinances/pensionssavingsandinvestments/bulletins/occupationalpensionschemessurvey/uk2017

ONS (2018a) Pension participation at record high but contributions cluster at minimum level, www.ons.gov.uk/employmentandlabourmarket/peopleinwork/workplacepensions/articles/pensionparticipatonatrecordhighbutcontributionsclusteratminimumlevels/2018-05-04

ONS (2018b) Profitability of UK companies: April to June 2018, www.ons.gov.uk/economy/nationalaccounts/uksectoraccounts/bulletins/profitabilityofukcompanies/apriltojune2018

Oude Nijhuis, D. (2013) *Labor divided in the postwar European welfare state: The Netherlands and the United Kingdom*, Cambridge: Cambridge University Press.

Parker, I. (2013) Defining ambitions: shaping pension reform around public attitudes, Institute for Public Policy Research, www.ippr.org/publications/defining-ambitions-shaping-pension-reform-around-public-attitudes

Paterson, J. (2013) Nest restrictions to be lifted in 2017, *Employee Benefits*, 9 July, www.employeebenefits.co.uk/issues/july-online-2013/nest-restrictions-to-be-lifted-in-2017/

Pemberton, H. (2012) The failure of 'nationalization by attraction': Britain's cross-class alliance against earnings-related pensions in the 1950s, *Economic History Review*, 65(4): 1428–49.

Pension Policy Institute (2013) The impact of the NEST contribution limits and restrictions to transfers, Briefing report 63, www.pensionspolicyinstitute.org.uk/research/research-reports/?year=2013&t=BriefingNotes

Pension Policy Institute (2014) The impact of the government's single-tier state pension reform, PPI Single Tier Series: Paper No. 1, www.pensionspolicyinstitute.org.uk/research/research-reports/?year=2014&t=Reports

Pensions Commission (2005) *A new pensions settlement for the twenty-first century. The second report of the Pensions Commission*, London: The Stationery Office, www.webarchive.org.uk/wayback/archive/20070801230000/http://www.pensionscommission.org.uk/index.html

Personal Accounts Delivery Authority (2009) Myth buster, www.padeliveryauthority.org.uk/documents/myth_buster_v3.pdf

Pitt-Watson, D., Stanley, N. and Wesbroom, K. (2014) Collective pension plans, briefing note, www.thersa.org/discover/publications-and-articles/reports/collective-pension-plans-briefing-notes

Sharp, T. (2017) Workers should be protected from pensions roulette, www.tuc.org.uk/blogs/workers-should-be-protected-pensions-roulette

Sinfield, A. (2000) Tax benefits in non-state pensions, *European Journal of Social Security*, 2(2): 137–67.

The Pension Regulator (2018) Check if your scheme is a master trust, www.thepensionsregulator.gov.uk/en/master-trust-pension-schemes/check-if-your-scheme-is-a-master-trust-

Thurley, D. (2018) Pensions guidance: pension wise, House of Commons Library briefing paper Number CBP-7042, 26 September, https://researchbriefings.parliament.uk/ResearchBriefing/Summary/SN07042

Tichá, V. (2018) DB closure to future accrual gathers pace as just 4% open to new members, finds research, *Professional Pensions*, 2 May, www.professionalpensions.com/professional-pensions/news/3031534/db-closure-to-future-accrual-gathers-pace-as-just-4-open-to-new-members-find-research

Timmins, N. (1995) *The five giants: A biography of the welfare state*, London: Harper Collins.

Titmuss, R. (1958) *Essays on the welfare state*, London: Allen and Unwin.

Townsend, P. (1979) *Poverty in the United Kingdom*, London: Penguin.

Trampusch, C. (2007) Industrial relations as a source of solidarity in times of welfare state retrenchment, *Journal of Social Policy*, 36(2): 197–215.

van der Zwan, N. (2014) Making sense of financialization, *Socio-Economic Review*, 12(1): 99–129.

Veit-Wilson, J. (1994) Condemned to deprivation? Beveridge's responsibility for the invisibility of poverty, in J. Hills, J. Ditch and H. Glennerster (eds) *Beveridge and social security. An international retrospective*, Oxford: Clarendon Press, pp 97–117.

Waine, B. (1995) A disaster foretold? The case of personal pension, *Social Policy and Administration*, 29(4): 317–34.

Watson, M. (2009) Planning for the future of asset-based welfare: New Labour, financialised economic agency and the housing market, *Planning, Practice and Research*, 24(1): 41–56.

Watson, M. (2013) New Labour's 'paradox of responsibility' and the unravelling of its macroeconomic policy, *British Journal of Politics and International Relations*, 15(1): 6–22.

World Bank (1994) *Averting the old age crisis. A World Bank policy research report*, New York, NY: Oxford University Press.

4

Towards a whole-economy approach to the welfare state: citizens, corporations and the state within the broad welfare mix

Kevin Farnsworth

Introduction

As welfare states have evolved, so their size, complexity, aims and functions have grown. Political systems and economies have similarly evolved and morphed into different forms so that it is increasingly difficult to capture what constitutes the welfare state and its interrelated forms without looking beyond the traditional social policy lens. In this chapter, it is maintained that we need to consider the complex ways in which a whole range of public and social policies and non-state provision (including, among other things, wages, taxation, regulations and private, occupational, third sector and informal welfare) come together and, in some cases, collide to shape and reshape the overall welfare mix. In addition, we need to examine how welfare funding, service provision and welfare receipts by one party within the welfare mix sit alongside other public policies and private (including citizens') provision, much of which does not appear on the social policy radar. In short, the focus of social policy needs to be broadened, going beyond the mixed economy towards a whole economy of welfare approach.

The structure of the chapter proceeds as follows. The first section examines the relevant literature that helps to shed light on the way in which social policy has been theorised, explored and explained. Existing literature is argued to be too narrow in focus and scope. The second section sets out and maps the whole economy of welfare approach advocated here. The third section draws on data in order to explore how different configurations of taxation, provision and regulation are distributed within different welfare states.

Section one: Pushing at the boundaries of the welfare state: considering the mixed economy of welfare

As is customary in work that seeks to look beyond the narrow frame of social welfare, our starting point is Richard's Titmuss (1958) conceptualisation of the social division of welfare approach. In carving out the emergent subject in the 1960s and 1970s, Titmuss perceived of social policy in a more radical, wide-ranging and less constrained way than many who have followed him. His *social division of welfare approach* recognised the important distinction between the different ways of funding and providing welfare and the implications that flow from this. In 1958, he mapped out what would later come to be known as the mixed economy of welfare or welfare pluralist approach, a typology that continues to have traction to this day. The importance of revisiting Titmuss's work is not so much that it contains the blueprint that helped to define the shape of the subject of social policy as it emerged, but the fact that it highlights the importance of looking beyond the immediate when it comes to the conceptualisation of the welfare state. Titmuss viewed social policy as being made up of social welfare (provided by the state in the form of direct benefits and services), fiscal welfare (also provided by the state, but in the form of tax breaks to purchase 'welfare'-related services, primarily from the private sector) and occupational welfare (mostly provided by employers). The most important contribution of Titmuss is that he forces us to look beyond direct state provision. A weakness is that it is far too citizen-centric, meaning that it neglects employers and businesses as political actors and as major beneficiaries within the welfare mix while recognising their role in occupational welfare.

In defining what was 'in' and 'out' as far as the conceptualisation of social policy was concerned, Titmuss was guided by his assessment of the 'effects' of different activities of the state and others (including employers) on citizens' incomes and well-being as defining features of 'welfare'. The argument here (see also Farnsworth, 2012, 2013) is that we need a much broader focus. This is becoming more, not less, important as welfare states and capitalism itself are subject to deeper crises and challenges and as the battle lines between Left and Right and rich and poor become more sharply drawn. Social policy scholars ought to take seriously Adrian Sinfield's (1978) challenge outlined 40 years ago: to move beyond the divisions that lie between occupational, social and fiscal welfare and towards an analysis of economic, political and social divisions in welfare more broadly. Titmuss himself grounds social policy in economic context more clearly in his *Commitment to welfare* in 1968 (Titmus, 1968), and Alan Walker developed this idea further in an important contribution to the debate in 1988. Walker argues that the erroneous separation of economy and social policy so that the latter is subservient to the former has tended to stifle welfare. His argument is that we need to bring the two together in order to more clearly see the connections between the two, in particular, the role of social policy in the distribution of resources and life chances (Walker, 1988: 2). The value of Walker's contribution, in particular, is that he argues that we need to focus on the interrelationship between economic and social policy. The two do not operate in isolation from each other, but have a bearing on each other. From a different starting point, Walker argues that economics has tended to dominate and shape social policy thinking so that the objectives of social policy play second fiddle to economic objectives. The dangers are all too obvious: restricting social policies to those that operate in the interests of the economy and restricting analysis of social policy to the narrow 'non-economic' (see Walker, 1988: 2–3). I would add that different elements and different forms of economic and social policy have an impact upon one another and so both disciplines, and others, need a broader, more thorough and more sophisticated grasp of each other. Where Walker focuses mainly on government policy, I argue that similar arguments need to be applied to the study and analysis of social policy.

Rein and Rainwater (1986) suggest that we can deal with such challenges by refocusing on 'welfare society' rather than the 'welfare state'. This would, they argue, enable a more meaningful discussion of how various actors and institutions contribute to the total delivery of welfare within different welfare systems. Similarly, Iversen (2005: 5; see also Iversen and Cusack, 2000) argues that 'Standard approaches to the welfare state fail to account for the relationship between production and social protection'. Perhaps a good summary of the previous arguments is that the sometimes arbitrary boundaries between the academic study of social, public and economic policy need to be broken down or, at least, constantly tested.

Some, of course, have already ventured into the terrain being argued for here. Michael Cahill's 'New Social Policy' approach sought to broaden the focus of social policy beyond 'service'-based categories to ask where and how social policies interact with other public policies and create welfare – or diswelfare – effects. Cahill (1994) is concerned with the third of society that are unable to consume in the same way as the wealthiest two thirds and are thus excluded from communications, transport, shopping, working and other economic and social categories by their relatively low incomes. The 'well-being' literature incorporates other variables, from job security to access to clean and affordable water (OECD, 2005). Food (Dowler, 2003: 698–717) has also been 'brought in', as has *corporate welfare* (Whitfield, 2001; Farnsworth, 2012, 2013, 2015). Furthermore, the critical social policy literature has examined wider structural inequalities and discrimination promoted by prejudice, ignorance and power, often linked to systemic problems found in social, economic and political spheres (Williams, 1989). Still others have urged us to look beyond economic distribution and redistribution towards predistribution (Hacker, 2011). Outside academia, the United Nations' (UN's) Sustainable Development Goals and the global business elite constituted as the World Economic Forum focus on the intricate relationship between social and public policies, work, consumption, inequality, and the environment: the former identifying the myriad range of unconnected goals that need to be addressed for human development to continue; the latter focusing on the range of factors that need to be in place in order for businesses and economies to prosper.

Various commentators have discussed the different categories of welfare and related public policies, some have discussed the economic and political functions of the welfare state, others have discussed the distribution of state provision to different individuals and organisations, and still others have discussed the ways in which competing interests shape public and social policies. However, few, if any, have tied these issues together. The challenge is not only to *bring such perspectives in* to social policy, but *to keep them in view* and examine how they interact with each other to shape welfare objectives, influence the distribution of resources and impact upon welfare outcomes. Furthermore, we should resist the temptation to carve up contributions to the mixed economy into isolated parts that often exist as isolated chapters in textbooks. The mixed economy of welfare contains various benefits, services and policies that make up a whole, that exist together in space and time, and that interact with each other. We have to examine the multiple social, political and economic interdependencies that exist, and Institutionalised Political Economy offers a theoretical framework to achieve this.

Towards an institutionalised political economy of welfare

Political economy approaches view the economy as having 'a special weight in explaining and properly understanding polity and politics'

(Gough, 2011: 50). As Iversen (2005) argues, economic production is key to the funding, aims and delivery of social policies. The inclusion of economic production can be further extended here to an analysis of the production of welfare services themselves. The distribution of power and the way in which it is distributed within welfare institutions are also important in setting the capacities, capabilities and overall shape of the welfare state (Korpi, 1989: 309–28).

As for the broader economy, productivity, employment, consumption, wages, tax revenues and the spending capacity of government are all central to overall levels of human welfare and well-being, but much more important are questions regarding the distribution of the costs and benefits of these activities and how the different players – employers, employees and governments – react and respond to the various risks they encounter. To give one example, governments may respond to factory closures in a particular area by boosting social protections (social welfare) or increasing subsidies and other protections for producers (corporate welfare), or a combination of the two. Producer subsidies, training subsidies, in-work subsidies, regulatory changes and tax breaks may all be utilised as part of a strategy to tackle the threat of unemployment, but the effects on employees, local communities and businesses could vary widely. The problem is that social policy research often fails to sufficiently examine how and why powerful actors and the prevailing economic and social challenges, as well as political institutional challenges, shape the choice of policy instrument (see also Cao et al, 2007).

As political economists focus on power within the context of economic structures, their interest in social policies tends to view social provision as reflecting the outcome of political struggle vis-a-vis capital and the state. Thus, James O'Connor (1973) incorporates within his analysis a discussion of the full range of public and social policies linked to the state. What is missing is sufficient attention paid to wages in kind (occupational welfare, employment 'perks' and general in-work benefits). Another problem associated with political economy approaches, at least the classical variety, is that the tendency to examine the big policy picture often gets in the way of policy detail.

Historical institutionalist approaches build upon political economy assumptions but place far greater emphasis on the importance of past politics, policy legacies, rules and actors. The work of Steinmo et al (1992), is helpful in broadening the focus to independent but connected institutions, operating according to their own internal logic, but also heavily influenced by their economic context, history, location, previous struggles and informal as well as formal constitutions. Institutional theories also illustrate how institutions bind the different players within capitalist economies in ways that are not always immediately obvious. Ebbinghaus and Manow (2001) point out, for example, that welfare states (operating through governments) and production regimes (operating through employers) respond to particular pressures by colluding together through complex institutional mechanisms to achieve particular goals. Collusion is the operative word here since responses do not necessarily operate in the interests of all. For example, by setting up social protection rules that enabled employers to shed older and more expensive employees through early retirement, especially during periods of economic stagnation, governments socialised the cost of redundancies.

Hall and Soskice's (2001) contention, in their work on different 'varieties of capitalism', is that we should place firms at the centre of social policy analysis. However, subsequent work within this framework tends to retreat into areas of specific focus in order to explain particular forms of public policymaking and so is rarely applied to the broader welfare mix. Nor do the existing classifications of welfare states based on liberal/coordinated market economies and the multiple worlds of welfare quite capture the complex relationships between different forms of welfare, different regulatory regimes, different industrial strategies, different growth strategies and different sized economies. The binary classification utilised in the varieties of capitalism literature in particular – between liberal and coordinated market economies – is too narrow and misses the point that liberal economies contain examples of very comprehensive and coordinated interventions within labour and production markets, especially when it comes to interventions to protect capital. While a lack of coordination within liberal economies may have led to the 2007 economic crisis, close, concerted and unprecedented levels of international and intra-national cooperation and coordination helped to limit the extent to which the crisis threatened to tear the very foundations of capitalism apart (Farnsworth and Irving, 2012).

Regarding the *worlds of welfare* or *welfare regime* literature, the core focus on the commodifying effects of markets and the potential decommodifying effects of social policies is important. While the contributions of Esping-Andersen (1990) and others that have followed his approach are useful in highlighting economic and political crises, class mobilisation, and political institutions as key factors in shaping welfare states, 'traditional' social policies offer only one of many ways in which capitalism may be managed and crises and conflicts resolved. Industrial policies, for instance, including industrial subsidies, may operate similarly by smoothing or managing the risks confronting capitalism and capitalists. However, industrial policy can also have positive welfare effects (Pfaller and Fink, 2011). Meanwhile, social welfare may decommodify labour, but corporate welfare may also operate to decommodify capital, including private markets.

Beyond the welfare state literature, work on competing regulatory regimes is useful in grasping the role of public policy in shaping welfare outcomes (Thelen, 1994). Kolberg and Esping-Andersen (2016), for instance, identify very different prevailing institutional regimes governing the interplay between social rights (within and outside the workplace), terms and conditions of work, and the engagement and involvement of the state in the policies (including the social policies) of firms. Also important here is the work on corporatism, social investment and industrial policies, which draws attention to the way in which a whole range of policy measures, from regulation, trade, taxation, grants and subsidies, are utilised to variously support local communities, workers and businesses. Industrial relations covers, among other things, terms and conditions of work, workplace representation, and rights at work, which, in turn, shape occupational welfare and overall levels of wage compensation. All of these issues are important to overall welfare. Moreover, because they are inextricably linked, they need to come under the social policy microscope.

Taken as a whole, these different perspectives point to a complex interrelationship of economic and political power (or forces) and political and economic institutions to policy outcomes. The Institutionalist Political Economy approach views institutions as important to shaping as well as constraining the behaviour of individuals operating within institutions, but also in maintaining a view of the economy as having 'special weight' as an explanatory force in the operation of capitalism and markets (Chang, 2001). The economy operates as a *structural* imperative that shapes and imposes constraints upon social and political institutions, and social policy is often shaped and constrained as much by the needs of the economy as the needs of citizens. Moreover, in determining the most desirable and effective way to deliver social welfare goals, policymakers often look beyond 'traditional' social policy entirely. Thus, social policies, public policies and economic policies are bound by multiple and complex threads to each other. The following section attempts to map the complex picture.

Section two: Mapping the whole-economy approach

The whole-economy approach invites us to look beyond the welfare activities of the state to other providers, to consider the importance of economic activities and production, to place the activities of businesses more at the heart of our analysis, to examine state largesse to businesses and other elite groups, and to focus on the terms and conditions of work and welfare and the regulatory sphere, as well as to reflect upon how power influences the distribution of resources and how the decisions of one actor or set of actors or policy measures in one area can influence the actions or decisions of other actors and other policy measures. Figure 4.1 maps out the 'whole economy of welfare'. Readers might observe that, for a whole economy, this is a relatively simple model. However, in capturing the whole economy, it does not pretend to be exhaustive. What it does do is capture and highlight the interrelated and complex picture of contributions and claims that accrue to, and are paid by, different actors – primarily citizens, business interests and state actors – within the whole economy of welfare. All transactions within the model have a major bearing on the ability of each agent to carry out even basic functions and coexist. Moreover, each agent within the whole economy directly and indirectly contributes to the overall capabilities of others. While commentators such as Nussbaum and Sen (1993) discuss the importance of the right conditions to increase the 'capabilities' of citizens within particular environments, it is possible to think of corporations and governments as similarly having capabilities enhanced or diminished by the particular set of conditions that prevail and are delivered or imposed by other actors within the whole.

The map in Figure 4.1 identifies the flow of resources – cash, services, commodities and taxes – between the four major actor-pillars of the welfare state: the state, businesses, citizens and the voluntary sector. It highlights the various forms that these flows can take and, in so doing, highlights the potential trade-offs and complex relationships between different forms of provision. In doing so, it raises important questions about the distribution and redistribution of resources within the whole economy, which is the subject of the following section.

Figure 4.1: The whole economy map

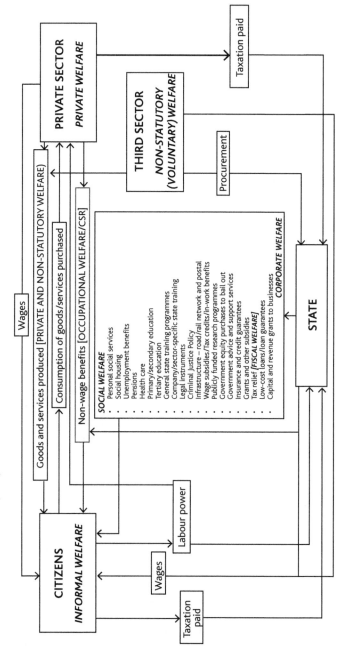

The distribution and redistribution of welfare within the whole economy

Many studies of distribution and redistribution focus on income and wealth transfers between one group or another. Studies that focus on income, gender, race or other inequalities in the distribution of cash or in-kind benefits are clearly important. However, so is the context within which such redistribution takes place. The argument here is that the contributions and benefits that are distributed and redistributed within the whole economy are interrelated. This is important not simply because power determines whether and how resources are redistributed, but also because of the effects of redistribution on incomes, profits or tax revenues. Complex relationships and multiple trade-offs exist between different policy options pursued within the public and private spheres. However, this is not to suggest that these are straightforward trade-offs pursued within a negative-sum game. The trade-offs are complex and shaped by politics and economic contexts, as well as other factors, such as policy legacies, the relative strength of employers and trade unions, the prevailing global politics of trade (which influences tariffs and subsidies, which also 'trade off' against each other) and the political complexion of government. A few examples can illustrate some of the key issues at stake.

First, as has been argued previously (O'Connor, 1973; Gough, 1979; Farnsworth and Holden, 2006; Hacker and Pierson, 2002), rival interests compete over public resources and, just as importantly, the distribution of the burden of paying for them. How governments raise and spend revenues has huge implications for the stability and sustainability of expenditure in future and on the distribution of income and wealth. Taxes may be progressive or regressive and fall differently between citizens and businesses, just as they fall disproportionately between different citizens and different businesses. Businesses may also bear different levels of tax burden – internationally mobile firms tend to face lower levels of taxation than immobile companies. Furthermore, the distribution of taxation has been as much of a battleground between competing interests as any other area of state governance (O'Connor, 1973). However, by imposing taxation in different ways on different constituents, or by reducing the tax burden through fiscal welfare, governments can dramatically alter income and wealth distributions – before they spend any of the money they have collected. Of course, how they subsequently spend these revenues will also have a big impact on final incomes. However, it is also clear that different interests struggle for different policy outcomes and solutions. Individuals may simultaneously fight for increases in National Health Service (NHS) spending while attacking unemployment benefits. Employers may call for increases in investment in higher education while arguing for cuts in corporation tax. To capture this complex picture, we need to look across social and public policies.

Second, Karl Polanyi (1957) and, later, Esping-Andersen (1990) drew attention to the decommodifying potential of social policies in providing protection to citizens in the wake of various social and economic problems (as already noted earlier). Corporate welfare operates in a similar way to decommodify markets for private businesses. In both instances, risks are socialised, leaving open the possibility that a range of policy options could have similar aims, most obviously in the decision of whether to act to prop up ailing businesses or act to protect citizens when businesses die. The two are not mutually exclusive, but there are complex complementarities, contradictions and trade-offs between a range of policies, only some of which tend to be the focus of social policy.

Third, social and public policies are often shaped as much by the needs of the economy as by the needs of citizens, and, of course, some of the core needs of citizens are a product of economic factors. This includes the negative impact of individual businesses and also the impact of endogenous macro and international economic factors. As Ruggie (1982) and Cao et al (2007) point out, policy responses are necessary to mediate the effects of international trade or the liberation of capital markets, but the actual policy instruments that are selected can vary widely. Although increased trade and globalisation may bring positive benefits for an economy overall, and some global businesses, they also bring risks to national industries, regions and citizenry. Significant numbers of individuals may bear real costs, especially in areas that are effectively devastated by the closure of old industries as former industrial centres are forced to close in the face of cheap imports (Iversen and Cusack, 2000). Social policies can (and should) compensate communities and individuals that, as a result, will bear disproportionate risks and costs, including higher unemployment, decimated local economies, poverty, falling property prices and ill health. Alternatively, states may seek to protect employees by increasing help and assistance to private companies. They may also try to offset the costs and risks that would otherwise be borne by employers through state subsidies, delivered directly (in cash or in kind) or indirectly (through tax breaks or wage subsidies). Here, politics matters: the extent to which governments intervene to compensate employers and employees for the effects of market liberalisation depends on whether government is dominated by parties of the Left or the Right (Garrett, 1998; Korpi, 1989).

Fourth, employers, whether in the public or private sector, rely heavily on the goodwill, cooperation, unpaid work and sacrifices of employees on a daily basis. Such efforts are often overlooked because the assumption is that workers are compensated for them through pay. Moreover, the day-to-day non-remunerated overtime, favours and kindnesses that are often necessary within work, especially when dealing with customers and/or service users, despite being hidden, are crucial to the functioning and profit-making of companies, just as they are important to effective public services.

Fifth, work, pay, community, environment and so on make up 'social quality', and taking each of these into account takes us beyond the social policy literature towards industrial relations and corporatist literatures, which transpose the analysis of power from macro-level national politics to the micro-level of the workplace with the concomitant and permanent struggles over the terms and conditions of work and the distribution of wages and occupational benefits (which increasingly extend to in-work state benefits) within the workplace. This is important because the outcome of such struggle may be as important to the welfare of (some) employees as state provision. The actions of others, the distribution of welfare and the distribution of power all play a part in shaping the overall welfare mix, a sentiment that is echoed by Kirk Mann (2009). Provision that is funded or delivered by one agent (whether employers, employees, citizens or the state), in various forms, helps to shape the decisions of other potential funders or delivery agents – and in the constant battle over resources, power and motivation matters.

Sixth, modern states rely on private companies to supply commodities and services that facilitate the operation of the state: private businesses contract with the state to build roads, bridges, railways, housing and other public buildings; they sell the technologies and medicines that underpin public health provision and run the care homes that provide 'public' care services to the elderly and disabled; and information technology (IT) companies provide the hardware and software that is so essential to the operation of the modern state. Some proportion of this contracting is essential – states could not efficiently produce all the infrastructure and materials they require in the delivery of state services – but governments often choose, for ideological or financial reasons, to contract with the private sector where they could deliver the outputs themselves.

Section three: What do the data tell us about the broad welfare mix?

This aim of this chapter so far has been to argue for a broadening and deepening of social policy approaches to move beyond the mixed economy of welfare to a whole economy of welfare approach. There are, of course, risks with such an approach, the major one being that focusing down facilitates subject discipline, precision and clarity. However, these risks are outweighed by the potential benefits. The approach advocated here does not suggest that all studies have to focus on every aspect of social policy, but suggests that researchers need to be aware of the broader context within which welfare is made, designed, delivered and interacts with other forms of provision. Within such a framework, it is possible to be selective in the variables and proxy measures that we draw together to better understand welfare societies or drill down on particular areas while maintaining some focus on the broader context.

Here, a limited range of indicative data that relate directly to some of the key forms of provision identified in the whole-economy map is drawn on. Data in four main areas are reviewed: taxation; corporate and social welfare; wages, occupational welfare and wage subsidies; and working conditions. Together, these areas provide some indication of the distribution of resources within the whole economy of welfare, but befitting a chapter that is as ambitious but space-limited as this, there is much that is left out. Remaining gaps will be filled in subsequent work.

Taxation and tax burdens

Governments raise revenues through imposing charges and profits on services, borrowing, and tax revenues. Of these, the only sustainable and realistic option in the long run is taxation. Taxes are levied on incomes (corporate and citizen), assets and consumption. The key taxes paid by individuals include income taxes, national insurance contributions, property taxes and taxes on consumption. Business taxes are levied on profits, capital gains and employment (in the form of payroll taxes and national insurance contributions). Of course, how governments tax and spend has huge implications for the stability and sustainability of expenditure in future, as well as on the distribution of income and wealth (see earlier).

As Figure 4.2 illustrates, the tax burden is distributed differently in various nations. It plots the tax take (as a percentage of gross domestic product (GDP)) for two different periods (2001–006 and 2011–16) and from two different sources (the key taxes levied on employers and employees, including income tax, national insurance and payroll taxes). The two periods lie either side of the 2007–08 economic crisis, which distorts the picture on many measures, and provides an illustration of the longer-term trends. Taking into account the major direct taxes on profits, capital gains and national insurance contributions (employer and employee) suggests that shifts in direct taxation have tended to reduce the amount levied on businesses and increase that levied on citizens. Taxes on businesses are relatively low, and taxation on citizens relatively high, in Canada, the US and the UK. In Germany, citizens similarly pay a relatively high proportion of the tax burden, although businesses also pay more compared with the UK, US and Canada. In Japan, the direct tax burden is balanced between businesses and citizens. In Sweden, Italy and France, the tax burden on businesses and citizens is relatively high. The period comparisons also point to small shifts in the tax burden in Canada, the US and UK, but larger shifts among the other nations. Italy, France, Japan and Germany all

Figure 4.2: The distribution of the tax burden (direct taxes as a percentage of GDP)

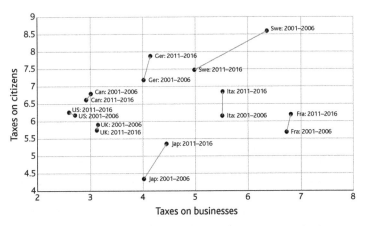

Source: Based on the Organisation for Economic Co-operation and Development's revenue statistics data series (stats.OECD.org)

increased the tax burden on citizens equivalent to around 1 per cent of GDP. France, Germany and Japan increased the burden on companies to a lesser extent. Only Sweden reduced the burden on both citizens and businesses, with a similar effect experienced by both groups.

Focusing in more detail on the UK, Figure 4.3 illustrates the relative tax burden placed on citizens and corporations. These figures are calculated by summing all taxes, direct and indirect, levied on individuals and businesses as compiled within the Organisation for Economic Co-operation and Development's (OECD's) revenue statistics. These data starkly reveal that since the 1970s, the relative tax burden on corporations has fallen and the tax burden on citizens has increased. In 1980, corporations paid 30 per cent of the overall tax burden, and citizens the remaining 70 per cent. By 2015, business' share had fallen to 23 per cent and citizens' share had risen to 75 per cent.

Tax expenditures and fiscal welfare are also important here. Both are provided to citizens and corporations by governments across most states, though, as Sinfield (2018) notes, they fulfil different functions at different times and across different states. Many tax breaks exist

Figure 4.3: The distribution of the tax burden, UK, 1970–2015

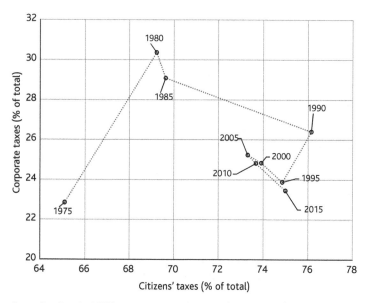

Source: Based on the OECD's revenue statistics data series (stats.OECD.org)

to support corporations, and some forms of fiscal welfare are not recognised as tax expenditures (see Sinfield, 2018).

As Titmuss and others have pointed out, it makes no difference to final incomes or profits whether state assistance takes the form of direct cash benefits or indirect tax benefits (Titmuss, 1958; Sinfield, 1978: 129–56; Howard, 1999). Furthermore, according to one of the few comparative studies of tax benefits, carried out by the OECD (2009), the UK has the most generous tax benefit systems of, and directs more assistance and support to businesses through tax expenditures than, the eight major economies it examined.

Two examples from the UK – Entrepreneur's Allowance and R&D tax credits – illustrate both the high costs of certain forms of provision and the ambiguities of the wider benefits to society. Entrepreneur's Relief is paid to a relatively low number of business owners who can dispose of businesses to avoid capital gains tax. The annual cost of this form of tax relief has expanded much faster than expected, and in 2017, was worth £4.2 billion. R&D tax credits, meanwhile, are considered to represent 'dead-weight' costs in that they make little or no difference to the level of research and development expenditure within firms. Her majesty's Revenue and Customs (HMRC), the Institute for Public Policy Research (IPPR) and the House of Common's Public Accounts Committee have all questioned whether these tax credits represent value for money. The IPPR (Cox and Schmuecker, 2010) estimated that 80 per cent of the costs of R&D tax credits, or £3 billion in 2017, are dead-weight costs. If we ignore evidence of the systematic abuse of tax allowances by businesses and the well-off (NAO, 2014), savings from ending R&D tax credits and Entrepreneur's Relief could more than pay for unemployment benefits. Considered another way, if the UK government raised the equivalent amount from corporation tax, employers' national insurance contributions and payroll taxes as France, it would be worth the equivalent of 6 per cent of GDP, or some £90 billion (though the exact amount would vary according to other intended and unintended behavioural effects).

Corporate versus social welfare

Next, I consider the relative generosity of business subsidies against unemployment benefits. Figure 4.4 charts the costs of both as a percentage of GDP. Here, business subsidies are made up of grants and other direct subsidies and exclude indirect subsidies (such as most

Figure 4.4: Business subsidies and unemployment benefits, various economies, 1995–2012

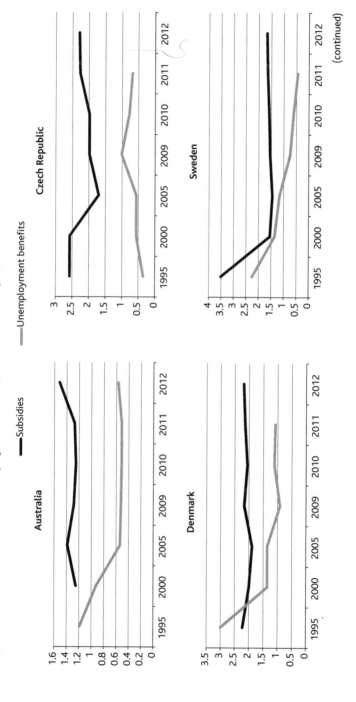

(continued)

Figure 4.4: Business subsidies and unemployment benefits, various economies, 1995–2012 (continued)

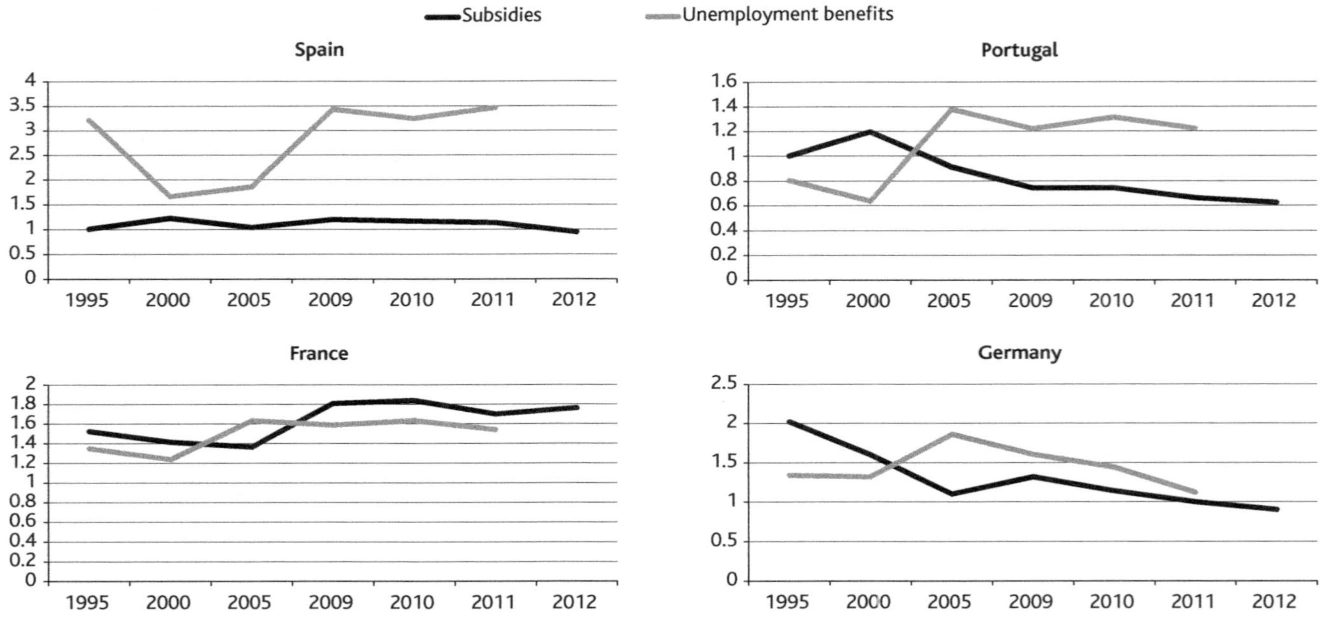

(continued)

Figure 4.4: Business subsidies and unemployment benefits, various economies, 1995–2012 (continued)

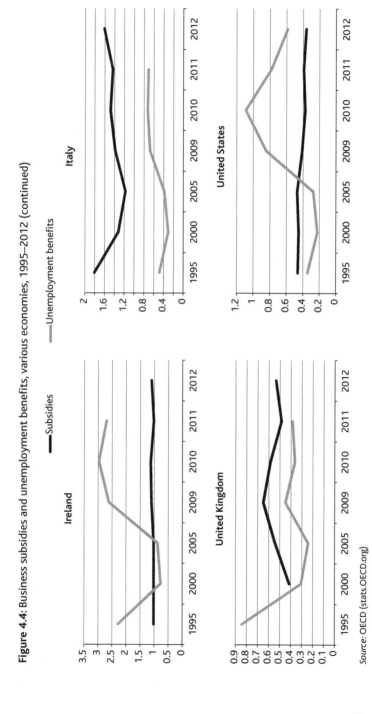

Source: OECD (stats.OECD.org)

business tax breaks and wage subsidies). What this illustrates is that, in many countries, including the UK, less is spent on unemployment benefits than is spent on business subsidies. This is an important point since far more attention is paid to the former than the latter. Moreover, far more negative attention is paid to unemployment benefit – some of it castigated as provision to the 'undeserving' poor. No such opprobrium is poured on wealthy recipients of state largesse, deserving or otherwise. Furthermore, there is a potential negative-sum relationship here between corporate and social welfare: provision made to private businesses may be provided instead of social welfare and for ostensibly social welfare reasons – perhaps because it might reduce food costs and/or increase food safety, or underpin industrial policy that is designed to increase skills, reduce unemployment and facilitate inclusive and/or sustainable growth within a region.

We can look at these potential trade-offs in another way. Figure 4.5 looks at different forms of provision within states along a commodifying–decommodifying continuum. At the top of this continuum, provision tends to have commodifying effects, preparing or pushing individuals into work. At the opposite end, provision tends to have decommodifying effects, not only supporting individuals out of work, but also providing benefits that support individuals who may find it more difficult to work. Not only do some states spend more on the range of benefits highlighted here, but they also have different priorities within their spending limits. Sweden and Denmark are not only outliers in spending more in total welfare than other economies, but they also spend most on active employment measures, including wage subsidies. The US is identified as a relatively low spending country on both forms of state welfare.

Relative wage costs are low in the UK, primarily because statutory and non-statutory occupational welfare is low. However, this only tells part of the story since the costs of occupational provision can be passed onto employees in lower wages and/or consumers in higher prices. Despite this, occupational welfare can bring real benefits to both employers and employees since businesses can exploit economies of scale when negotiating deals (on insurance or other provision) for employees, thus allowing them to deliver benefits with higher than face value. For employers, this means that they can find more cost-effective ways than cash wages for compensating employees, which might also bring productivity gains. The ability of employers to deliver such benefits is also aided by the fact that many forms of occupational provision attract tax exemptions; thus, some of the

Figure 4.5: State provision by purpose, various countries

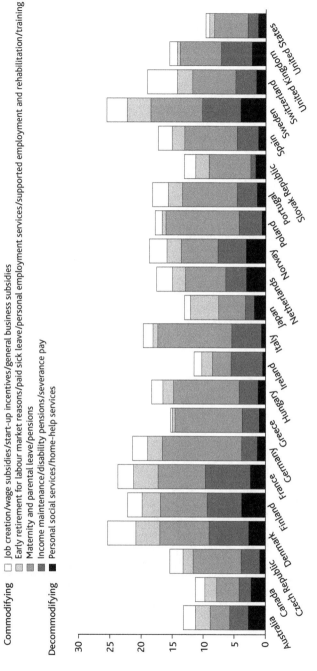

Source: Compiled from the OECD's social expenditure database (stats.OECD.org)

costs of occupational welfare are borne by general taxpayers while the benefits may accrue to employers and employees.

There is also quite a difference between different states regarding wage costs and non-wage costs. Figure 4.6 compares total hourly wage rates in industry across a number of economies, broken down into pay, social insurance costs and non-wage (directly paid) benefits. Wages and non-wage benefits are high in Switzerland and Belgium, but in the latter case, wages are lower and non-wage benefits are higher. Comparisons between France and the UK reveal that wages in both countries are very similar, but non-wage costs are much higher in the former than the latter. These data are, of course, collected in order to examine the costs that employers face, but it reveals that some citizens in some states not only are paid less, but also receive less in additional benefits from employers, a situation that will result in lower overall social welfare for citizens unless it is made up for by the state.

Next, we turn to in-work state benefits. As wages have fallen and/or unemployment has risen in recent decades, governments in many states have turned to state-funded wage supplements as a way of ensuring

Figure 4.6: Hourly compensation costs, US$, 2012

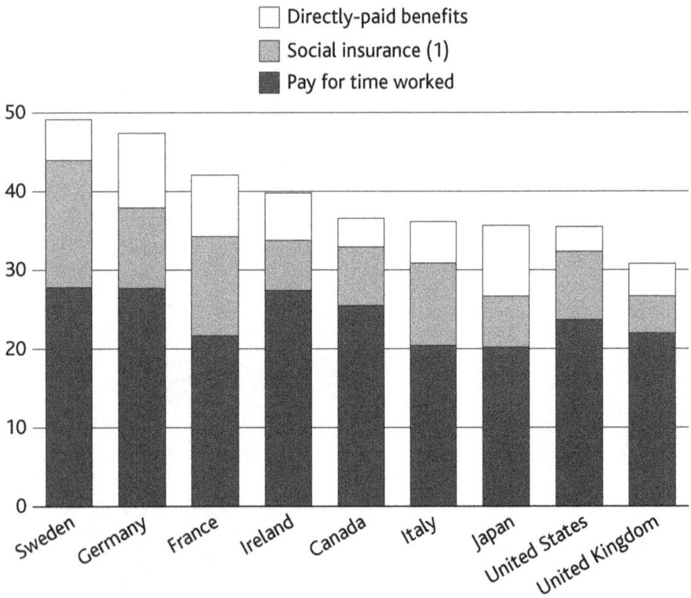

Source: Bureau of Labor Statistics, hourly wage costs

that individuals are better off in work than they are on state benefits. Such benefits are also a way of encouraging businesses to employ more workers at the lower end since, by providing benefits to individuals in work, they socialise the costs of paying what might be deemed to be an adequate or 'living' wage. They may also operate to reduce wage-inflation pressures at the bottom since, for workers, the effects of pushing wages higher will, to some extent, erode the relative support that they obtain from the state. The value of such in-work benefits across a number of economies is shown in Figure 4.7. This reveals that, in Japan, almost half the wage of a working family is provided by the state. In the UK, the equivalent figure is around one third. On this measure, the US government is a more generous provider of 'welfare', spending more on supporting the lowest paid than either Germany or Sweden. Of course, there is another way of perceiving of such benefits: as they are paid in order to increase wages to the levels that support the poorest families, such benefits operate as wage subsidies, with significant benefits to employers as well as employees.

Figure 4.7: Total value of state contribution to working families as a percentage of gross wages, including tax benefits (two children, two adults, one in work earning 40 per cent of the average wage)

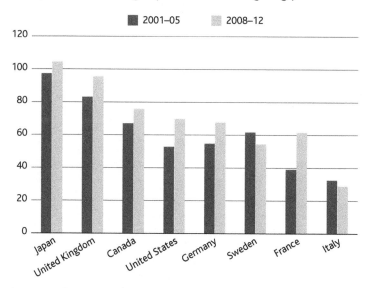

Source: OECD (stats.OECD.org)

Lastly, we turn to regulations. Labour market regulations can be as important in protecting workers as more direct forms of social provision, but they are seldom discussed by social policy academics. The OECD collects data on labour market protections in two forms. First, it surveys general regulations on labour markets, covering state controls over hiring policy and dismissals. Second, since 2010, it has provided data on Labour Market Security, which brings together measures of the incidence of labour market insecurity and the risks of unemployment, and 'Job Strain', which looks at the gap between what is expected of workers and the extent to which they are provided with the resources to do their job effectively. These data are summarised in Table 4.1. On both measures, the lower the number, the better the quality of the working environment and the greater the level of labour market security. On this measure, the quality of the working environment is highest in Sweden, but job security is highest in Japan. The US and UK perform badly in terms of the quality of the working environment, but reasonably well in terms of labour market security.

Table 4.1: Labour market conditions

	Quality of the working environment (higher value = poorer quality environment)	Labour market insecurity (higher values = greater security)
Canada		5.69
France	27.05	8.01
Germany	28.52	4.64
Italy	22.58	11.15
Japan	30.19	2.71
Sweden	27.61	6.33
United Kingdom	30.79	4.18
United States	37.65	4.79

Source: OECD (stats.OECD.org)

Discussion of data

While they represent only a narrow snapshot from across the whole economy of welfare, the preceding data nonetheless provide an interesting and informative picture. On taxation, they suggest wide variations across states. They reveal that direct taxes, measured as a percentage of GDP, are relatively low in the UK. Perhaps more interestingly, the key difference between direct taxes levied in the UK and France is that in the latter, business taxes are much higher (the equivalent of 4 percentage points). This, in turn, is an outcome of a higher rate of contributions by French employers towards national insurance. Tax expenditures, which effectively reduce the tax burden, also tend to be more generous in the UK. Meanwhile, in many states, the costs of subsidies to private businesses often outpace the costs of unemployment benefits. In GDP terms, they are highest in Sweden. If we consider subsidies and other 'employer-friendly' corporate welfare measures, the UK and US look relatively low, suggesting that, on the basis of these data alone, these countries tend to protect businesses through lower taxes rather than higher subsidies (though this misses the point that targeted subsidies to major corporations tend to be relatively high in the US). In the UK, a nation that has embraced austerity and deep cuts to unemployment benefits, business subsidies look relatively generous. More generally, welfare states clearly deliver core benefits for businesses (corporate welfare). Regarding employer-provided in-work, expressed as a percentage of hourly wage rates, the US looks like less of a welfare laggard than is often revealed when we look simply at social welfare spending, but average hourly pay overall looks low when compared to other, non-UK, European countries. As for state-provided in-work benefits (or wage subsidies), the picture here is again interesting, with the US government spending more on this form of provision than either Germany or Sweden. Lastly, regarding regulations and the working environment, regulations are relatively low in the UK and US, working environments are of relatively poorer quality, and labour market insecurity is relatively high.

Taken together, such data suggest that our understanding of welfare states would benefit from a wider and broader focus. They also suggest that discussions about state largesse, generosity and/or spending need to take into account the fuller distribution of benefits between different interests and groups. A more detailed analysis of any of these measures would reveal much more about the welfare state. This is what the whole-economy approach advocates.

Conclusion: towards a whole economy of welfare

One of the key strengths of social policy lies in its multidisciplinarity over its relatively short history. It also tends to be broad, flexible and accommodating in terms of its focus. As it has evolved, however, there has been a tendency for social policy scholarship to retreat to its core (primarily social welfare) and/or to deviate towards niche areas as if they are disconnected from mainstream welfare. The purpose of this chapter was to revisit the valuable contribution of those who have pushed at the boundaries of the subject and to argue that it is necessary to build on such traditions to extend its focus still further. This chapter has not been able to cover all bases, but rather argued that real and important connections between a range of state and non-state provision are hugely important to welfare systems and the study of welfare systems. However, there is more to do. Available data – on social, corporate, occupational, private, voluntary and third sector welfare – have to be improved, made more transparent and more systematically analysed. The whole-economy approach outlined here argues for the adoption of a broader analysis in social policy, and resistance to restrictive and sometimes arbitrary subject boundaries that can get in the way of a deeper analysis and understanding of the positions, role and purpose of key actors and key services. The risk in arguing for a whole-economy approach is that readers may rightly point to key omissions in both the map and data presented here. However, the argument for the adoption of a whole-economy approach is not to try to argue that in specific studies or discussions of the welfare state, we should include everything. Rather, it is an argument for the principle of the inclusion of political and economic factors that directly and indirectly shape social policies and welfare but are often neglected or ignored in mainstream social policy.

References

Cahill, M. (1994) *New social policy*, London: Wiley.

Cao, X., Prakash, A. and Ward, M.D. (2007) Protecting jobs in the age of globalisation: examining the relative salience of social welfare and industrial subsidies in OECD countries, *International Studies Quarterly*, 51: 301–27.

Chang, H.-J. (2001) *Breaking the mould: An institutionalist political economy alternative to the neoliberal theory of the market and the state*, Social Policy and Development Programme Paper Number 6, Geneva: United Nations Research Institute for Social Development.

Cox, E. and Schmuecker, K. (2010) *Well north of fair: The implications of the spending review for the North of England*, London: IPPR.

Dowler, E. (2003) Food and poverty in Britain: rights and responsibilities, *Social Policy & Administration*, 36(6): 698–717.

Ebbinghaus, B. and Manow, P. (eds) (2001) *Comparing welfare capitalism: Social policy and political economy in Europe, Japan and the USA*, London: Routledge.

Esping-Andersen, G. (1990) *The three worlds of welfare capitalism*, Cambridge: Polity Press.

Farnsworth, K. (2012) *Social versus corporate welfare: Competing needs and interests within the welfare state*, London: Palgrave.

Farnsworth, K. (2013) Bringing corporate welfare in. *Journal of Social Policy*, 42(1): 1–22.

Farnsworth, K. (2015) *The British corporate welfare state*, Sheffield: SPERI.

Farnsworth, K. and Holden, C. (2006) The business–social policy nexus: corporate power and corporate inputs into social policy, *Journal of Social Policy*, 35: 473–94.

Farnsworth, K. and Irving, Z. (2012) Varieties of crisis, varieties of austerity: social policy in challenging times, *Journal of Poverty and Social Justice*, 20(2): 133–47.

Garrett, G. (1998) *Partisan politics in the global economy*, Cambridge: Cambridge University Press.

Gough, I. (1979) *Political economy of the welfare state*, London: Palgrave.

Gough, I. (2011) 'From financial crisis to fiscal crisis' in K. Farnsworth and Z. Irving (eds) *Social policy in challenging times*, Bristol: Policy Press.

Hacker, J.S. (2011) The institutional foundations of middle-class democracy, working paper, Policy Network, www.policy-network. net/pno_detail.aspx?ID=3998&title=The+institutional+foundatio ns+of+middle-class+democracy

Hacker, J.S. and Pierson, P. (2002) Business power and social policy: employers and the formation of the American welfare state, *Politics and Society*, 30(2): 277–325.

Hall, P.A. and Soskice, D. (eds) (2001) *Varieties of capitalism: The institutional foundations of comparative advantage*, Oxford: Oxford University Press.

Howard, C. (1999) *The hidden welfare state: Tax expenditures and social policy in the United States*, Princeton, NJ: Princeton University Press.

Iversen, T. (2005) *Capitalism, democracy and welfare*, Cambridge: CUP.

Iversen, T. and Cusack, T.R. (2000) The causes of welfare state expansion: de-industrialization or globalization?, *World Politics*, 52(3): 313–49.

Kolberg, J.E. and Esping-Andersen, G. (2016) Welfare states and employment regimes, *International Journal of Sociology*, 20(3): 3–36.

Korpi, W. (1989) Power, politics and state autonomy in the development of social citizenship: social rights during sickness in eighteen OECD countries since 1930, *American Sociological Review*, 54: 309–28.

Mann, K. (2009) Remembering and rethinking the social divisions of welfare: 50 years on, *Journal of Social Policy*, 38(1): 1–18.

NAO (2014) *The effective management of tax reliefs*, London: National Audit Office.

Nussbaum, M.C. and Sen, A. (1993) *The quality of life*, Oxford: Oxford University Press.

O'Connor, J. (1973) *The fiscal crisis of the state*, New York, NY: St Martin's Press.

OECD (Organisation for Economic Co-operation and Development) (2005) *Extending opportunities: How active social policy can benefit us all*, Paris: OECD.

OECD (2009) *Tax expenditures in OECD countries*, Paris: OECD.

Pfaller, A. and Fink, P. (2011) *An industrial policy for social democracy: Cornerstones of an agenda for Germany*, London: Friedrich-Ebert-Stiftung.

Polanyi, K. (1957) *The great transformation: The political and economic origins of our time*, Boston, MA: Beacon Press.

Rein, M. and Rainwater, L. (1986) The public/private mix: the institutions of social protection, in M. Rein (ed) *Public/private interplay in social protection: A comparative study*, New York, NY: M.E. Sharpe.

Ruggie, J.G. (1982) International regimes, transitions, and changes: embedded liberalism in the postwar economic order, *International Organization*, 36(2): 379–415.

Sinfield, A. (1978) Analyses in the social division of welfare, *Journal of Social Policy*, 7(2): 129–56.

Sinfield, A. (2018) Fiscal welfare, in B. Grieve (ed) *Routledge handbook of the welfare state*, London: Routledge.

Steinmo, S., Thelen, K. and Longstreth, F. (1992) *Structuring politics: Historical institutionalism in comparative analysis*, Cambridge: Cambridge University Press.

Thelen, K. (1994) Beyond corporatism: toward a new framework for the study of labor in advanced capitalism, *Journal of Comparative Politics*, 27(1): 107–24.

Titmuss, R.M. (1958) *Essays on 'the welfare state'*, London: Unwin Books.

Titmuss, R.M. (1968) *Commitment to welfare*, London: Allen and Unwin.

Walker, A. (1988) Social policy versus economic policy: the future of social planning, Peter Hodge Memorial Lecture, Hong Kong, Department of Social Work.

Whitfield, D. (2001) *Public services or corporate welfare: Rethinking the nation state in the global economy*, London: Pluto Press.

Williams, F. (1989) *Social policy: A critical introduction*, London: Polity.

5

From welfare state to participation society: austerity, ideology or rhetoric?

Menno Fenger and Babs Broekema

Introduction

On 19 July 2010, then Prime Minster David Cameron delivered his so-called 'Big Society' speech in Liverpool (Cameron, 2010). He stated that:

> For a long time, the way government has worked – top down, top-heavy, controlling – has frequently had the effect of sapping responsibility, local innovation and civic action. It has turned many motivated public-sector workers into disillusioned, weary puppets of government targets. It has turned able, capable individuals into passive recipients of state help with little hope for a better future. It has turned lively communities into dull, soulless clones of one another. So we need to turn government completely on its head. The rule of this government should be this: if it unleashes community engagement, we should do it; if it crushes it, we shouldn't. (Cameron, 2010)

Cameron's ideas got a mixed reception at the time. Whereas some critics considered it an admirable and genuine attempt to unite a conservative communitarian agenda with social aspirations, other critics dismissed it as 'just another argument for austerity' or 'a fig-leaf for neo-liberalism' (see Kisby, 2010; Jordan, 2011; Corbett and Walker, 2013). According to Kisby (2010), the ideas of the Big Society never came to full realisation as the 'Great Recession' reached the UK in 2010 and turned the political and economic landscape upside down. This may be one of the reasons why the ideas of the Big Society have not fundamentally rebalanced the responsibilities between the state and society in the UK. An audit by non-profit agency Civil Exchange in 2015 even claimed that the results of the Big Society programme were largely negative (Civil Exchange, 2015).

However, Cameron's ideas of the Big Society were part of a bigger ideology that Wiggan (2011) refers to as a 'civic conservative' perspective. This ideology emphasises that social problems and the decline of civil society are exacerbated by a big state (see also Sage, 2012: 371). Therefore, elements of the Big Society ideology also found their ways to other countries. One of these countries is the Netherlands.

In his first annual address to Parliament in September 2013, after succeeding his mother in April 2013, the Dutch King Willem-Alexander announced the end of the era of the welfare state and proclaimed the 'Participation Society'. He claimed that:

> The mutual involvement of citizens in our country traditionally is strong. To make sure that this will remain that way, we need to face the fact that public regulations and services need to be adjusted. It is unmistakably the case that people in our current network- and information society are more outspoken and independent than in the past. Combined with the necessity to reduce the government's deficit, this leads to a slow transition of the classical welfare state into a Participation Society. Everyone who is able to do so, is asked to take responsibility for his or her own life and environment. When people shape their own future, they not only create added value for their own life, but also for society. (Rijksoverheid, 2013)

Just like in the UK, the reception in the Netherlands was mixed. Even though there was support for the idea of increasing social cohesion and individual responsibility, the critics focused specifically on two issues. First, the Participation Society might further increase inequalities. High-income groups may benefit from community initiatives that are developed within the ideology of the Participation Society and have extensive social networks to call upon in times of need, whereas low-income groups lack these skills and networks (see Tonkens, 2014). Second, a shift towards the Participation Society might imply a shift from public services delivered by professionals to public services delivered by amateurs (Trappenburg, 2016; see also Verhoeven and Bochove, 2018).

However, different from the UK, five years after the introduction of the concept, the Participation Society is still 'alive and kicking' in the Netherlands (Rusman and van der Wiel, 2018). The ideas have been actively included in the revisions of long-term care, social support and social assistance. Also, in a survey from the Social and Cultural Planning Office, it appeared that the percentage of citizens that consider care for the elderly as only a state task decreased between 2014 and 2016, whereas the share of people that think that people should support family members in need has slightly increased (De Klerk et al, 2017).

This chapter discusses the background of the Dutch Participation Society and analyses how and to what extent the ideas of the Participation Society have actually been translated into the implementation of social policies. In doing so, it shows how the Dutch social model has changed over the last five years, based on an analysis of policy documents, policy evaluations and academic literature. From this analysis, we might learn valuable lessons from the Dutch experience about the possibilities, limitations and consequences of increasing the responsibility of citizens in the welfare state. These lessons may also have important implications for other European countries, including the UK.

The chapter is structured as follows. In the next section, the ideas of the Participation Society are elaborated on and presented as an alternative model of organising the welfare state. Then, the chapter turns to three practical examples of the Participation Society 'in action': the mandatory civic contribution in social assistance; the role of informal care; and the rise of community initiatives for social welfare. In the final section, the experiences in these three domains are reflected on and conclusions are made as to whether the self-proclaimed shift towards a Participation Society in the Netherlands is only a matter of rhetoric, just another argument for austerity or a significant ideological turn in the attitude towards the welfare state.

The Participation Society in perspective

In this section, the emergence of the ideas of the Participation Society is shown to have marked a new era in the development of the Dutch welfare state. Even though the ideas have not fully matured and their implementation is still in their infancy, the key ideas of the Participation Society and the ways in which it differs from other eras in the development of the Dutch welfare state are summarised in Table 5.1. In Table 5.1, first, the social risks that seem to be perceived

Table 5.1: The development of the Dutch welfare state in different stages

	Rise	Expansion	Reform	Social investment	Participation Society
Period	1900–45	1946–80	1981–2000	2001–13	2014–
Social risks	Ageing, unemployment, need, sickness	Inequality, exclusion	Exhaustion of the welfare state, abuse and fraud of benefits	Unequal distribution of opportunities, new social risks	Dependence, inactivity, limited solidarity
Cause of risks	Industrialisation and modernisation	Capitalist economy	Unintended consequences	Inadequate individual choices	Crowding out
Governance strategy	Address the consequences	Plan and control	Reform	Prevent	Stimulate self-organisation
Organisation	Local, non-profit, charity, gradually supplemented by central public arrangements	Central, public, corporatist	Central, privatisation and competition	Local, public	Local, community organisation

as most important in each period are briefly presented Then, the perceived causes of these risks, the strategies that are used to address these risks and the modes of organisation that are used to implement these strategies are outlined. Table 5.1 will be elaborated on in the remainder of this section, thus giving a bird's-eye view on the history of the Dutch welfare state.

In general, the year 1901 is considered the year of birth of the Dutch welfare state. In that year, the 'Accidents Law' was introduced, a compulsory social insurance against accidents at the workplace (Cox, 1993; Schuyt, 2013). In reality, other forms of social protection started to develop as early as the 16th century (Slokker, 2010) and gradually evolved into predecessors of unemployment benefits and sickness benefits in the 18th and 19th centuries (van Genabeek, 1999; van Leeuwen, 2000). After the Accidents Law of 1901, the Dutch welfare state took off somewhat hesitantly in comparison with other European countries. Therefore, most scholars consider the Dutch welfare state a laggard in the pre-Second World War period (Bannink, 1999). Social protection in these years was aimed at the protection against the traditional social risks of ageing, unemployment, sickness and need, by means of providing income or in-kind benefits to those affected by these risks. To a large extent, social risks were considered to be unavoidable consequences of the processes of modernisation and industrialisation that could affect any worker. Traditional non-profit and charity organisations also continued to play an important role, for instance, in education, health care and poverty relief, so the Dutch welfare state was characterised in these early days by a mix of non-profit and public governance.

In the post-war period, the Dutch welfare state turned from laggard into front-runner, with the introduction of a rather generous system of social provisions, including sickness benefits, disability benefits, social assistance and pensions (Rigter et al, 1995; Bannink, 1999). The political landscape in this period was dominated by the Social-Democratic Party and the centre-left Catholic Party. The introduction of the capitalist economy brought great wealth in the post-war years, but potentially also great inequality. Therefore, the Social-Democratic and Christian-Democratic Parties aimed for a fair distribution of the post-war prosperity throughout all groups in society, which resulted in a radical increase in the coverage and level of benefits in this period (van Kersbergen, 1995). This increase was fuelled by the dominant position that trade unions managed to take in the post-war period (Cox, 1993).

In the 1980s, the expansion of the welfare state came to a radical halt. Just like in many other European countries, the financial sustainability of the welfare system was questioned (see Bannink, 1999; Pierson, 2001). This led to extensive reforms of the welfare state by tightening eligibility, cutting benefits and creating incentives for efficient implementation through privatisation and the creation of semi-autonomous implementation agencies. More specifically for the Netherlands, attention to large-scale abuse and fraud in disability and social assistance benefits – resulting in a series of parliamentary inquiries – further triggered the reform of the Dutch welfare state (see Fenger et al, 2013).

Towards the end of the 1990s, a new perspective on social policies emerged in Europe as an alternative to both the Keynesian extensive welfare state and the neoliberal austerity welfare state: the social investment state (Morel et al, 2012). The social investment state aimed to address post-industrial labour market risks, improve labour market inclusion and boost economic growth (van Kersbergen and Hemerijck, 2012). Instead of viewing social policies as an economic burden, the social investment paradigm highlighted the potential contribution of social policies to the competitive position of a country in the global knowledge-based economy. Therefore, the social investment state emphasised the importance of training and education policies throughout the life course to upskill the labour force. Moreover, the removal of labour market rigidities to ensure the efficient and effective match of demand and supply on the labour market was regarded as an important goal in this paradigm (Benda, 2018). The social investment state also emphasised individual responsibility in risk and care management (Ellison and Fenger, 2013).

The ideas of the social investment state built upon the capability approach, as developed by Sen and others (see Sen, 2005). The capability approach basically posed that a just society should try to reduce inequalities in the capabilities of people in order to reduce inequalities in their well-being and welfare. Therefore, the social investment state highlighted the importance of high-quality childcare, education, training and other services that advanced people's opportunities throughout the life course (Benda et al, 2017). It also entailed a shift from passive to active labour market policies. In doing so, the social investment state tried to create an environment in which individuals were enabled to take responsibility for their own welfare. Policy instruments were aimed at stimulating people to show 'appropriate' behaviour. Finally, policies were aimed at covering the social risks of people that were not well covered by the traditional welfare state, the so-called new social risks groups (see Bonoli, 2005). These groups included lone parents, people that combine informal care for a frail relative with a job on the regular labour market and people with non-standard forms of employment and/or careers. In the social investment paradigm, government played an important role in the welfare state, which was reflected in relatively high levels of social spending. More specifically, a relatively large share of spending on active labour market policies in relation to total spending on labour market policies is considered a good indicator of the shift towards social investment (Benda, 2018).

Even though the social investment paradigm is still under development (Hemerijck, 2018), the introduction of the Participation Society demarcates a step further on the road from collective to individual responsibility. As we saw earlier, the social investment paradigm focuses on individual responsibility for individual welfare. The Participation Society paradigm highlights individual responsibility for collective welfare. Therefore, the shift towards the Participation Society is considered as a newly emerging era in the development of the Dutch welfare state.

The Participation Society paradigm highlights the role of civil society in tackling social problems. As we saw earlier, civil society has traditionally played an important role in the delivery of welfare services in the Netherlands. The assessment of the role of civil society in the welfare state has been rather ambiguous: its call upon cohesion and solidarity and its ability to produce tailor-made solutions are often praised; whereas its particularism and paternalism are often criticised, just like the fragmented welfare landscape that results from a patchwork of non-profit organisations (see Streeck and Schmitter, 1985; Fenger, 2006). As argued earlier, there was a reappraisal of the role of civil society in the early 2010s, not only in the Netherlands and the UK, but also, for instance, in the US, with President Obama stating the following after winning the 2012 election: 'The role of citizens in our democracy does not end with your vote. America has never been about what can be done for us; it is about what can be done by us together, through the hard and frustrating but necessary work of self-government' (Obama, 2012).

The emergence of the Participation Society paradigm in the Netherlands may be understood as the meeting of four different streams: first, the search for a common ideology by the coalition of liberals and social democrats – a remarkable coalition even in the

Dutch tradition of coalition governments – which also coincided with the inauguration of a new king; second, the renewal of international attention to the ideas of communitarianism by people like Philip Blond in the UK and – somewhat earlier – Robert Putnam in the US (see Putnam, 2001; Blond, 2010); third, the long-standing tradition of self-governance that was supported from different ideological and religious positions in the Netherlands; and, fourth, even though the Dutch economy was showing signs of recovery in the aftermath of the Great Recession, the need for efforts to reduce the government's deficit. The ideology of the Participation Society, with its emphasis on 'modest' government, suited these circumstances better than the social investment ideology, which favours government spending.

The ideas of the Participation Society as they have been introduced in the Netherlands refer to the advantages of non-profit governance. It has not yet developed into a full ideology, but in Table 5.1, we have included some of its core elements. At the heart of the Participation Society perspective seems to be the idea that people in communities are intrinsically motivated to take care of themselves and others. External incentives and regulation are considered to drive out the intrinsic motivation (see Ostrom, 2000). This effect is known as the crowding-out effect. In the area of the welfare state, this implies that social expenditure and comprehensive social programmes crowd out informal caring relations and social networks. Due to the state taking responsibility for this kind of care, familial, communal and occupational systems of self-help and reciprocity seem unnecessary. As a consequence, the welfare state might foster social isolation, anomie and self-centredness. This may lead to a general decline of commitment to civil norms, participation in civil society and trust in fellow citizens and social institutions (van Oorschot and Arts, 2005).[1] The Participation Society aims to reverse crowding out by facilitating and incentivising social and altruistic behaviour. Therefore, rather than addressing social needs, government interventions are aimed at stimulating and facilitating citizens' self-organisation. Moreover, government calls upon the altruistic behaviour of individual citizens. This implies that the availability of alternative sources of service provision by, for instance, relatives or community members becomes part of the needs-based assessment: people are expected to ask their neighbours, family members or friends for help before they turn to government. The facilitation and stimulation of self-organisation requires a close connection to local communities, just like the assessment of the social network of service users requires detailed interactions with service users. Therefore, according to the Participation

Society paradigm, the implementation and design of social policies should take place as close to service users as possible, preferably on the level of communities and neighbourhoods.

As already discussed in the Introduction of this chapter, the Participation Society paradigm in the Netherlands is not without criticism, to put it mildly. Words like 'inhumane' and 'modern slavery' can be found among the critics (see Tonkens, 2014; Simons, 2016; van Ditmars, 2017). However, this chapter does not aim to provide a moral assessment of the ideology of the Participation Society, but shows how the Dutch government has tried to implement this ideology and with what consequences. To do so, three domains of the welfare state in which the government has implemented specific measures to put the underlying ideas of the Participation Society into practice are focused on: the mandatory civic contribution in social assistance; informal care; and community initiatives for social welfare. For each of these cases, the chapter discusses what they entail, what their objectives are, why they fit into the Participation Society ideology and what the experiences are. The case descriptions are based on an analysis of the available literature and evaluations by government bodies, independent organisations and media reports.

The Participation Society in action

In the Netherlands, the development of the Participation Society has gone hand in hand with the decentralisation of social care, social assistance and labour market policies (Bannink, 2014; Pommer and Boelhouwer, 2016). Since January 2015, Dutch municipalities have held the legal capacity and responsibility for the formation and implementation of these policies. The transfer of responsibilities to municipalities was accompanied by significant budget cuts, arguing that the implementation of tailor-made solutions and the active involvement of citizens would make the policies significantly cheaper (Pommer and Boelhouwer, 2016). In this section, three specific examples of how this active involvement of citizens has been shaped are discussed, thus providing an image of the Participation Society in action: mandatory civic contribution; informal care; and community services.

Mandatory civic contribution

One of the most prominent examples of the Participation Society in action results from the Dutch Participation Act, the so-called mandatory civic contribution (Rijksoverheid, 2018). As of 2015, social assistance recipients are expected to carry out unpaid socially useful activities in return for their social assistance benefits if their personal circumstances allow them to do so (Municipality of Rotterdam, 2017; Rijksoverheid, 2018). These activities can take different forms like community work and volunteer work, as well as attending a language course or sorting out financial debts (Municipality of Rotterdam, 2017). For claimants who do not meet the requirements or refuse to carry out a mandatory civic contribution, social assistance payments may temporarily be cut (Kampen, 2014; Programmaraad, 2015; Rijksoverheid, 2018).

Although the idea of requiring specific tasks or actions in return for a benefit is not a new phenomenon, the inclusion of the obligation to do so by law is. Some of the requirements regarding civic contributions are determined at the national level, but the actual formulation and implementation are the responsibility of municipalities. In particular, a civic contribution is mandatory but may not suppress paid labour or impede the recipient's reintegration into the labour market (TK 32 815, no 3, 2010/11: 28–9). Furthermore, the contribution should fit personal circumstances, be adjusted to the best of the recipient's ability and have legal exceptions to its obligatory nature for single parents with young children (Kampen, 2014; Rijksoverheid, 2018). In addition to these general requirements, the Participation Act provides each individual municipality with substantial legal capacity and responsibility to develop and implement the new mandatory civic contribution legislation in their own way. Consequently, local policy variation in the application and content of the mandatory civic contribution can be observed.

The main objective of the mandatory civic contribution is that claimants who 'appeal to the solidarity of society' give something in return and thereby fulfil their social involvement (TK 32 815, no 3, 2010/11: 14). In other words, it is assumed that the general public's support for the welfare state increases if those on benefit perform civic duties in exchange for their benefits (Corra and Bosselaar, 2013; Kampen, 2014). In accordance with this redistribution objective, 'quid pro quo' seems to be the new credo of social assistance (Corra and Bosselaar, 2013). The secondary objective of the mandatory civic contribution policy includes the activation of the unemployed, thereby increasing opportunities for reintegration into the workforce (Programmaraad, 2014).

The objectives of the mandatory civic contribution policy relate directly to the core aims of the Participation Society on both the collective and individual level. On the collective level, voluntary community work is considered as a valuable activity. The discourse about the mandatory civic contribution highlights the values of voluntary community work for the individual as well as for the community. So, paradoxically, in the official discourse, the intrinsic values of voluntary work are transposed to involuntary voluntary work. Hence, in the official discourse, the mandatory civic contribution for social assistance recipients is a good illustration of the Dutch Participation Society. However, how does the implementation work in practice?

As might be expected from the devolution of policymaking responsibilities, the first answer to this question is: this differs between municipalities. In particular, what municipalities consider satisfactory civic contributions and how much of it they expect from benefit recipients varies (Limburg, 2015). Even though there have been no systematic comparisons yet, we can offer some typical examples to illustrate the local variation. For instance, the number of hours that have to be devoted to the mandatory civic contribution by a benefit recipient ranges from 20 hours a week in the city of Rotterdam to a negligible four hours a year in Nijmegen (Limburg, 2015), whereas in the city of Utrecht, the voluntary nature of the mandatory civic contribution is emphasised, even despite the obligation of requiring some form of mandatory civic contribution stipulated by national government (College voor de Rechten van de Mens, 2016; Limburg, 2016). There is also variation in the level of conditionality for those not conforming to the obligation. For instance, the municipality of Rotterdam stresses the mandatory nature and imposes sanctions if requirements are not fulfilled, whereas the municipality of Arnhem does not require a mandatory civic contribution at all (Kampen, 2014; Limburg, 2016).

This variation in implementation leads, in turn, to a variation in the experiences of policymakers as well as social assistance recipients across the Netherlands. The civic contribution is perceived as a positive experience by some recipients due to the fact that: it provides recipients with the opportunity to give something back in return for their benefits; they feel useful to society; their daily rhythms are reinforced; and their social network increases, resulting in enhanced mental and physical health (Municipality of Rotterdam, 2017). Other recipients, however, perceive the legal obligation to perform a mandatory civic contribution as a sign of distrust (Kampen, 2014: 211). Furthermore, many others emphasise the danger of repressing paid labour by voluntary work, or the grey area between 'mandatory civic contributions' and 'enforced labour' (Tonkens, 2014; Limburg, 2015; College voor de Rechten van de Mens, 2016).

In conclusion, the case of the mandatory civic contribution shows a rather coercive way of enforcing the ideas of the Participation Society. Moreover, the large amount of variation at the local and individual levels presents clear risks for the fair and equal implementation of the Participation Society ideals.

Informal care

A second prominent example of the Participation Society in action results from the Dutch Social Support Act 2015 (WMO) and is related to the position of informal care in the implementation of social support. Informal caregivers provide voluntary, long-term and unpaid care to a chronically ill, disabled or dependent partner, parent, child or other family member, friend or acquaintance (Mezzo, 2018a, 2018b; Pommer and Boelhouwer, 2016; TK 32 620, no 27, 2011/12). This informal care includes, for example, the support of an acquaintance's self-sufficiency, social companionship, help with household chores or other services (van Groenou and De Boer, 2016).

The WMO transfers the responsibility for policy formulation and implementation in the area of social support to municipalities. The transfer of responsibilities is accompanied by considerable cutbacks in residential and professional home care (Pavolini and Ranci, 2008; Dijkhoff, 2014: 277; van Groenou and De Boer, 2016). As a result, a new vibrant discourse arises 'on civic responsibility and civic values with regard to self-care and helping others' (van Groenou and De Boer, 2016: 272), and appeals are increasingly made on informal caregivers 'to compensate for these cutbacks' (van Groenou and De Boer, 2016: 272). 'Only when problems get too big or complicated to be solved by the (social and familial network of the) person in question, do the municipalities have to organise the support' (Dijkhoff, 2014: 278). Consequently, although providing informal care to kin or non-kin is no new phenomenon, Dutch municipalities increasingly appeal to informal caregivers.

While the governance arrangement and the policy substance of informal care differ from that of the mandatory civic contribution, the general philosophies of the two arrangements show similarities (Bannink, 2014). In particular, the Participation Society's core aim of increasing social cohesion among citizens is expressed by the increasing appeal to informal caregivers. Hence, theoretically, the increasing appeal on informal care is a good illustration of the Dutch Participation Society. However, in practice, defining the balance between informal and formal care proves to be a challenge.

In the first years after the implementation of the WMO, various municipalities have implemented rather far-reaching attempts to oblige informal care by relatives. For instance, the municipality of Etten-Leur ended the provision of a personalised care budget to a disabled woman who used the budget to pay her daughter to perform household tasks. The municipality claimed that these tasks were part of a regular family relation, but the Court of Appeal decided that under no circumstances could informal care be obliged (De Koster, 2017). In another example, in 2015, the municipality of Montferland decided to reject all applications for household support for less than three hours a week. The municipality argued that arranging three hours a week of household support is the responsibility of citizens themselves, either through arranging informal care or hiring a paid household cleaner. Again, the Court of Appeal ruled that if citizens need care, municipalities are obliged to provide it (*Omroep Gelderland*, 2016). These two examples show how these municipalities have tried to stretch the boundaries of the Participation Society paradigm even beyond the level of what the national government intended by making self-sufficiency and informal care obligatory but have been limited in doing so by the judiciary.

Alternatively, instead of trying to replace formal care by informal care, other municipalities have started pilots to voluntarily increase self-reliance and informal care, while decreasing demand for professional care. Verhoeven and Bochove (2018) report on two of these pilots. The first entails the 'living-room' projects in the municipality of Eindhoven. These living rooms provide day-care activities for people with disabilities and people suffering from social isolation (Verhoeven and van Bochove, 2018). These living-room activities are run by informal caregivers and volunteers with one or more front-line workers at arm's length (Verhoeven and Bochove, 2018). The second example they discuss concerns the aftercare of multi-problem families and people with psychiatric or psychosocial problems who have been on a welfare programme in the municipality of Dordrecht. In contrast to 'living rooms', the first 70 hours of aftercare in Dordrecht are still provided by front-line workers, who are succeeded by informal caregivers after the initial 70 hours (Verhoeven and Bochove, 2018). Despite the substantial differences in implementation, both examples show that emphasising self-reliance and informal and/or volunteer aid does not imply that professional care is completely substituted, but rather how both forms of care may be combined (Ministry of Public Health, Welfare and Sport, 2009; Verhoeven and Tonkens, 2013).

Even though the formal appeal to perform informal care is prohibited, in the ideology of the Participation Society, there is a strong moral appeal to citizens to perform informal care. De Klerk et al (2017) show that between 2014 and 2016, the amount of informal care has remained stable in the Netherlands. In the public discourse, however, there is increasing attention to the negative consequences of informal care. This relates, for example, to the difficulties of combining informal caring with paid work, the extent of the care that they have to provide or the social exclusion experienced by caregivers due to the intensiveness of their caring activities (European Parliament, 2010). Additionally, an unintended consequence of increasingly appealing to informal caregivers is that it decreases the time they dedicate to 'regular' voluntary work (Movisie, 2017). Furthermore, front-line professional caregivers experience an increased workload since working with volunteers can create extra tasks and responsibilities (Verhoeven and Bochove, 2018). Also, there is a challenge to the quality of care. Informal care carries 'the potential of a threat to professionalism, particularly if the aim of social policies is that citizens take over tasks from care and social workers' (Verhoeven and van Bochove, 2018: 787), because the question is unanswered as to who determines the informal caregiver's suitability to perform these care tasks. Finally, Benda et al (2017) highlight the new inequalities that may be related to a larger role for informal care: citizens with extensive social networks may receive more and better care than people without these networks. Moreover, as women tend to be more involved in informal care than men, this may also reinforce gender inequalities.

The central lesson in this case is that the severe budget cuts have forced municipalities to turn to the possible contribution of informal and voluntary care, irrespective of whether or not they agreed with the Participation Society paradigm. Whereas on the national level, the Participation Society and budget cuts go hand in hand, on the local level, the budget cuts seem to be an important driver of change. As the Court of Appeal has blocked the road to obligating citizens to perform informal care tasks, they are now looking for innovative ways to combine formal and informal care. The informal caregivers' capacities seem to be an important factor that should be taken into account when implementing the ideas of the Participation Society.

Social welfare community initiatives

Finally, the Participation Society in action is indissolubly linked to the final example of this chapter, namely, social welfare community initiatives (Dekker et al, 2007: 86). Such initiatives are voluntarily initiated by and for one or multiple citizens to improve the local quality of life by addressing problems, or create innovative care and welfare services in a local community (Vilans, 2014, 2015), for example, citizens initiating the development of a local nursing home or care cooperative. These initiatives are characterised by the absence of an institutionalised established organisation. Hence, they function fully on citizen ideas and efforts (Vilans, 2015; Movisie, 2017). However, they can only operate in accordance with the principles of solidarity and reciprocity (Vilans, 2014).

Just like mandatory civic contributions and informal care, citizen initiatives are no new phenomenon: 'The current government appreciation for the citizens' initiative is in a sense a revaluation of a strong tradition in the Netherlands' (van de Wijdeven et al, 2013: 9–10). However, community initiatives as a policy objective can be discerned from the former two examples because they are not legally institutionalised and cannot be imposed by government. Nonetheless, this does not mean that the Dutch government does not try to do so (Movisie, 2016). The Social and Cultural Planning Office (SCP) has already observed that the national government has been investing in citizen initiatives and participation with renewed vigour over the last decade (Dekker et al, 2007: 86). In particular, the introduction of the WMO is a striking example of how civil servants at the top increasingly promote the development of these initiatives from citizens at the bottom (van de Wijdeven et al, 2013: 8; Movisie, 2014). As a result, citizen initiatives in care and welfare services are advancing fast, from 30 initiatives in 2013 to well over 300 initiatives in 2016 (De Jong, 2016).

The main objectives of community initiatives are threefold. The first objective is to improve the local quality of life by providing and innovating services or by adjusting elements of welfare services to local needs. Second, the initiatives aim to play a connecting role in improving this local quality of life (Fischer, 2009). This connecting role is either reflected in the involvement of many citizens in the implementation of the initiative or in the broad accessibility of the initiative's services to the widest possible range of citizens. This also applies to people who are usually sidelined by the government (Movisie, 2015). The third objective is to reduce the workload of municipalities. As citizens solve multiple welfare problems locally, municipalities can increasingly focus on other core tasks (Fischer, 2009). These aims correspond perfectly with the aims of the Participation Society.

Citizens' social welfare initiatives can be found in many shapes, sizes and judicial forms. However, in the era of the Participation Society, the citizens' cooperative is one that has become increasingly popular. We will discuss two examples here. The first is the citizens' initiative in the municipality of Lierop: the village cooperative 'Lierop Lives' (Vilans, 2014). The initiative was a response to the decentralisation in 2015, being aimed at maintaining the quality of life despite the increased workload of the municipality in providing social services (Lierop Leeft, 2018a). This initiative is broad in several ways: half of the local population is a member of the initiative as a volunteer; it is directed at all local inhabitants; and it focuses on multiple welfare domains, such as home care and education (Vilans, 2014; Lierop Leeft, 2018b). A second example can be found in the municipality of Zoetermeer. This example is much more specific (Vilans, 2014). It was initiated by a small number of citizens and specifically directed at all citizens trying to organise their own welfare support concerning household chores, jobs in and around the house, or personal care (Vilans, 2014). The cooperative serves solely as a digital intermediary between providers and recipients, without providing care of any sort themselves.

Due to the immense diversity in what is considered to be a citizen initiative, reported experiences show contrasting perceptions (Movisie, 2017). On the one hand, the number of citizens' social welfare initiatives has increased, resulting in solutions specifically designed to solve local problems (Vilans, 2014; Igalla and van Meerkerk, 2015). This increase can be attributed to the facilitating roles of municipalities, as well as to the favourable discourse of the Participation Society. On the other hand, research shows that those participating in initiatives are mainly highly educated, native inhabitants, who are physically and mentally healthy (Igalla and van Meerkerk, 2015; Movisie, 2017), and that those inhabitants usually sidelined by the government are equally sidelined in community initiatives (Movisie, 2016).

Conclusions

This chapter has shown how the communitarian ideals that inspired Cameron's 'Big Society' ideology can also be found in the current ideas about the Participation Society in the Netherlands. The Dutch

Participation Society emphasises the virtues of self-sufficiency and social solidarity. On the base of this – necessarily brief – overview, four conclusions can be made.

The first conclusion also refers to the title of this contribution. Through the three different policy domains that have been discussed, it has become clear that the ideas of the Participation Society in the Netherlands are well beyond the stage of rhetoric. The ideas have been translated into several legal reforms that are at the heart of the Dutch welfare state, most notably, social assistance and social support. Deconstructing the causal interference between budget cuts and the ideology of the Participation Society is beyond the scope of this article, but it is clear that these two are interrelated. Cutting budgets for welfare services undeniably creates incentives and institutional space for citizens to participate in the production of welfare services, but such arguments fit within a conservative neoliberal political agenda, as well as within a more progressive social- or Christian-democratic agenda. Just as the Big Society discourse played a role in morally founding the UK's Coalition government, the Participation Society discourse may have played a role in ideologically uniting the uncommon Liberal–Social-Democratic coalition in the Netherlands.

Second, using the virtue and power of individual and organised citizens requires policy formulation and implementation at an administrative level that is easily accessible to these citizens. Therefore, decentralisation is an important governance strategy in the ideology of the Participation Society. However, with decentralisation comes local variation, as has clearly been shown in our empirical examples. This leads to a normative question: to what extent are local and/or regional differences acceptable within an advanced welfare state like the Netherlands?

The third conclusion deals with the motivations of citizens to participate in the Participation Society. Each of the three cases shows different levels of coercion. In the case of the mandatory civic contribution, the level of coercion is very strong, even though some local variation can be found. In contrast, in the case of social welfare initiatives, the voluntary action seems to be genuinely voluntary, even though municipalities may – and often do – facilitate or even trigger voluntary action. The case of informal care shows both sides of the coercion coin. However, the idea of crowding out – which morally underpins the Participation Society – clearly builds on the importance of intrinsic motivation rather than extrinsic motivation (see Ostrom, 2000). Therefore, it is at least contested as to what extent coerced participation actually meets the aims of the Participation Society.

The final conclusion is perhaps also the most important one. In all three cases, the issue of 'new inequalities' has clearly been raised by scholars, politicians and in the public discourse. These new inequalities may concern the subjects of policies, as well as those participating in the Participation Society. Specifically in the case of informal care, these inequalities may also be gender-related: as women still perform a larger share of informal care tasks than men, a moral appeal to extend these activities may also affect them more than men. This may further increase the gender gap despite all the efforts in other policy domains to contain this gap. Moreover, in all three cases, the shift towards the Participation Society seems to increase the division between low-educated and high-educated citizens.

Therefore, we may conclude that the ideas of the Participation Society in the Netherlands do not form a coherent, matured set of policy guidelines. In contrast, what we observe is a large-scale policy experiment in which an advanced welfare state is seeking to address the problems of financial sustainability, ideological sustainability and popular support. Two lessons may already be drawn from the early stages of this experiment: coercion is not the solution; and creating or widening inequalities is the largest pitfall. Therefore, the Participation Society should be considered not as an alternative to the welfare state, but as an addition to it.

Note

[1] The ideas of the Participation Society are morally embedded in the idea of crowding out. However, it is important to note that there are also scholars who put forward the idea of 'crowding in': a country with a well-developed welfare state is fertile ground for an extensive civil society with high levels of solidarity and reciprocity. Van Oorschot and Arts (2005) show that the evidence is not conclusive in one direction or the other.

References

Bannink, D. (1999) Het Nederlands stelsel van sociale zekerheid. Van achterblijver naar koploper naar vroege hervormer, in W.A. Trommel and R.J. van der Veen (eds) *De Herverdeelde Samenleving: Ontwikkeling en herziening van de Nederlandse verzorgingsstaat*, Amsterdam: Amsterdam University Press, pp 51–81.

Bannink, D. (2014) Decentralised integration of social policy domains, in K. Farnsworth, Z. Irving and M. Fenger (eds) *Social policy review 26: Analysis and debate in social policy, 2014*, Bristol: Policy Press, pp 221–38.

Benda, L. (2018) *Understanding active labour market policies. An institutional perspective on intended and unintended consequences*, Rotterdam: Erasmus University.

Benda, L., Fenger, M., Koster, F. and van der Veen, R.J. (2017) Social investment risks? An explorative analysis of new social risks in the social investment state, *Corvinus Journal of Sociology and Social Policy*, 8(2): 25–42.

Blond, P. (2010) *The red Tory. How Left and Right have broken Britain and how we can fix it*, London: Faber.

Bonoli, G. (2005) The politics of the new social policies: providing coverage against new social risks in mature welfare states, *Policy and Politics*, 33(3): 431–49.

Cameron, D. (2010) Big Society speech in Liverpool, 19 July, www.number10.gov.uk/news/speeches-and-transcripts/2010/07/big-society-speech-53572

Civil Exchange (2015) *Whose society? The final Big Society audit*, London: Civil Exchange.

College voor de Rechten van de Mens (2016) Tegenprestatie voor de Bijstand, 26 January, www.mensenrechten.nl/nl/toegelicht/tegenprestatie-voor-de-bijstand

Corbett, S. and Walker, A. (2013) The Big Society: rediscovery of 'the social' or rhetorical fig-leaf for neo-liberalism?, *Critical Social Policy*, 33(3): 451–72.

Corra, A.D.R. and Bosselaar, J.H. (2013) *De Maatschappelijk Nuttige Tegenprestatie: Schipperen tussen Sociale Integratie en Repressie*, Amsterdam: Vrije Universiteit Amsterdam.

Cox, R. (1993) *The development of the Dutch welfare state: From workers' insurance to universal entitlement*, Pittsburgh, PA: University of Pittsburgh Press.

De Jong, F. (2016) 320 Burgerinitiatieven in de zorg in kaart gebracht, 15 December, www.vilans.nl/artikelen/320-burgerinitiatieven-in-de-zorg-in-kaart-gebracht

Dekker, P., Hart, J. and De Faulk, L. (2007) *Toekomstverkenning vrijwillige inzet 2015*, The Hague: Sociaal en Cultureel Planbureau.

De Klerk, M., De Boer, A., Plaisier, I. and Schyns, P. (2017) *Voor elkaar. Stand van de informele hulp 2016*, The Hague: Sociaal en Cultureel Planbureau.

De Koster, Y. (2017) Mantelzorg-uitspraak van Belang voor Alle Gemeenten, 17 January, www.binnenlandsbestuur.nl/sociaal/nieuws/mantelzorg-uitspraak-van-belang-voor-alle.9556276.lynkx

Dijkhoff, T. (2014) The Dutch Social Support Act in the shadow of the decentralization dream, *Journal of Social Welfare and Family Law*, 36(6): 276–94.

Ellison, M. and Fenger, M. (2013) Social investment, protection and inequality within the new economy and the politics of welfare in Europe, *Social Policy and Society*, 12(4): 611–24.

European Parliament (2010) European Parliament resolution of 6 May 2009 on the active inclusion of people excluded from the labour market, C2010/212/EC, Official Journal of the European Union, https://eur-lex.europa.eu/LexUriServ/LexUriServ.do?uri=OJ:C:2010:212E:0023:0031:EN:PDF

Fenger, M. (2006) Shifts in welfare governance: the state, private and non-profit sectors in four European countries, in P. Henman and M. Fenger (eds) *Administering welfare reform. International transformations in welfare governance*, Bristol: Policy Press, pp 73–92.

Fenger, M., van der Steen, M. and van der Torre, L. (2013) *The responsiveness of social policy in Europe. The Netherlands in comparative perspective*, Bristol: Policy Press.

Fischer, F. (2009) *Democracy and expertise: Reorienting policy inquiry*, New York, NY: Oxford University Press.

Hemerijck, A. (2018) Social investment as a policy paradigm, *Journal of European Public Policy*, 25(6): 810–27.

Igalla, M. and van Meerkerk, I. (2015) De Duurzaamheid van Burgerinitiatieven, *Bestuurswetenschappen*, 69(3): 25–53.

Jordan, B. (2011) Making sense of the 'Big Society': social work and the moral order, *Journal of Social Work*, 12(6): 630–46.

Kampen, T. (2014) Verplicht vrijwilligerswerk: de ervaringen van bijstand cliënten met een tegenprestatie voor hun uitkering, PhD thesis, University of Amsterdam, The Netherlands.

Kisby, B. (2010) The Big Society: power to the people?, *The Political Quarterly*, 81(4): 484–91.

Lierop Leeft (2018a) Hoe zijn we begonnen?, www.lieropleeft.nl/?a=2&b=5

Lierop Leeft (2018b) Werkvelden, www.lieropleeft.nl/?a=4

Limburg, M. (2015) Adviesraad Rotterdam ziet toe op verdringing, 21 May, www.binnenlandsbestuur.nl/sociaal/nieuws/adviesraad-rotterdam-ziet-toe-op-verdringing.9475675.lynkx

Limburg, M. (2016) 20 Gemeenten Blijven Verplichte Tegenprestatie Weigeren, 23 February, www.binnenlandsbestuur.nl/sociaal/nieuws/20-gemeenten-blijven-verplichte-tegenprestatie.9520810.lynkx

Mezzo (2018a) Dit is Mantelzorg, www.mezzo.nl/pagina/voor-mantelzorgers/thema-s/dit-is-mantelzorg

Mezzo (2018b) WMO en mantelzorg, www.mezzo.nl/pagina/voor-mantelzorgers/thema-s/wetten-en-regels/wmo-en-mantelzorg

Ministry of Public Health, Welfare and Sport (2009) Naast en met elkaar: brief over de relatie tussen informele en formele zorg, 19 February, http://docplayer.nl/428070-Datum-27-oktober-2009-betreft-naast-en-met-elkaar-brief-over-de-relatie-tussen-informele-en-formele-zorg.html

Morel, N., Palier, B. and Palme, J. (2012) *Towards a social investment state? Ideas, policies and challenges*, Bristol: Policy Press.

Movisie (2014) Succesvolle Burgerinitiatieven in Wonen, Welzijn en zorg, 24 December, www.movisie.nl/artikel/succesvolle-burgerinitiatieven-wonen-welzijn-zorg

Movisie (2015) De Voordelen van de Participatiesamenleving, 8 December, www.movisie.nl/artikel/voordelen-participatiesamenleving

Movisie (2016) Kwaliteitseisen aan Burgerinitiatieven: Meerwaarde of Dooddoener?, 21 April, www.movisie.nl/artikel/kwaliteitseisen-aan-burgerinitiatieven-meerwaarde-dooddoener

Movisie (2017) Participatiesamenleving anno 2017: volop kansen. Hoe staat het ervoor met de participatiesamenleving?, 27 September, www.koepeladviesradensociaaldomein.nl/nieuws/participatiesamenleving-anno-2017-volop-kansen-hoe-staat-het-er-voor

Municipality of Rotterdam (2017) *De zin en onzin van Vijf jaar Tegenprestatie in Rotterdam*, Rotterdam: Municipality of Rotterdam.

Obama, B. (2012) Election Night Speech, Chicago, 6 November, www.theguardian.com/world/2012/nov/07/barack-obama-speech-full-text

Omroep Gelderland (2016) Gelderse gemeenten moeten voldoende huishoudelijke hulp geven, 18 May, www.omroepgelderland.nl/nieuws/2110253/Gelderse-gemeenten-moeten-voldoende-huishoudelijke-hulp-geven

Ostrom, E. (2000) Crowding out citizenship, *Scandinavian Political Studies*, 23(1): 1–16.

Pavolini, E. and Ranci, C. (2008) Restructuring the welfare state: reforms in long-term care in Western European countries, *Journal of European Social Policy*, 18: 246–59.

Pierson, P. (2001) Coping with permanent austerity: welfare state restructuring in affluent democracies, in P. Pierson (ed) *The new politics of the welfare state*, Oxford: Oxford University Press, pp 410–56.

Pommer, E. and Boelhouwer, J. (2016) *Overall Rapportage Sociaal Domein 2015*, The Hague: Sociaal en Cultureel Planbureau.

Programmaraad (2014) *Werkwijzer Tegenprestatie*, The Hague: Programmaraad.

Programmaraad (2015) *Participatiewet*, The Hague: Programmaraad.

Putnam, R. (2001) *Bowling alone. The collapse and revival of American community*, New York, NY: Simon and Schuster.

Rigter, D., van den Bosch, E., van der Veen, R. and Hemerijck, A. (1995) *Tussen sociale wil en werkelijkheid. Een geschiedenis van het beleid van het Ministerie van Sociale Zaken*, 's-Gravenhage: VUGA.

Rijksoverheid (2013) Troonrede 2013, The Hague, www.rijksoverheid. nl/documenten/toespraken/2013/09/17/troonrede-2013

Rijksoverheid (2018) Wat is de tegenprestatie in de bijstand?, www. rijksoverheid.nl/onderwerpen/bijstand/vraag-en-antwoord/wat-is-de-tegenprestatie-in-de-bijstand

Rusman, F. and van der Wiel, C. (2018) Het p-woord raakte goed ingeburgerd, *NRC*, 17 September, www.nrc.nl/nieuws/2018/09/17/het-p-woord-raakte-goed-ingeburgerd-a1616833

Sage, D. (2012) A change to liberalism? The communitarianism of the Big Society and Blue Labour, *Critical Social Policy*, 32(3): 365–82.

Schuyt, K. (2013) Noden en wensen: De verzorgingsstaat gezien als een historisch fenomeen, 24 June, www.eur.nl/sites/corporate/files/FSW_-_13_oratie_binnenwerk_Schuyt_20jun_0.pdf

Sen, A. (2005) Human rights and capabilities, *Journal of Human Development*, 6(2): 151–66.

Simons, G. (2016) De moderne slavernij van de participatiesamenleving, *Joop*, 17 June, https://joop.bnnvara.nl/opinies/het-morele-vacuum-van-de-participatiesamenleving

Slokker, N. (2010) *Ruggengraat van de stad: De betekenis van gilden in Utrecht 1528–1818*, Amsterdam: Aksant.

Streeck, W. and Schmitter, P.C. (1985) Community, market, state – and associations? The prospective contribution of interest governance to social order, *European Sociological Review*, 1(2): 119–38.

TK 32 815, no 3 (2010/11) *Wijziging van de Wet werk en bijstand en samenvoeging van die wet met de Wet investeren in jongeren gericht op bevordering van deelname aan de arbeidsmarkt en vergroting van de eigen verantwoordelijkheid van uitkeringsgerechtigden*, The Hague: Documents Second Chamber of Dutch Parliament.

TK 32 620, no 27 (2011/12) *Beleidsdoelstellingen op het gebied van Volksgezondheid, Welzijn en Sport*, The Hague: Documents Second Chamber of Dutch Parliament.

Tonkens, E. (2014) *Vijf misvattingen over de participatiesamenleving*, Amsterdam: Universiteit van Amsterdam, www.actiefburgerschap. nl/wp-content/uploads/2014/04/Afscheidsrede-16april14.pdf

Trappenburg, M. (2016) *Helpen als ambacht. Arbeidsdeling in de participatiemaatschappij*, Utrecht: Universiteit voor Humanistiek.

van de Wijdeven, T.M.F., De Graaf, L.J. and Hendriks, F. (2013) *Actief Burgerschap: lijnen in de literatuur*, The Hague: Ministry of Interior and Kingdom Relations.

van Ditmars, A. (2017) De participatiesamenleving is een armoedig ideaal, *Trouw*, 21 September, www.trouw.nl/religie-en-filosofie/-de-participatiesamenleving-is-een-armoedig-ideaal-~adc055e5/

van Genabeek, J. (1999) *Met vereende kracht risico's verzacht. De plaats van onderlinge hulp binnen de negentiende-eeuwse particuliere regelingen van sociale zekerheid*, Amsterdam: Stichting Beheer IISG.

van Groenou, M.I.B. and De Boer, A. (2016) Providing informal care in a changing society, *European Journal of Ageing*, 13(3): 271–9.

van Kersbergen, K. (1995) *Social capitalism. A study of Christian democracy and the welfare state*, London: Routledge.

van Kersbergen, K. and Hemerijck, A. (2012) Two decades of change in Europe: the emergence of the social investment state, *Journal of Social Policy*, 41(3): 475–92.

van Leeuwen, M. (2000) *De rijke Republiek: gilden, assuradeurs en armenzorg 1500–1800*, Den Haag: Verbond van Verzekeraars.

van Oorschot, W. and Arts, W. (2005) The social capital of European welfare states: the crowding out hypothesis revisited, *Journal of European Social Policy*, 15(1): 5–26.

Verhoeven, I. and Bochove, M. (2018) Moving away, toward, and against: how front-line workers cope with substitution by volunteers in Dutch care and welfare services, *Journal of Social Policy*, 47(4): 783–801.

Verhoeven, I. and Tonkens, E. (2013) Talking active citizenship: framing welfare state reform in England and the Netherlands, *Social Policy & Society*, 12: 415–26.

Vilans (2014) Het verhalenboek: Waarin mensen een boekje open doen over hun eigen burgerinitiatief, www.vilans.nl/vilans/media/documents/producten/waarde-burgerinitiatief.pdf

Vilans (2015) Burgerinitaitieven in zorg wel welzijn, www.vilans.nl/docs/vilans/publicaties/burgerinitiatieven-in-zorg-en-welzijn.pdf

Wiggan, J. (2011) Something old and blue, or red, bold and new? Welfare reform and the Coalition government, in C. Holden, M. Kilkey and G. Ramia (eds) *Social policy review 23: Analysis and debate in social policy, 2011*, Bristol: Policy Press, pp 25–44.

Part II
Developments in social policy and contributions from the Social Policy Association Conference 2018

James Rees and Catherine Needham

The limitations of public policy can often be exemplified by high-profile scandals and news stories, which contain within them multiple policy failings. In 2017, that was the Grenfell fire. In 2018, it could be argued that it was the treatment of people from the so-called Windrush Generation – people who arrived from the Caribbean in the post-war era and were facing detention or deportation due to recent changes to immigration law. This exemplified the 'hostile environment' that had been a deliberate aspect of recent Home Office policy, and for many people, it was also linked to the broader rise of racist incidents that have been recorded since the 2016 Brexit referendum, as well as the rise of populist and anti-immigrant politics more broadly.

It is therefore timely that Andy Jolly's chapter, which starts this section, focuses on a related issue that has received much less attention in the public and academic debate: the treatment of people from what he calls the Air Jamaica generation, who came to the UK from the Commonwealth after the Immigration Act 1971. As Jolly explains, 'families in the post-Windrush era did not come as British passport holders, but were "subject to immigration control", with no recourse to public funds' and thus risked becoming undocumented if they overstayed the length of their visa. He shows that children of this generation are often invisible in social policy discussions because they lack the legal right to paid employment and are subject to the no recourse to public funds (NRPF) rule. This excludes them from accessing welfare provision, including most social security benefits, council housing and homelessness assistance. The chapter draws on a unique empirical analysis of data relating to support under section 17 of the Children Act 1989, one of the few welfare entitlements that children and families with NRPF retain, finding that support varies widely and is 'all but invisible' in policy debate. Ultimately, he argues that without access to mainstream social security, section 17 is an inadequate safety net to prevent poverty. This, in turn, stems from discriminatory legislation and policy, resulting in a situation that can reasonably be called 'statutory neglect'.

In their chapter on the Alt-Right, Julia Lux and John David Jordan explore the impact of the Alt-Right on social policy discourse in the UK, highlighting what they argue is a mainstream extremism. They argue that intensive media focus on young, working-class – usually American – white supremacists sharing extremist material over the Internet masks incidences of closely related racist, conspiracist, misogynist and 'anti-elitist' ideology in wider, often middle-class, mainstream media, politics and social policy discourse. Drawing partly on the work of Mary Douglas and Antonio Gramsci, they contribute to ongoing national and international 'Alt-Right' debates with an interdisciplinary, political-anthropological model of what they call 'mainstremeist' belief and action.

Two of the contributions in this section focus on the third sector. Rob Macmillan and Jeremy Kendall discuss the significance of the third sector within the discipline and core texts of social policy. They argue that social policy has tended to underplay the significance of the third sector, treating it as a residual category (non-bureaucratic and non-profit) that is understood only by its relationship to the state and the market. The chapter sets out an approach to exploring the moving boundaries between the third sector and the state that moves beyond the notion of a single frontier. It also challenges the very notion of 'sector' thinking, which they argue risks reifying activities behind untested assumptions, and solidifying boundaries that are otherwise emergent and contested.

Similarly, Rebecca Ince sets out to understand the place of third sector organisations in a contemporary process of localised experimentation by coalitions of actors, including local authorities, third sector organisations and private sector companies, in the Green New Deal implemented between 2011 and 2016. In this period, the UK government encouraged owner-occupied households to 'retrofit' their properties in order to improve energy efficiency and contribute to reducing carbon emissions, as well as improving energy security, through complex mechanisms, including a finance mechanism and accreditation scheme, in the context of the Coalition government's Localism agenda. The chapter investigates place-based variations in responses to Green Deal policy using three case studies in Bristol, Birmingham and Manchester, and explores in detail the contribution that third sector organisations made to each response. The emerging messages are relevant not only for energy policy, but also for other fields delivering policy through localised networks, with often contested interests and priorities.

As issues around the retirement age and compulsory versus optional retirement continue to be live within a number of sectors, including academia, Jacques Wels and John Macnicol's chapter provides a timely contribution. They discuss the 'lump of labour' fallacy, which has been used for over a century and posits that the number of jobs in an economy is fixed. They point to a lack of empirical data to support the claim, despite it being influential in debates about raising the retirement age. Their chapter concludes that more work needs to be done to understand how and why the number of jobs varies, including looking at the evolution of working time.

In the final chapter, Theo Papadopoulos and Antonios Roumpakis also tackle major themes in social policy. After years of neoliberal restructuring of social welfare, families are under pressure to act more strategically in absorbing the social risks and costs associated with social reproduction. They argue that it is imperative to extend theoretical understanding of the family as a socio-economic actor whose agency extends beyond the realm of care provision. Drawing upon Karl Polanyi's work on the variety of moral rationalities of economic action and upon critical realist sociological literature on the family as a relational subject, the chapter conceptualises the family as a collective socio-economic actor that deploys a portfolio of moral 'rationales' and practices to enhance the welfare of its members. They conclude by arguing for a new research agenda that treats the terrain of families' collective agency as a separate level of analysis, where intersections of class, racial, gender and generational inequalities can be re-imagined in studying how different welfare regimes institutionalise the conditions for families to act as socio-economic agents.

6

From the Windrush Generation to the 'Air Jamaica generation': local authority support for families with no recourse to public funds

Andy Jolly

Introduction

Over the past year, immigration has been a continued focus of policy debates in the Global North, with governments in Hungary and Italy elected on openly anti-immigration and 'welfare chauvinist' platforms. On the other side of the Atlantic, the US federal government's family separations policy has also been a source of fierce dispute. In the UK, the potential implications of Brexit for European Union (EU) migrants in the UK and the treatment of the children of the 'Windrush Generation' under the hostile (or 'compliant') environment have caused particular controversy and precipitated the resignation of the Home Secretary.

However, there has been less discussion of the rights of the next generation of migrants who came to the UK from the Commonwealth after the Immigration Act 1971. Often from the same Caribbean countries as the Windrush Generation (Price and Spencer, 2015; Jolly, 2018), they could be described as the 'Air Jamaica generation' after the former national carrier's regular flights from Kingston's Norman Manley Airport to London Heathrow between 1974 and 2007. In contrast to those migrating to the UK in the immediate post-war period, families in the post-Windrush era did not come as British passport holders, but were 'subject to immigration control', with no recourse to public funds (NRPF) and the risk of becoming undocumented if they overstayed the length of their visa.

As the children of the 'Air Jamaica generation' have NRPF and restrictions on the right to take up paid employment, they do not have the access to the welfare state or social security system that children with British citizenship have. They therefore run an increased risk of destitution, defined in section 95 of the Immigration and Asylum Act 1999 as lacking adequate accommodation (or any means of obtaining it), or as not being able to meet other essential living needs. This has serious consequences for child welfare. There have been three serious case reviews into child deaths in England reported in the past year involving children with NRPF, all of which referred to their NRPF status as an exacerbating factor (NSPCC, 2018).

One of the few state welfare entitlements for families with NRPF is support from local authority children's services under section 17 of the Children Act 1989. Section 17 was intended to give local authorities the power to provide 'a range and level of services' for children who were in need because of disability or if 'a reasonable standard of health or development' would not be achieved without the local authority providing a service. It was not intended as a replacement for social security benefits or homelessness assistance. However, section 17 does give provision for 'providing accommodation and giving assistance in kind or in cash'. In the absence of any other means of welfare support, families with NRPF who present to children's services can be given subsistence support and accommodation under section 17, often on a long-term basis. This has subsequently resulted in the emergence of an improvised and contingent branch of social work aiming to provide financial and housing support to families that have become destitute as a result of the NRPF rule. Unlike other fields of social work practice, this parallel system of support for destitute migrant families exists without statutory guidance from central government under section 7 of the Local Authority Social Services Act 1970.[1] Additionally, unlike other areas of social care, local authorities do not receive an allocation from central government for the costs of supporting families with NRPF, resulting in services that are under-resourced and separate from mainstream welfare support.

Context

Child migrant destitution and the provision of section 17 support to mitigate its effects take place against the backdrop of renewed concern about the social welfare implications of austerity, and the re-emergence of extreme poverty in the UK. This is exemplified by the criticisms from the United Nations (UN) Special Rapporteur on extreme poverty and human rights of the effect of austerity on poverty in the UK (OHCHR, 2018), as well as by the growth of foodbanks and increasing food insecurity since 2010 (Lambie-Mumford and Dowler, 2014; Dowler and Lambie-Mumford, 2015; Loopstra et al, 2015; Garthwaite, 2016).

Narratives of deservingness in relation to welfare, and the removal of welfare entitlements as a punishment for actions that do not comply with standards or expectations of behaviour, have become a familiar feature of the welfare state in recent years. This emphasis can be traced back to the New Labour belief in rebalancing 'rights and responsibilities' (Dwyer, 2004), which was extended through the Coalition government's introduction of Universal Credit, with its system of sanctions and fines (Dwyer and Wright, 2014; Reeve, 2017).

Welfare chauvinism based on immigration status has often evolved in parallel with welfare conditionality based on social class (Guentner et al, 2016), but it is immigration welfare chauvinism that has been the most pervasive form of welfare conditionality in the UK, having developed incrementally under Labour and Conservative governments alike since the 1970s, and pre-dating other forms of welfare conditionality. However, for Taylor-Gooby (2016), migrant exclusions from the welfare state form part of a wider programme of reducing the amount of national resources that are spent on recipients of social security spending, including changes to taxation and reductions in working-age benefits, which contributes to exacerbating and embedding social divisions. Nonetheless, for migrants, welfare conditionality has usually taken a distinctive form, with the almost complete removal of rights to work for asylum seekers and undocumented migrants contrasting sharply with the wider policy of labour market activation, where social security is conditional on entering the labour market or making efforts to become more employable (Dwyer, 2004).

The issue of access to social security benefits has informed debates across Europe on 'welfare tourism', particularly in the years immediately before and after EU enlargement to include the A2 (Bulgaria and Romania) and A8 (the Czech Republic, Estonia, Hungary, Latvia, Lithuania, Poland, Slovakia and Slovenia) states (Shutes, 2017). More recently, the impact of immigration on public services featured prominently in the Leave campaign during the Brexit referendum (Gietel-Basten, 2016), with a correlation between negative attitudes towards immigration and EU enlargement and voting for Brexit (Arnorsson and Zoega, 2018), and higher support for leaving the EU in areas that had experienced higher immigration in the period leading up to the vote (Goodwin and Milazzo, 2017).

Statutory neglect

Previous research (Jolly, 2018) has suggested the concept of statutory neglect as a way of framing the form of welfare conditionality experienced by migrant children who are excluded by statute from the welfare safety net of social security and homelessness assistance. Statutory neglect is not a result of poor practice on the part of individual local authorities or social workers, but rather a structural form of neglect as a result of welfare chauvinist policy and/or legislation that does not have regard for the health and well-being of particular types of children.

Most definitions of child neglect take an individual, rather than a structural or collective, perspective, and focus on the actions of parents or legal guardians (US Department of Health and Human Services, 2010; HM Government, 2015). However, ideas of what constitutes neglect evolve over time and in different contexts (Corby et al, 2012). Erikson and Egeland (2002) recognise that a failure to provide support so that parents can meet their children's needs can be a form of neglect, and Sethi et al (2013) take an ecological perspective on neglect that includes structural factors such as law and policy. The concept of statutory neglect draws on these acknowledgements of the broader societal factors that contribute to neglectful situations by including situations where neglect is a direct result of law or policy.

Statutory neglect occurs when children have experiences as a result of law or policy that would meet the definition of neglect if they were as a result of action by a parent or carer. It could include: lack of food, clothing and shelter; physical or emotional harm or danger; or emotional needs (HM Government, 2010: 38). As such, it differs from the legal concept of wilful neglect in the Criminal Justice and Courts Act 2015, where a person is treated neglectfully in the care of a medical professional in a hospital, care home or domiciliary care service. Statutory neglect is structural, only occurring when the structures and policies themselves, rather than an individual substandard care worker or care service, neglect the needs of children.

This chapter uses the concept of statutory neglect as a lens to critically examine subsistence support given to children and families with NRPF by local authorities in England under section 17 of the Children Act 1989. The focus is on English local authorities because child welfare legislation differs in the other three nations of the UK. In Wales, the relevant legislation is section 37 of the Social Services and Well-being (Wales) Act 2014. In Scotland, support is provided under section 22 of the Children (Scotland) Act 1995, and in Northern Ireland, article 18 of the Children (Northern Ireland) Order 1995 is the relevant legislation. Nevertheless, although child welfare law differs across the UK, immigration control is a reserved matter to the UK government and, consequently, the NRPF rule applies across the UK. Therefore, there are examples from across the four nations of the UK of how the NRPF rule impacts at a local authority level, such as: Farmer's (2017) account of social work with families with NRPF in Glasgow; Mackenzie and Stephens' (2015) research into how NRPF status affects those experiencing gender-based violence in Wales; and, finally, research for the Belfast Area Domestic and Sexual Violence and Abuse Partnership on domestic abuse and women with NRPF (Dudley, 2014). Mindful of the danger of methodological nationalism (Wimmer and Glick Schiller, 2002), it is not the intent here to reduce analysis to the boundaries of the nation-state as processes of statutory neglect can be observed in other contexts beyond the borders of the UK, such as the Trump administration's 'Zero Tolerance' protocol that separated the children of undocumented migrants from their parents after crossing into the US. However, it is useful to study processes within the boundaries of a nation-state as the specifics of how laws and policies are constructed and interact with the lives of those who are subject to them is particular to the national context.

Methods

Freedom of information requests were made to all 33 London borough councils in recognition of the fact that a majority of families supported under section 17 are likely to be in London (Price and Spencer, 2015). In addition, in order to provide a regional comparison with experiences outside the capital, a second set of freedom of information requests were made to nine English local authorities. This sample was chosen to include one local authority from each of the English regions. Local authorities with the largest number of non-British residents according to the 2011 census were chosen from each region. The sample was not intended to be representative of the whole population of families with NRPF, but was geographically representative of the local authorities in each region that were likely to have the largest number of children with NRPF. Local authorities were asked to provide: the number of children and families who were supported under section 17 in October 2018; the numbers of referrals received in the previous financial year; and the weekly subsistence rates paid to families with NRPF. Freedom of information requests were supplemented by information in the public domain from local safeguarding children's board and local authority websites.

Findings

Numbers supported

The lowest number of families with NRPF supported by a local authority was eight, and the highest was 156, with a mean number of families being supported across all local authorities being 41. Three out of the five local authorities with the highest numbers of families were in London. However, despite the likely high proportion of families with NRPF who live in London, the authority that was supporting the largest numbers of families was Birmingham City Council, and there were families with NRPF supported by local authorities in all the English regions. This suggests that the issue of families with NRPF becoming destitute is not an issue solely confined to London and the South-East of England.

Refusal of section 17 support

Most of the local authorities did not record the number of referrals received for families with NRPF or the number of refusals of support. It is therefore difficult to track what happens to families who present as destitute to local authorities but are refused section 17 support. This in itself is a child welfare concern because without a means to other welfare support, and without the legal entitlement to paid employment in many cases, families with NRPF are left at risk of various forms of labour or sexual exploitation (Pinter, 2011). However, 12 local authorities did disclose the numbers of families that were referred (or self-referred) for section 17 support. From this, it is possible to work out how many referrals resulted in section 17 support being provided. Three local authorities supported all of the families who were referred to them between April 2017 and March 2018. However, the majority had some form of pre-assessment screening for immigration status and eligibility, which resulted in families with NRPF being refused financial assistance or housing. In half of the local authorities, fewer than half of the total number of referrals resulted in a family being given section 17 support. It is not possible to know the reasons for refusal as this was not recorded in many cases, but five local authorities did record when support was refused due to immigration status. These amounted to 347 families across five local authorities, all in London, ranging from 6 per cent of all referrals to 67 per cent. As screening for immigration status takes place before an assessment of need (NRPF Network, 2018), it is not known whether these families would otherwise have been assessed as destitute and provided with section 17 support. Nonetheless, it is indicative of what Humphries (2004) describes as the 'unacceptable role for social work' in implementing immigration control, and of the various ways in which immigration control can conflict with, or even take precedence over, child welfare (Barn and Kirton, 2015).

The proportion of referrals that resulted in a service being provided under section 17 varied widely. The mean number of refusals across the local authorities was 40 per cent, but this conceals a broad range – from the two authorities who supported all of those who were referred, to one authority, at the other extreme, who refused 80 per cent of those who were referred to them. The five local authorities who received the highest number of referrals were also in the top five for the highest number of refusals.

Supported out of borough

A total of 22 local authorities disclosed the numbers of families that were provided with accommodation under section 17 of the Children Act outside of the local authority area. For local authorities outside of London, this was typically a small minority of the total, although Newcastle was unusual in that the majority of families were given housing outside the city. London boroughs were far more likely to support families out of the area: in outer London, six out of 13 boroughs supported a majority of families out of the area; five out of the six inner London boroughs who responded housed a majority of families with NRPF outside of the borough; and Westminster supported all of the families outside of the area.

There may be individual welfare reasons for families to be housed outside of the area, such as to protect them from the risk of trafficking or exploitation (Department for Education, 2018a), and one authority housed a number of families outside of the area at the request of the family. However, it does have the effect of moving families away from support networks and has been identified in a serious case review as a risk factor in the death by starvation of Lynne Mutumba, who was supported with her mother out of the area by Croydon Borough

Council (Smith, 2018). It is also notable that the practice of housing families out of the area, while common for families with NRPF, is now increasingly also used for families that are not subject to immigration control. Under powers introduced in 2012, local authorities can discharge their duty to homeless families by offering them a year's tenancy in the private sector, a power that has been extensively used to move families outside London and into cheaper accommodation in the West Midlands and other areas of the South-East (*The Independent*, 2015). This practice resonates with Guentner et al's (2016) observation that restrictions on welfare in the UK have historically been trialled on migrants before being extended to other groups who are perceived as 'undeserving'.

Support given

In the absence of guidance from central government under section 7 of the Local Authority Social Services Act 1970 on subsistence support rates, support levels varied widely (see Table 6.1). Of the 38 local authorities where information was available, just over half published guidance for social workers about the rates of support given to families. London boroughs were far more likely to have NRPF policies that included subsistence rates than other authorities. Only three out of the eight representative authorities of the English regions had subsistence policies, but 18 of the 33 London boroughs had published policies. The range of subsistence support rates for a family with one parent and two children varied from £65 per week to £225.14 per week. The mean weekly payment across all 21 local authorities with published policies was £120.29.

Seven local authorities did not specify rates of support, but based them on an individual assessment of needs, as required by the *Working together to safeguard children* guidance (Department for Education, 2018b). However, without any guidelines as to how subsistence should be assessed and calculated, it is difficult to know how consistent and equitable they were in practice. Some authorities offered guidance about the criteria that should be used by social workers when deciding rates of support during assessments. Merton varied the rate they paid to families 'depending if food [was] included and water rates [and] other income received from charity and family network' (Merton Borough Council, 2018). Redbridge also varied their rate according to family circumstance: 'some families have no other support, whereas some do have other support, for example from friends, church, or benefits that

Table 6.1: Weekly rates for one parent and two children

Local authority	Weekly amount for a family of one parent and two children	Notes
Inner London		
Camden	–	Based on assessment of needs
Hackney	–	No published policy
Hammersmith and Fulham	£111.90	
Haringey	–	No published policy
Islington	£134	
Kensington and Chelsea	£225.14	Benefit rate
Lambeth	£106.17	Section 4
Lewisham	£105	
Newham	£106.17	Section 4
Southwark	–	No published policy
Tower Hamlets	£77.50	
Wandsworth	–	No published policy
Westminster	£202.63	90% benefit rate
Outer London		
Barking and Dagenham	£105.22	Between £70.78 and £176 depending on size of family
Barnet	–	No published policy
Bexley	£102.56	
Brent	£149.86	In line with S4/S95 rates
Bromley	–	Based on assessment of needs
Croydon	£110.78	
Ealing	£158.98	
Enfield	–	No published policy
Greenwich	£105.78	
Harrow	£110.85	
Havering	£114.98	
Hillingdon	£135	
Hounslow	–	No published policy
Kingston upon Thames	–	No published policy
Merton	–	Based on assessment of needs
Redbridge	–	Based on assessment of needs
Richmond upon Thames	–	No published policy
Sutton	£65	
Waltham Forest	–	Based on assessment of needs

(continued)

Table 6.1: Weekly rates for one parent and two children (continued)

Local authority	Weekly amount for a family of one parent and two children	Notes
Regional local authorities		
Leicester	–	No published policy
Luton	–	Based on assessment of needs
Manchester	–	Based on assessment of needs
Southampton	–	No published policy
Bristol	–	No published policy
Birmingham	£105.30	Policy currently under review but rates reviewed on a case-by-case basis at discretion of team manager
Leeds	£113.25	Based on asylum support rates
Newcastle	£100	

other family members are claiming for them' (Redbridge Borough Council, 2018). In contrast, Waltham Forest calculated the amount by estimating a budget that included 'cost for food for the entire family; cleaning materials, essential products for babies and young children – nappies and formula milk (plus additional payments on a case by case basis)' (Waltham Forest Borough Council, 2018).

For the authorities who specified a weekly subsistence rate for families under section 17, it was not always clear what these rates were based on, and there were large variations in the amounts paid. However, a minority of local authorities did specify how their rates were calculated. Two used the equivalent rate that the family would receive if they were eligible for mainstream social security benefits, with one subtracting 10 per cent (for reasons that were not explained). Four mentioned asylum support rates as a starting point for calculating subsistence rates, and a further nine, although not mentioning asylum support, paid rates that appeared to be derived from Home Office asylum support rates.

Currently, asylum support rates are £37.75 for each person in a household (or £35.39 in a voucher card for section 4 'hard case' support to refused asylum seekers). Additionally, pregnant mothers receive an additional £3 per week, and there are payments of £5 for a baby under one year old, and £3 for a child aged one to three years. This would equate to £113.25 per week, and 14 of the 21 authorities who specified a rate paid less than this.

Using these rates, it is possible to calculate the amount of support for a notional household of one parent and two children of school age (see Table 6.2). Despite the fact that many subsistence support rates appeared to mirror asylum support rates, there was also a tendency for subsistence rates to not be uprated to keep pace with increases in asylum support. Hence, over time, these fell below the rates paid to asylum seekers. There was also confusion about their levels, particularly between the standard asylum support rate and the lower, 'section 4' rate for refused asylum seekers. Some authorities offered extras such as a one-off winter clothes payment, payments for utility bills and weekly additional payments to pregnant mothers and pre-school children in line with asylum support. However, others paid less for subsequent children in the household after the first child.

This can also be compared with what the same family would receive if they were eligible for public funds. Working on the assumption of a family with no savings, in a Universal Credit area, a comparable family who were not subject to immigration control would be entitled to £225.14 per week after housing costs, comprised of £190.74 from Universal Credit and child benefit of £34.40. A family would also be entitled to Local Housing Allowance (LHA) for housing costs, as well as free prescriptions, dental care, eye tests and free school meals for the children, and would be eligible for the National Health Service (NHS) Low Income Scheme for help towards prescriptions for the parent. All but one authority who used a standard rate of subsistence support were paying less than the amount that the family could expect if they were eligible for mainstream social security benefits, and an average paid just 52 per cent of the amount that the family would receive through mainstream social security.

Table 6.2: Comparison of weekly payments to families with poverty lines

	Inner London mean	Outer London mean	Regional mean	Total mean
Weekly section 17 payment for parent and two children	£133.56	£115.90	£106.18	£118.55
Percentage below HBAI poverty line	56%	62%	65%	61%
Percentage below minimum income standard	68%	72%	74%	71%

Note: HBAI = households below average income.

Discussion

Are subsistence rates sufficient to live on?

Using the households below average income (HBAI) measure of relative poverty, the poverty line is currently £306 per week after housing costs for a family with one parent and two children aged five and 14 (DWP, 2018). Rates of subsistence support were, on average, 61 per cent below the poverty line (see Table 6.2), with inner London boroughs paying the highest, and the non-London authorities paying the lowest. The majority of rates were lower than other mainstream social security or asylum support: the lowest weekly amount of the surveyed local authorities corresponded to only £3.10 per day per household member, and the highest was £10.72 – all rates were below the HBAI poverty line.

An alternative indicator of deprivation is the Joseph Rowntree Foundation (JRF) minimum income standard (Davis et al, 2018). This measure is based on a consensus of the cost of everything that a household needs in order to 'achieve an acceptable living standard'. The standard is similar in intent and wording to the threshold for section 17 support under the Children Act of 'maintaining a reasonable standard of health or development'. Section 17 rates for families with NRPF were even further below the minimum income standard than the HBAI. In 2018, a household of one parent with two school-age children would need £412.35 per week after housing costs, excluding the cost of council tax and childcare, to achieve an acceptable living standard. However, the mean weekly rate of support across all authorities was 71 per cent below the minimum income standard. Overall, authorities outside London were further below the poverty line than those in the capital, with inner London authorities having rates that were the closest to the poverty line and minimum income standards.

Are support rates neglectful?

In order to be indicative of statutory neglect, subsistence rates of support would have to, first, meet the criteria of neglect and, second, be a result of policy and/or legislation. Howarth's (2007) taxonomy of child neglect includes four types of neglect: physical, educational, emotional and medical. Educational neglect does not apply to children with NRPF as a matter of policy because schooling is not classed as a public fund in the immigration rules and they are therefore not excluded as a matter of policy. The restrictions on secondary medical care and lack of access to prescription costs for children with NRPF could fall into the category of medical neglect, or, as Howarth (2007: 28–29) phrases it, 'Failing to provide appropriate health care … and refusal of care'. NHS health care is not the responsibility of local authorities and so is not relevant to section 17 support rates. However, physical neglect particularly resonates with the low support rates that families with NRPF are paid under section 17: 'failing to provide for a child's basic needs such as food, clothing or shelter' (Howarth, 2007: 16–17). Certainly, rates of support paid by local authorities around the country are far below the level of support reasonably expected by those who are not subject to immigration control. They are significantly lower than the equivalent rates of Universal Credit and child benefit that families with access to public funds would be paid. They are also consistently lower than the poverty line of 60 per cent of median income and the JRF minimum income standards, and would therefore be unlikely to be high enough to consistently meet a child's 'basic physical needs'. Although it is beyond the scope of this chapter to assess the extent to which below-poverty-line support rates would be 'likely to result in the serious impairment of the child's health or development', a parent or carer who consistently provided for some of the children in their care at a level that was knowingly below the minimum income for an adequate standard of living could reasonably meet the threshold for neglect.

The second criterion for statutory neglect is that it is as a result of policy/legislation rather than 'wilful ineptitude or negligence by a care service or individual'. Certainly, there are examples of individual ineptitude and negligence in some cases (see, for instance, North East London Migrant Action's (NELMA) accompanying work in London; Pinter, 2011). However, there is also evidence of positive attitudes and supportive relationships with social workers (Jolly, 2018). Nonetheless, the reason why families with NRPF approach local authorities for subsistence support and housing under section 17, rather than seeking employment or support through the mainstream social security system, is due to the NRPF policy itself. Most strikingly, the government's stated aim is to use immigration law and policy 'to create here in Britain a really hostile environment' for those subject to immigration control, which suggests deliberate intent behind exclusionary policies towards families with NRPF (Kirkup and Winnet, 2012).

The welfare needs of families with NRPF are therefore neglected by the government in at least two ways: first, in the exclusionary policies themselves, which remove the right to access welfare; and, second, the lack of statutory guidance on meeting the needs of children with NRPF, itself a symptom of the way in which the welfare needs of families with NRPF are neglected by the government. This results in a contradictory and ambivalent approach from local authorities (Thomas et al, 2019). On the one hand, authorities have duties to safeguard child welfare and are often critical of the Home Office for leaving 'families in limbo at a great emotional cost to them' (Lewisham Borough Council, 2015). On the other hand, in the context of austerity that has seen budgets cut, local authorities sometimes reduce the financial burden of support by paying below-poverty-line subsistence rates to families, or reducing the numbers of people who request support through the aggressive 'gatekeeping' of services.

The local authority response

In the absence of national guidance from government, some local authorities have responded with 'robust front door' gatekeeping, an approach that was pioneered by Lewisham Borough Council:

> It ... means establishing eligibility for NRPF in a robust and fair way. Without the intervention of this successful pilot we found that costs of NRPF may have increased to as much as £15,719,000 by 2018. We support the robust front door approach that has been taken by the NRPF pilot project and recommend that the pilot approach is mainstreamed and made a permanent approach.

This approach entails restricting access in order to prevent families claiming the support that they would be entitled to, and the impact of the policy can be seen in the fact that only 20 per cent of families who were referred to Lewisham in the 2017/18 financial year received section 17 support. This was the lowest percentage of all local authorities, and compares with an average of 59 per cent across all of the local authorities surveyed. This policy has been taken up by other local authorities across London – Lambeth Borough Council is on record as wanting to 'drive down the cost of this service through a range of measures we are taking to narrow our front door and to expedite the closure of "open cases" through a variety of means' (Lambeth Borough Council, 2015). Merton Borough Council have also taken on this 'robust' approach, coupling it with support to regularise families' immigration status: 'We need to maintain a robust front door response and speed up the process of families lodging their applications and case management through the legal systems' (Merton Borough Council, 2017).

Other local authorities did not appear to have a formal policy of gatekeeping to prevent families accessing support, although the large numbers of families with NRPF who were referred to children's services but did not receive section 17 support, and the testimony of advocacy organisations such as NELMA (nd) and Project 17 (Dickson, 2019), are perhaps indicative of similar processes at work on a more informal 'street-level bureaucracy' basis.

Why do local authorities respond in this way?

Local authorities respond with this ambivalent approach towards families with NRPF for a number of reasons. First, in the context of austerity, local authorities have increasing budgetary constraints, while facing competing priorities for support. Children with NRPF are, by the admission of some local authorities themselves, not a priority compared to more 'desirable' groups. In evidence to the Clue judgment on support for families with NRPF, Birmingham City Council admitted that: 'The stark reality is that costs for people with no recourse to public funds is at the expense of other services the local authority is either required or expected to provide' (R. Clue v Birmingham 2010 EWCA Civ 460).

Similarly, the Chair of the Public Accounts Select Committee for Lewisham Borough Council acknowledged that the vulnerability of children with NRPF had to be balanced against financial constraints: 'Due to their circumstances, children from such families are particularly vulnerable. However, there is no government grant available to authorities for their support and no provision within the Council's base budget. The need to balance these issues is a considerable challenge' (Lewisham Borough Council, 2015).

Second, the costs to local authorities of supporting families with NRPF are increasing. The best estimates are that the numbers of undocumented migrant families are growing (Dexter et al, 2016; Jolly et al, 2019), and more families are consequently approaching local authorities for support. In one particularly striking example, Lewisham Council's 'Overview and scrutiny' report on the cost of NRPF support found that in 2008, the annual cost of support for families with NRPF was £242,000. However, by 2012, the costs had increased to £2,244,000, and by 2013, had increased again to £5,368,000 (Lewisham Borough Council, 2015).

Third, Home Office decisions, such as granting people discretionary leave to remain in the UK without recourse to public funds (Guentner et al, 2016), and the continuing 'backlogs' of immigration applications, considerably increase costs to local authorities by passing costs that would be met by the national social security system onto local government. Again, Lewisham Borough Council (2015) were particularly blunt about where they considered that the blame lay for the rising costs of supporting families with NRPF:

> The conclusions of this committee were clear; that Home Office incompetence directly contributes to council overspends.
>
> In addition, we hope [this scrutiny report] will go some way to informing the public as to the vast sums councils are forced to spend to cover up Home Office chaos. It cannot be right that the never-ending saga of Home Office disarray drags local councils down with it and if I were permitted to make one personal recommendation it would be that the Home Secretary make an urgent statement as to her plans for remedying this latest costly failure.

Conclusions

Despite often being from the same Commonwealth countries as the Windrush Generation, migrants from the Air Jamaica generation have featured less in policy discussions about the impact of the hostile environment, or in conversations about the impact of austerity and welfare conditionality on levels of poverty in the UK. Without the entitlement to access mainstream welfare services, families can experience destitution, and are often reliant on section 17 support from local authority children's services. In the absence of guidance to local authority children's services on section 17 support for families with NRPF, a parallel, ad hoc benefits system has developed that is independent of mainstream social security and all but invisible in the social policy literature. While this system goes further than other forms of welfare conditionality, it resonates with other trends in welfare and social security towards a more informal, discretionary, localised welfare system.

Analysis of subsistence support indicates that rates are too low to lift children out of poverty, or to achieve the section 17 aim of maintaining a 'reasonable standard of health or development'. Rates of subsistence support that are paid to families vary widely by local authority but are consistently below the amount needed to maintain an adequate standard of living, as measured by the equivalent social security benefit entitlement, the HBAI poverty line or the minimum income standard.

It is therefore reasonable to conclude that based on the definition of child neglect in England, a parent or caregiver who consistently provided a standard of support for some of the children in their care that was less than adequate for a reasonable standard of living would be viewed as neglectful. Furthermore, as the reason that families are approaching local authorities for section 17 support is the NRPF restrictions on mainstream social security, the neglect is statutory in nature.

Although this parallel system is a result of national policies of welfare conditionality, such as the NRPF rule, it is administered and enforced at a local authority level through bordering practices such as 'robust front door' policies. These policies employ gatekeeping to prevent access to subsistence support and undermine both the Children Act principle of the welfare of the child being paramount and the social work values of 'empowerment and liberation of people' (IFSW, 2014). Local authorities are in a conflicted position of having safeguarding duties towards children irrespective of immigration status but without the resources to do so in a context of austerity and a hostile environment towards people who are subject to immigration control.

Note

[1] See: www.legislation.gov.uk/ukpga/1970/42/section/7

References

Arnorsson, A. and Zoega, G. (2018) On the causes of Brexit, *European Journal of Political Economy*, http://dx.doi.org/10.1016/j.ejpoleco.2018.02.001

Barn, R. and Kirton, D. (2015) Child welfare and migrant families and children, in M. Skivens, R. Barn, K. Kriz and T. Pösö (eds) *Child welfare systems and migrant children: A cross country study of policies and practice*, Oxford: Oxford University Press.

Corby, B., Shemmings, D. and Wilkins, D. (2012) *Child abuse: An evidence base for confident practice* (4th edn). Maidenhead: Open University Press.

Davis, A., Hirsch, D., Padley, M. and Shepherd, C. (2018) *A minimum income standard for the UK 2008–2018: Continuity and change*, York: JRF.

Department for Education (2018a) What is a suitable placement for an unaccompanied asylum seeking child? Information for local authorities to accompany the national transfer protocol for unaccompanied asylum seeking children, London, www.local.gov. uk/sites/default/files/documents/Suitable%20placements%20for%20 UASC%20updated%20April%202018%20Final.pdf

Department for Education (2018b) *Working together to safeguard children: Statutory guidance on inter-agency working to safeguard and promote the welfare of children*, London: The Stationery Office.

Dexter, Z., Capron, L. and Gregg, L. (2016) *Making life impossible: How the needs of destitute migrant children are going unmet*, London: The Children's Society.

Dickson, E. (2019) *Not seen, not heard: Children's experiences of the hostile environment*, London: Project 17, www.project17.org.uk/policy/ campaigns/seen-and-heard/

Dowler, E. and Lambie-Mumford, H. (2015) How can households eat in austerity? Challenges for social policy in the UK, *Social Policy and Society*, 14(3): 417–28.

Dudley, R. (2014) *Domestic abuse and women with no recourse to public funds: Where human rights do not reach*, Belfast: Belfast Area Domestic & Sexual Violence and Abuse Partnership.

DWP (Department for Work and Pensions) (2018) Households below average income, 1994/95 to 2016/17, Table 2.4ts: equivalent money values of overall distribution mean, median, and 60 per cent of median income for different family types in 2016/17 prices, United Kingdom, www.gov.uk/government/statistics/hbai-199495-to-201617-incomes-data-tables

Dwyer, P. (2004) Creeping conditionality in the UK: from welfare rights to conditional entitlements?, *The Canadian Journal of Sociology*, 29(2): 265–87, http://dx.doi.org/10.1353/cjs.2004.0022

Dwyer, P. and Wright, S. (2014) Universal credit, ubiquitous conditionality and its implications for social citizenship, *The Journal of Poverty and Social Justice*, 22(1): 27.

Erikson, M. and Egeland, B. (2002) Child neglect, in J.B. Klika and J.R. Conte (eds) *The ASPSAC handbook on child maltreatment*, Thousand Oaks, CA: Sage, pp 3–20.

Farmer, N.J. (2017) 'No recourse to public funds', insecure immigration status and destitution: the role of social work?, *Critical and Radical Social Work*, 5(3): 357–67.

Garthwaite, K. (2016) *Hunger pains: Life inside foodbank Britain*, Bristol: Policy Press.

Gietel-Basten, S. (2016) Why Brexit? The toxic mix of immigration and austerity, *Population and Development Review*, 42(4): 673–80, http://dx.doi.org/10.1111/padr.12007

Goodwin, M. and Milazzo, C. (2017) Taking back control? Investigating the role of immigration in the 2016 vote for Brexit, *The British Journal of Politics and International Relations*, 19(3): 450–64.

Guentner, S., Lukes, S., Stanton, R., Vollmer, B.A. and Wilding, J. (2016) Bordering practices in the UK welfare system, *Critical Social Policy*, 36(3): 391–411.

HM Government (2015) Working together to safeguard children: a guide to inter-agency working to safeguard and promote the welfare of children, HM Government, https://assets.publishing.service. gov.uk/government/uploads/system/uploads/attachment_data/ file/592101/Working_Together_to_Safeguard_Children_20170213. pdf

Howarth, J. (2007) *Child neglect: Identification and assessment*, Basingstoke: Palgrave Macmillan.

Humphries, B. (2004) An unacceptable role for social work: implementing immigration policy, *British Journal of Social Work*, 34(1): 93–107.

IFSW (International Federation of Social Workers) (2014) Global definition of the social work profession, www.ifsw.org/what-is-social-work/global-definition-of-social-work/

Jolly, A. (2018) No recourse to social work? Statutory neglect, social exclusion and undocumented migrant families in the UK, *Social Inclusion*, 6(3): 190–200, http://dx.doi.org/10.17645/si.v6i3.1486

Jolly, A. Thomas, S. and Stanyer, J. (2019) *London's children and young people who are not British citizens: A profile*. Wolverhampton: Institute for Community Research and Development/Greater London Authority.

Kirkup, J. and Winnet, R. (2012) Theresa May interview: 'We're going to give illegal migrants a really hostile reception', *The Daily Telegraph*, 25 May, www.telegraph.co.uk/news/uknews/ immigration/9291483/Theresa-May-interview-Were-going-to-give-illegal-migrants-a-really-hostile-reception.html

Lambeth Borough Council (2015) Cabinet member delegated decision: increase in subsistence payments paid to families with no recourse to public funds, https://moderngov.lambeth.gov.uk/documents/s72437/Final_uplifting%20NRPF%20subsistence%20rates%20docx%2019%2002.pdf

Lambie-Mumford, H. and Dowler, E. (2014) Rising use of 'food aid' in the United Kingdom P. Martin Caraher and Dr Alessio Cavic, ed, *British Food Journal*, 116(9):1418–25, http://dx.doi.org/10.1108/BFJ-06-2014-0207

Lewisham Borough Council (2015) Overview and scrutiny, no recourse to public funds review, Public Accounts Select Committee, http://councilmeetings.lewisham.gov.uk/documents/s33873/No%20Recourse%20to%20Public%20Funds%20Review.pdf

Loopstra, R., Reeves, A., Taylor-Robinson, D., Barr, B., McKee, M. and Stuckler, D. (2015) Austerity, sanctions, and the rise of food banks in the UK, *BMJ*, 350: h1775.

Mackenzie, D. and Stephens, A. (2015) *Research into how 'no recourse to public funds' status affects those experiencing gender based violence, domestic abuse and sexual violence in Wales*, Cardiff: Local Government Data Unit, www.wsmp.org.uk/documents/wsmp/No%20Recourse%20to%20Public%20Funds/No%20Recourse%20to%20Public%20Funds%20Research%20report%202015%20FINAL%20v4.pdf

Merton Borough Council (2017) Financial Monitoring Task Group (FMTG), briefings on UASC, NRPF, SIA expenditure and key issues, https://democracy.merton.gov.uk/documents/s16472/CSF%20deepdive%2020.02.17.pdf

Merton Borough Council (2018) Freedom of Information Act 2000/Environmental Information Regulations 2004 Information request 27 September, Information Governance Team, London: Merton Borough Council.

NELMA (North East London Migrant Action) (nd) Our Manifesto, https://nelmacampaigns.wordpress.com/nelma-manifesto/

NRPF (No Recourse to Public Funds) Network (2018) *Practice guidance: Assessing and supporting children and families with NRPF*, London: Islington Borough Council, http://guidance.nrpfnetwork.org.uk/reader/practice-guidance-families/

NSPCC (National Society for the Prevention of Cruelty to Children) (2018) National case review repository, https://learning.nspcc.org.uk/case-reviews/national-case-review-repository/

OHCHR (Office of the United Nations High Commissioner for Human Rights) (2018) Statement on visit to the United Kingdom, by Professor Philip Alston, United Nations Special Rapporteur on extreme poverty and human rights, www.ohchr.org/Documents/Issues/Poverty/EOM_GB_16Nov2018.pdf

Pinter, I. (2011) *'I don't feel human': Experiences of destitution among young refugees and migrants*, London: Children's Society.

Price, J. and Spencer, S. (2015) *Safeguarding children from destitution: Local authority responses to families with 'no recourse to public funds'*, Oxford: COMPAS, www.nuffieldfoundation.org/sites/default/files/files/PR-2015-No_Recourse_Public_Funds_LAs.pdf

Redbridge Borough Council (2018) Freedom of Information Act 2000 request Ref. 3449840 11 October, Children's Services team, London: Redbridge Borough Council.

Reeve, K. (2017) Welfare conditionality, benefit sanctions and homelessness in the UK: ending the 'something for nothing culture' or punishing the poor?, *Journal of Poverty and Social Justice*, 25(1): 65–78, http://dx.doi.org/10.1332/175982717X14842281240539

Sethi, D., Bellis, M., Hughes, K., Gilbert, R., Mitis, F. and Galea, G. (2013) *European report on preventing child maltreatment*, Geneva: World Health Organisation.

Shutes, I. (2017) Controlling migration: the gender implications of work-related conditions in restricting rights to residence and social benefits, in J. Hudson, C. Needham and E. Heins (eds) *Social policy review 29: Analysis and debate in social policy, 2017*, Bristol: Policy Press.

Smith, F. (2018) Serious case review 'Ellie': Overview report, Chatham: Medway LSCB.

Taylor-Gooby, P. (2016) The divisive welfare state, *Social Policy and Administration*, 50(6): 712–33.

The Independent (2015) Over 50,000 families shipped out of London boroughs in the past three years due to welfare cuts and soaring rents, *The Independent*, 29 April, www.independent.co.uk/news/uk/home-news/over-50000-families-shipped-out-of-london-in-the-past-three-years-due-to-welfare-cuts-and-soaring-10213854.html

Thomas, S., Jolly, A. and Goodson, L. (2019) *Undocumented children in London and their heath and wellbeing*. Birmingham: University of Birmingham/Barnardo's.

US Department of Health and Human Services (2010) *The Child Abuse Prevention and Treatment Act 2010: Including Adoption Opportunities & the Abandoned Infants Assistance Act*, CAPTA P.L. 111-320 Booklet, Washington, DC: US Department of Health and Human Services, https://www.acf.hhs.gov/sites/default/files/cb/capta.pdf

Waltham Forest Borough Council (2018) FOI Response FOI87896886 'emotional health and wellbeing of undocumented migrant children'. 11 October, Information Officer, London: Waltham Forest Borough Council.

Wimmer, A. and Glick Schiller, N. (2002) Methodological nationalism and beyond: nation-state building, migration and the social sciences, *Global Networks*, 2(4): 301–34.

7

Alt-Right 'cultural purity', ideology and mainstream social policy discourse: towards a political anthropology of 'mainstremeist' ideology

Julia Lux and John David Jordan

Introduction

According to a well-rehearsed media trope, the 'Alt-Right' ('alternative right') burst into a shocked public consciousness in the run-up to the 2016 US presidential election (Caldwell, 2016; Collins, 2016). Curiously, this phenomenon materialised in *media* consciousness as a nebulous interconnectivity of white supremacists incubated in the obscure 'dark web' before spreading into the minds of poorly educated people via the unfiltered medium of the mainstream Internet (Cook, 2016; Caldwell, 2016). This definition was rapidly deployed by presidential candidate Hillary Clinton to attack Donald Trump's supporters as a 'paranoid fringe' (Ohlheiser and Dewey, 2016). Explaining the ability of this racist 'fringe' to somehow capture the White House similarly defaulted to the deeply classist, technophobic and socially convenient narrative of uneducated poor people exposed to bad ideas on the Internet (Ember, 2016; Weigel, 2016; Marwick and Lewis, 2017; Bartlett, 2018; Daniels, 2018).

A series of books and articles exploring the Alt-Right have been published since 2016. Perhaps due to the different publication timelines involved in academic output, this material is primarily journalistic. This literature provides detailed empirical data critical to understanding the underpinning social networks of the Alt-Right. However, intensive media focus on young, working-class – usually American – white supremacists (Neiwert, 2017) sharing extremist material over the Internet (Nagel, 2017) masks incidences of closely related racist, conspiracist (ie belief in/promotion of conspiracy theories), misogynist and 'anti-elitist' ideology in wider, often middle-class, mainstream media, politics and social policy discourse (Mondon and Winter, 2018). This mainstream extremism – or, as we will call it, 'mainstremeism' – is often couched in terms of 'refreshingly un-politically correct' hard truths (see Harris, 2015). This article problematises current narratives surrounding the 'Alt-Right'. We then draw on the work of anthropologist Mary Douglas – who argues that ideologies of purity, impurity and purge recur in numerous cultures, helping to mask social inequalities, shore up group identity and legitimise and rationalise access to group resources (Douglas, 2003) – and Antonio Gramsci's insights about the role of 'organic intellectuals' to contribute to ongoing national and international 'Alt-Right' debates by presenting an interdisciplinary, political-anthropological understanding of 'mainstremeist' belief and action. This approach highlights the links between 'fringe' and 'centre'. This kind of reasoning is crucial to understanding the impact of the Alt-Right on social policy in the UK. Key figures seek to deploy social policy as a tool of misogynist, patriarchal, racist and classist retrenchment.

The remainder of this article is structured as follows. The second section introduces the literature on the Alt-Right and its current strengths and weaknesses. The third section outlines a political-anthropological approach that links Alt-Right ideas to 'mainstremeist intellectuals'. The fourth section offers a schematic practical application of this approach to immigration, education and gender equality. The fifth section concludes the article by drawing together each of the preceding themes into the argument that while the 'Alt-Right' is widely presented as fringe, working class and generally uneducated, there are numerous examples of mainstream, highly educated, middle-class individuals promoting similar discourses.

The Alt-Right in public and academic discourse

Many commentators characterise the Alt-Right as a sanitising self-description used to hide connections with violent white supremacy and other forms of oppressive ideology (Michael, 2017; Bezio, 2018; Blodgett and Salter, 2018; Hartzell, 2018; Salazar, 2018). Nevertheless, the Alt-Right is usually defined as a 'movement', albeit retaining ambiguity as to what defines adherence (Heikkilä, 2017; Atkinson, 2018; Bezio, 2018). For example, while several commentators assume that the Alt-Right are mostly young, white men (Hawley, 2017; Bezio, 2018), others point out that this may be a myth (Wendling, 2018) or a proud self-description to be considered with caution (Salazar, 2018). Given that the key features of the Alt-Right are white supremacy and misogyny, it may target white males whose ethnic and gender identity are fragile (Kelly, 2017; Neiwert, 2017), but there are also female adherents (Kelly, 2018).

The term 'Alt-Right' distinguishes the current character of the extreme Right from previous instalments, and many commentators see novelty in the movement's use of cyberspace. The Internet's low cost and minimal regulation of speech offers an attractive and exploitable battleground for extreme right-wing organising (Adams and Roscigno, 2005; Barkun, 2015; Hawley, 2017). While Internet use might not be that new for white supremacists after all (Adams and Roscigno, 2005), its role as an amplifier of Alt-Right messages and community building is well documented (Hawley, 2017; Heikkilä, 2017; Love, 2017; Salter, 2017; Bezio, 2018; Blodgett and Salter, 2018; Daniels, 2018; Massanari and Chess, 2018; Wendling, 2018). Beyond using websites to disseminate information, Alt-Right Internet users have also been active in specific online communities, such as Reddit, 4chan, Gab and news comments sections, where they have creatively adapted their modes of communication, often using memes, humour, irony and 'trolling' (Hawley, 2017; Heikkilä, 2017; Salter, 2017; Bezio, 2018; Blodgett and Salter, 2018; Massanari and Chess, 2018; Salazar, 2018).

The ability to employ often-overlooked racist and sexist lilts in social media structures is a key feature of Alt-Right activism, while the desire to do so indicates that its roots and ideology are characterised by white supremacy *and* misogyny (Wilkinson, 2016). The Alt-Right is militantly sexist – and closely associated with the 'Men's Rights' movement, the 'menosphere', 'incel' (involuntary celibate) groups and the misogynist 'pick up artists' scene (Hawley, 2017; Kelly, 2017; Salter, 2017; Bezio, 2018; Blodgett and Salter, 2018; Massanari and Chess, 2018). Most analyses assume that the Alt-Right has been tech-savvy while Internet platform providers have been unaware of how their services are being misused. Some claim that the realisation of the white supremacist character of the movement following the 2017 Charlottesville events will lead to online providers 'deplatforming' extremists (Atkinson, 2018). However, Daniels (2018: 63) argues that 'the ideology of color-blindness in technology – both in the industry and in popular understandings of technology – serves [as] a key mechanism enabling white nationalists to exploit technological innovations'. A similar point has been made about the gendered dimension of the Internet (Salter, 2017; Bezio, 2018).

Reflecting the nebulous nature of the Alt-Right, commentators have pointed to its ideological influences as including palaeo-conservatism, neo-reactionism, neo-Nazism, radical libertarianism, European right-wing movements – particularly identitarianism – and anti-immigration movements (Hawley, 2017; Heikkilä, 2017; Lyons, 2017; Michael, 2017; Wendling, 2018). These ideologies all espouse, or imply, racism, including Islamophobia and, in numerous cases, anti-Semitism. They are often used to legitimise or incite violence, and it is notable that hate crimes have increased in line with the growth of Alt-Right activism (Lyons, 2017; Atkinson, 2018; Wendling, 2018), leading Reid and Valasik (2018) to characterise the Alt-Right as, effectively, a violent street gang. Forscher and Kteily (2017) further suggest that members of the Alt-Right are likely to admit to aggressive behaviour online and to holding extreme prejudices, often linked to evolutionary theories regarding the inferiority of non-white, non-males and people who believe in contrary perspectives, particularly social justice.

Most of the links between ideological currents and the Alt-Right are established through analysing online content, as well as by tracing the ideas of key figures such as Richard Spencer, Steve Bannon and Andrew Anglin to thinkers in older rightist philosophies. They further link the Alt-Right to the work of academics like Kevin MacDonald, Aleksandr Dugin, Paul Gottfried and Charles Murray (Gray, 2017; Michael, 2017; Atkinson, 2018; Hartzell, 2018; Wendling, 2018). The precise mix of ideologies underpinning the Alt-Right remains fuzzy and, to a certain extent, contradictory, leading to internal inconsistencies and divisions within the movement (Hawley, 2017; Wendling, 2018). Such internal divisions are reflected in the ambivalent relationship between the Alt-Right and conservatism. Nevertheless, the Alt-Right shares several common views and talking points with mainstream conservatism, particularly the 'fight' against political correctness (Atkinson, 2018; Hartzell, 2018). There is also an overlap in terms of media and other conspiracy theories (Neiwert, 2017). However, mainstream conservatism, and in particular the established institutions of the US Republican Party, is widely argued to be despised by the Alt-Right, being viewed as its most significant obstacle to seizing power (Hawley, 2017). The relationship between the Trump presidency and the Alt-Right is thus discussed in the literature with some ambivalence. Hawley (2017) argues that the presidential election is a stepping stone to Alt-Right political supremacy due to Trump's apparent destabilisation of the Republican Party. Others have argued that the election of Trump, and Steve Bannon's time as National

Security Advisor, signify the Alt-Right being in power (Lyons, 2017; Hartzell, 2018; Wendling, 2018).

Either way, a widely recognised effect of the political rise of the Alt-Right is a poisoning of the discursive climate of politics, and an attempted undermining of the legitimacy of the media with potentially serious – and negative – implications for democracy (Harris et al, 2017; Bennett and Livingston, 2018). There has been some recent discussion of the Alt-Right's links to European populism, but when the political and policy influence of populist radical-right groups is discussed, this focuses on parties as they get into parliament (Minkenberg, 2017) yet says little on their impact *without* a party-political organisation – a key identifying feature of the Alt-Right. A more concrete discussion of the European Alt-Right's impact on policy beyond immigration debates (Mudde, 2017) is also absent from existing scholarship.

Problematisation of existing narratives

We find four key problems with these primarily US, extremist and/ or technophobic narratives in media and academic discourse. First, while new communications technologies often play an amplifying role in political discourse, the Internet has been overemphasised as the Alt-Right's progenitor. The Internet is clearly *a* medium, the specific characteristics of which produce empirically identifiable phenomena (anonymity, hyper-real content, democratisation and speed of dissemination), but 'cyber-causality' masks the role of broader economic and social factors, and downplays the continued influence, and real power, of traditional political and media platforms to spread, enact and entrench ideology. Cyber-causality also fails to explain the success of non-Internet-based populist phenomena, such as much of the debate surrounding Brexit, and the emergence of populist personalities into public fame outside of the Internet. Additionally, 'fringe', generally powerless, individuals have little retort to accusations of trolling, whereas the personal gravitas of mainstream figures helps to skew perception of their actions, transforming them in the minds and analyses of their social media followers into waggish scientific wit. This is not to say that the Alt-Right does not troll, but rather, that trolling as a tactic is often ascribed to Alt-Right working-class 'resentment' but rarely linked to middle-class *advantage* when middle-class often highly educated people do it.

Second, the current literature quarantines analyses far too narrowly. White supremacists exist, but explicitly articulating the retrenchment of white power in a racially striated US economic system (see Neiwert, 2017) is not the same phenomenon as European populist ethno-nationalism, with its focus on excluding and/or expelling migrants – or, indeed, isolationism (eg Brexit), which partially leverages resentment against broadly white-majority states, and even more problematically 'institutions' *per se*, perceived somewhat abstractly, for example, 'the European Union'. Additionally, save for notable exceptions (including Blodgett and Salter, 2018; Salter, 2017; Kelly, 2017), overemphasis on the macro-political agenda of white supremacism regularly analytically overwhelms recognition and analysis of the equally important Alt-Right focus on the meso-institutional and micro-cultural retrenchment of misogyny, patriarchal power, hetero-normativity and, in many cases, extreme socially conservative and free market capitalist ideology.

Third, focusing on a supposed militant hatred of traditional conservatism seems analytically delinked from numerous instances of traditional right-wing parties succumbing to increasing populist ideological capture, a phenomenon experienced in both America and beyond. Fourth, the notion of the Internet bringing bad ideas to uneducated people, and, indeed, the overall notion of uneducated people constituting the Alt-Right, is classist, patronising and feeds the resentment at elite disdain that it attempts to explain. Relatedly, the aphasic sense of real geographical locations embedded in the constant implication of 'fringe', relative to 'mainstream', which is discursively reproduced in the repeated linkage of the Alt-Right to housing estates, 'rust belt' US states or even 'redneck' swamps (Gawrylewski, 2016; MacBain, 2017; Marwick and Lewis, 2017), contrasts poor locations not with any real 'centre', but with the ideological centre of 'normalness'. 'Centre' is, in this regard, a code for 'middle-classness'.

Towards a political anthropology of 'mainstremeism'

While the current literature provides a detailed account of people, events and networks, this work is analytically problematic and overwhelmingly descriptive, as argued earlier. In this section, we thus conceptualise two indicative structures – 'conspiracy entrepreneurs' and 'cultural Marxist conspiracism' (CMC) – in order to more systematically understand the impact of the Alt-Right on social policy, particularly through the output of its organic intellectuals. These concepts spring from Douglas's work on 'cultural purity' and Gramsci's insights into the role of intellectuals in political organising.

Cultural purity

Anthropologist Mary Douglas (2003) argues that purity/impurity narratives, including ritualised purges, help to structure numerous cultural practices. Drawing on Douglas's work, a broader sociocultural, socio-political agenda can be identified within 'alt' social narratives, based on five key purity meta-nodes:

1. There is a pure ethnic 'in-group'.
2. Structural inequalities and advantages within the in-group are natural, but the civilisational norms that separate the in-group from 'savagery', both internal and external, are ancestral.
3. This overall social structure is threatened by external impurity and internal deviance.
4. Deviance and inequality are proxies for individual bodily impurity/ purity statuses.
5. A purge is necessary to restore social purity.

This is an adaptive structure, idiosyncratically malleable by conspiracy entrepreneurs to do everything from swelling the ranks of populist movements through to justifying resentment and violence over loss of privilege, inability to form a relationship or perceived personal slights. To understand the function and position of these entrepreneurs, Gramscian insights on organic intellectuals are helpful.

Organic intellectuals, common sense and the mainstream

Italian Marxist Antonio Gramsci highlights the role of 'organic intellectuals' in organising political movements. He states that everyone is an intellectual but not all perform the function of one (Gramsci and Forgacs, 1988: 304). This function is to give homogeneity and awareness to the social group that they organically come from (Gramsci and Forgacs, 1988: 301) or seek to link into (Gramsci and Forgacs, 1988: 302). When Gramsci employs the term 'organic', this refers to the social class that these intellectuals stem from and are trying to organise.

In order to organise homogeneity and awareness, intellectuals need to connect with common sense and integrate it into a world view. This is a fundamentally never-ending and contradictory process given that 'common sense' is diffuse and contradictory, as well as context-specific (Gramsci and Forgacs, 1988: 331). For our purposes, this is to be distinguished from the mainstream, which we understand as a more streamlined, self-proclaimed centrist and majority position. Within this so-called 'centrist' civil society, however, Alt-Right ideas have an identifiable presence. Moreover, there is significant middle-class and well-educated support for these ideas. While many Alt-Right ideas are promulgated via cyberspace, the Internet is a classic 'weapon of the weak'; a tool used by poorer, less influential people. Analyses therefore risk replicating a classist skew by focusing primarily on Internet dissemination and ignoring that mainstream intellectuals have access to instruments of power, such as politics, media, publishing and lawyers, and can deflect and contend claims of extremism in a way that disadvantaged people find much more difficult.

Conspiracy entrepreneurs

Conspiracism is highly active and creative. One way of thinking about this is with regard to 'conspiracy entrepreneurs', that is, competitive content providers offering maps to the centre of the maze. The centre often transpires to be the 'entrepreneur' itself, as the central arbiter and dot-to-dotter of relevant conspiracy fragments, so much so that conspiracy entrepreneurs will often denounce one another for failing to adhere to their own idiosyncratic map.

Conspiracy entrepreneurialism can be defined by the implausible creative linkage of facts, ideas and prejudices to claims that society is under threat from subversion – often coupled with claims of personal social martyrdom for revealing the 'truth' (Jay, 2011; Perkins, 2018). This latter technique transforms even the most devastating criticism into an advantage, hence the sociological phenomenon of many conspiracy entrepreneurs, particularly famous ones, being criticised for spreading false information and then claiming that those criticisms are themselves part of a subversive conspiracy (Penny, 2018) and the entrepreneurs themselves 'free-speech martyrs' (Garavelli, 2018; Pettigrew, 2018; Perkins, 2018).[1]

Drawing on Gramsci insights, the entrepreneurs need to be understood as 'organic intellectuals' who take a more central position in political organising than their adherents. This conceptualisation of embedded class power relations forms the backdrop of our empirical discussion in the following sections. We provide examples of intellectuals who are disseminating and 'sanitising' Alt-Right ideas, most crucially, Cultural Marxist Conspiracism.

Cultural Marxist Conspiracism

The essentials of Cultural Marxist Conspiracism (CMC) are that following the failure of political Marxism in the West, the Frankfurt Institute Marxists and their 'allies' attempted to destroy white, Western culture 'from the inside'. They attacked all family and social institutions, undermined the role and status of men, created feminism, invented children's individual rights and aggressively promoted divorce, perversion, bestiality, homosexuality, extramarital sex and paedophilia. As the blurb for Alt-Right conspiracist W. August Mayer's (2016) book puts it: 'Western Civilization is being intentionally destabilized by a process of cultural subversion. Leading the charge in this below the radar, stealth war is an alliance between the hard, Marxist left and the Jihadist Muslims who have been chipping away at traditional Western liberal values and mores for decades'. While these ideas might seem absurd, their internal logic can be explained with reference to Douglas' work as a perceived 'purity threat' introduced by external actors ('Marxist Jews' and more recently 'Jihadist Muslims'), aided by internal malefactors ('elites', socialists, 'deviants', university lecturers). It also highlights the role of the intellectual to construct an awareness of a pure and threatened 'in-group', in this case, by presenting a threatening other.

CMC further alleges that this project of cultural destabilisation subsequently 'promoted' the civil rights agenda and anti-racism, while simultaneously defaming all attempts to celebrate white, Western culture as 'fascist'. It undermined 'honest' capitalism by engineering human rights legislation, globalisation and 'corporate capitalism', as well as by 'infecting' economies with ecological ideology, 'health and safety', 'social justice' and 'political correctness'. Political correctness is a key CMC concept. While always vague, this term broadly refers to the idea that criticism of chauvinism, racism or capitalist operation is itself an affront to the free speech and civil rights of the Right, and of white males in general. Feminism is characterised as a 'hysterical' attack on male rights and status. As sociology professor Anthony Synnott (2010) puts it: 'This new sexism, reverse sexism, is widespread in feminist and pro-feminist literature – or propaganda, one might say – but largely ignored'. In other words, Professor Synnott is repeating the commonplace Alt-Right claim that feminism is anti-male sexism. Patriarchy and racial, age and class inequality are alleged to be encoded within nature, whether this be a spiritual or a genetic nature, or both. Cultural Marxist-encouraged deviance is characterised

159

as a deviation from this natural order, leading to social catastrophe. Criticism of this sentiment is deemed to be 'political correctness', Marxist brainwashing, an attack on 'Western values' and a denial of evolutionary science. Universities, schools, the entertainment industry, the media and even entire governments are all allegedly controlled by 'Marxists' deploying 'postmodernism' to destroy critical thinking. As key Alt-Right ideologue Jordan Peterson warns: 'I don't think its dangers can be overstated. And I also don't think the degree to which it's already infiltrated our culture can be overstated' (quoted in Phillipp, 2017). Additionally, CMC alleges that climate change is a hoax, and that Western governments are introducing 'Islamification' as a form of cultural doomsday device.

When presented as an overarching narrative, CMC might seem ridiculous and linkable only to the extreme social 'fringe'. Nevertheless, despite this seeming absurdity it does have clear, definitive elements: misogynist anti-feminism, neo-eugenic science (broadly defined as various forms of genetic determinism), genetic and cultural white supremacy, McCarthyist anti-Leftism fixated on postmodernism, radical anti-intellectualism applied to the social sciences, and the idea that a purge is required to restore normality. Seen in this way, as a set of ideas rather than an ideological absurdity definable only be location with in a putative social fringe, we find all of these items supported, proselytised and academically buoyed by intellectuals, politicians and media figures with extremely credible educational backgrounds. A major source of intellectual justification for CMC, for example, comes from philosopher Stephen Hicks (2004).

In the following, we will apply these theoretical and conceptual insights to social policy, primarily in the UK. In order to provide more evidence for the role of intellectuals and CMC, we provide specific examples of individuals' public speech acts, like publications or Twitter postings, as well as reported statements and interviews, that illustrate the prevalence of major elements of CMC among a well-educated and influential group of people. This allows us to link these ideas in the Anglo-Saxon language area with social policies in the UK. It is important to note that our methodology is schematic and interpretive, that is, we have selected relevant quotes to map the conceptualisation of entrepreneurs and CMC, as well as the purity/impurity meta-nodes outlined in more abstract form earlier.

Analysis: cultural purity political anthropology applied to social policy

In the following, for each of three selected policy fields (immigration, education, gender equality), we discuss key intellectuals and their organic power resources, highlight their ideas from a purity/impurity perspective, and suggest specific social policies that can be linked to these ideas.

Linking the Alt-Right to immigration policy

Media pundit, journalist and conspiracy entrepreneur Douglas Murray is a prime example illustrating the influence of an 'organic intellectual'. Murray has written passionately in support of British fascist Tommy Robinson (Murray, 2018) and describes Islam as an 'opportunistic infection' (Hasan, 2013) linked to the 'strange death of Europe' (Murray, 2017a). Murray's ideas are entangled not only with the Far Right (working class or otherwise), but with wider social connections. He is organic not to the working class, but to the middle class, and his books and comments find echoes in the output of a range of middle-class politicians and intellectuals, like biologist Richard Dawkins (2013b), who comments that Murray 'sees through David Cameron's ingratiating Islamophilia'. Militant atheism, of which Dawkins is the leading figure, has played a pre-eminent role in promoting and scientising crypto-racist narratives of religious believers as a savage, ignorant threat to white cultural purity (Robbins, 2013; Arel, 2017; Gray, 2018). Both Dawkins and Murray are atheists, yet both invoke the notion of 'cultural Christianity' to underpin their claims that Islam is a threat to progressive 'European values', such as lesbian, gay, bisexual and trans (LGBT) and women's rights, as, indeed, do several European Far Right groups. Murray, for example, has provided support for European Far Right activist Geert Wilders on the grounds of his putative defence of European liberalism (Murray, 2017b), as has Dawkins (Jones, 2013). The invocation of an entirely imaginary 'progressive' Christian past ('ancestral values' meta-node) serves to 'other' another religion, Islam, which Dawkins (2013a) describes as 'the greatest force for evil in the world today' and a putative threat to the white European in-group's cultural purity.

Despite significant differences over the truth of religion, as opposed to its cultural importance, both militant atheism and the Alt-Right proffer the same purity narrative: that multiculturalism is a critical and deadly threat to Western society (see Wax and Alexander, 2017; Zubatov, 2018). Dawkins, for instance, describes multiculturalism as a 'code for Islam' (Robbins, 2013); that is, an external impurity threat. Professor of Law Amy Wax's homophobic and racist comments on the putative destruction of US 'Judeo-Christian' culture (Zagoria-Moffet, 2014), and fundamental conclusion that 'all cultures are not equal' (Wax and Alexander, 2017), reflect this cultural purity claim (see also Harris, 2015: 1). Dovetailing these claims is an allegation of a cultural betrayal by the 'liberal elite' (Dawkins, 2007; Harris, 2015) – in Douglas's conceptualisation, the *internal* 'purity threat'.

In the UK, 'immigration conspiracy' allegations have focused on assertions of a Labour Party conspiracy to change the cultural face of Britain (Green, 2016: 1; Murray, 2017a). Allegations of 'the liberal elite' betrayal is now also a key Alt-Right *and* mainstream allegation levied against the European Union's leadership, as well as the US 'deep state'. Wax and Alexander (2017) have similarly attempted to stoke populist ire with claims of a deviant 'bourgeois political hegemony'. Cultural purity narratives and Islamophobia ideologically buoy a wide range of immigration policy and political events, including Brexit (Virdee and McGeever, 2017), the revalorisation of 'stop and search', the Windrush scandal and the 'hostile environment' policies more generally, and several pieces of so-called anti-terrorist action, including the PREVENT agenda (Abbas and Awan, 2015).

Linking the Alt-Right to education policy

As argued earlier, CMC is crucial to understanding the Alt-Right and has significant implications for education policy – given the assumption that teachers and lecturers indoctrinate pupils and students. Both Richard Dawkins (2007) and fellow militant atheist, philosopher Steve Harris (2015) explicitly denounce postmodernism, or putative cultural Marxism, as rotting the intellectual culture of the West, as do several other of their key intellectual allies, including Steve Pinker (2018) and Christopher Hitchens (2005), who blames postmodernism for the 'abysmal state of mind that prevails in so many of our universities'. Wax and Alexander (2017) blame 'the expansion of higher education' for rotting culture *per se*. Echoing ideas promoted by one-time UK Education Secretary Michael Gove, Wax and Alexander extol educational systems that are geared towards 'gainful employment', productivity and 'social coherence', and reflect a broader and emerging rightist anti-intellectualism that views higher education as unacceptably subversively critical of white, capitalist social order.

Crucially, this is a major project of extreme anti-intellectualism prosecuted against mainstream sociology, feminism, postmodernism, Marxism and critical race theory *by*, primarily, academics, including several militant atheists, plus Murray and Peterson, but also hundreds of others, particularly in the field of 'evolutionary psychology' (Evans, 2018). This purge ideology extends to a significant and growing 'parallel academy' of institutes, books, blog-sites, discussion boards and related media. Most recently, it revolves around the online magazine *Quillette* (whose associate London editor is currently Toby Young), promoting CMC, anti-feminism and genetic determinist 'science'.[2] The Alt-Right *and* the mainstremeist 'parallel academy' have promoted a purge of the 'rotten' academy for several years, on and off the Internet. *Quillette* author and social psychologist Lee Jussim's 'Heterodox Academy' (Heterodox Academy, 2018), for example, has hundreds of academic members and finds its reason for existence in the claim that the US academy has gone from 'leaning left to being almost entirely on the left'.

Calls for a purge achieved wider prominence in 2018 when three individuals revealed that they had published four hoax articles in feminist and 'postmodern' journals. Jussim (2018a) tweeted 'Like most evidence of radical leftist corrupt intolerance in academia, this will be dismissed as a small number of anecdotes', while Peterson (2018) commented that 'The grievance studies disciplines are fraudulent to the core.... And the core disciplines of the humanities are disappearing down the same black hole'. This 'purge' meta-node is explicitly articulated by the Alt-Right conspiracy entrepreneurs in *precisely* the same terms, against precisely the same disciplines (eg RockingMrE, 2015). The purge focus on sociology, feminism and critical race theory is not coincidental; these disciplines are a bulwark against patriarchy, racism and class privilege. The Hungarian decree to remove gender studies, for example, may seem 'fringe' politically, geographically and phenomenally, but it indicates the growing influence and potential trajectory of this project. Even the manner of reportage of this event in the UK helps to push this agenda, for example, the *Daily Mail*'s (2018) reproduction of tropes such as 'gender-ology' and 'George Soros-funded university'. Speculatively, one might argue that gender studies are viewed as an easy first target, following which the 'purge' can be spread into critical sociology and related subjects.

Mainstream newspapers, including the *Daily Mail* and *The Spectator*, have run several articles claiming that 'cultural Marxists' have infiltrated universities and other cultural institutions. This includes allegations by *Daily Mail* columnist Peter Hitchens (2017; see also Hitchens, 2018) that primary school teachers are indoctrinating children with Marxist ideology. Most recently, Toby Young, who was briefly appointed to the board of the UK's university system, claimed a widespread conspiracy of 'hard Left' teachers indoctrinating children was likely responsible for Jeremy Corbyn's youth vote. Young (2018) asks 'Who will stop them brainwashing our children?'. Senior UK cabinet member, and one-time Education Secretary (2010–14), Michael Gove (2013), meanwhile, has described high-school teachers as a 'Marxist blob' and announced that he will 'refuse to surrender to the Marxist teachers hell-bent on destroying our schools'. This may be linked with the Conservative government's intention to extend grammar schools and academies, which have been shown to reproduce socio-economic inequalities (Gorard and Siddiqui, 2018), and changes to the UK's school curriculum, introduced by Gove, which have been widely described as ideological in nature (Bousted, 2017). By tracing who voices elements of CMC, we see clear links between politicians in (or almost in) powerful positions, their organic intellectuals including well-established professors and the wider group of Alt-Right thinkers and adherents. The first two groups are more in a position to directly change policies. The PREVENT agenda, for example, can be seen as a measure to not just police pupils' and students' 'radicalisation', but also to police their teachers (O'Donnell, 2015). Conservative government whip Chris Heaton-Harris's attempt to force universities to reveal the names of lecturers teaching about Brexit, as well as the content of their lectures (Fazackerley, 2017), demonstrates the potential for harnessing public opinion towards the policing of knowledge by political actors.

Douglas's insights on deviance and inequality help understand this aspect of legitimising education policy reform. The Alt-Right and its more mainstream versions share this understanding that deviance and inequality are proxies for individual bodily impurity/purity. In most cases, this is *reactive*, through arguing that genes are responsible for inequality, success, human behaviour, unemployment, health, patriarchy, crime, national success and 'superior' Western culture. Genetic explanations for inequality are the most widespread and significant concepts within the mainstream, scientised Right (Evans, 2018). Charles Murray's arguments regarding putative average intelligence differences between 'races' are perhaps the most well-known example (Hernstein and Murray, 1994). British genetic determinists focus largely on class and economic inequality. That 'IQ', or other inherited features, might account for social inequality is a long-standing claim. Yet, as with much 'evolutionary psychology', the science is broadly imaginary. Nevertheless, the idea of genetically inherited intelligence re-emerged in British sociological debate in the 1990s with Peter Saunders's (1995) claims that the structure of social mobility in the UK appeared largely explicable by intelligence. Critically, this argument relies on defending the putative science behind the IQ concept, namely, claims of genetically inherited intelligence.[3] As Young (2015: 3) puts it: 'it's probable that in the next few years genetic research scientists will produce even more evidence that important aspects of people's personalities – including those that determine whether they succeed or fail – are linked to their genes'. The message being sent is that inequality is natural, and based on graduations of internal, that is, genetic, purity/impurity. In other words, it presents a scientised description *of* inequality masquerading as an explanation *for* inequality. Constant testing of pupils' and students' achievements and the consequential rankings of schools and universities partly reflect the idea that performance is related to capability and the quality of teaching rather than socio-economic background and resources – and, indeed, the social and psychological processes involved in testing that can skew results.

Linking the Alt-Right to gender-equality policies

The claim that welfare states prevent evolution from weeding out 'genes for having too many children' appears most famously in Dawkins's (2006: 117) *The selfish gene*. More recently, Dawkins's argument has been reanimated by neuroscientist Adam Perkins (2016), who claims that genes for being 'disagreeable' help to explain why the long-term unemployed cannot find work, and, moreover, that there is a demonstrable empirical link between rising welfare benefits and having 'extra' children who will, in turn, be disagreeable and need more welfare. Perkins calls this the 'welfare trait'. Perkins is an advocate of CMC, and has been forced to apologise for racist comments (Apostolakis, 2017). He played a major role in ideologically justifying the UK's two-child benefit cap – which affects children born after 2017 and their families.

The potential descent of Perkins's arguments into forced individual purge has already happened, *in the mainstream*, with the *Daily Mail* publishing an article in 2010 mooting the potential sterilisation of poor women (Clarke, 2010). The disciplining of poor women is not just reflected in suggestions, however; it is a feature of much recent social policy. The targeting of single mothers as responsible for society's ills has a well-known history and continues with the 'Troubled Families Programme' (Nunn and Tepe-Belfrage, 2017) and a wider misogyny-creep into UK social policy. It has now been well evidenced that austerity disproportionately affects women (Karamessini and Rubery, 2013; Rafferty, 2014), thus drawing on the public–private divide to hide some significant social and gendered effects of austerity (Hajek and Opratko, 2015).

The scientisation of misogyny is a primary means of justifying, explaining and promoting gender inequality. Perkins seeks to control poor women's alleged genetically pathologised fertility. Dawkins (2006) presents women's wider social behaviour as driven by genetic impulses towards reproduction and childcare. Pinker – who describes feminism as 'an academic clique committed to eccentric doctrines' – argues that women are born with fundamentally different minds (note *minds*, not brains) to men (Pinker, 2003: 371). Peterson (amongst a host of egregiously misogynist claims) argues that women are genetically programmed to be have lower intellectual capacity than men (Peterson, 2017), that patriarchy is a beneficial epiphenomena of this 'reality', and 'politically correct' intellectual opposition to patriarchal structures can only end in social catastrophe (Bowles, 2018). Reprising ancient purity panics, Peterson also claims that witches are real in the sense of culturally signifying actual female behaviours (Bowles, 2018).

The 'science' behind these misogynist claims is asinine, often relying on no more than an appeal to pre-existing prejudices and stereotypes as superior sources of information to those outputted by a supposedly deviant intellectual elite. Jussim's (2012: 308) primary work has been to establish that there are 'extraordinary levels of accuracy in social stereotypes', stating that 'I have been pointing out for years that the full scope of evidence shows that stereotypes usually *reflect* [sic] reality far more than they cause it' (Jussim, 2018b). Seen another way – as a scientised anthropological purity myth – the socio-genetic 'science' behind Jussim's, Dawkins's, Pinker's and Perkins's claims all turn out to have already been known, recognised and fully understood by society – or at least by one part of it because these claims are merely social prejudice re-presented as science.

Conclusion

By emphasising white nationalist individuals and groups, analytic, media and public interest in the so-called Alt-Right has been artificially fixated on a social 'fringe' as the putative 'patient zero' of a racist, misogynist cultural epidemiology. This is generally framed in terms of poorer, less educated people, and linked to the unique characteristics of the Internet permitting the unfettered spread of 'egregious nonsense' to the resentful and disenfranchised. Using a model of political anthropology based partly on Mary Douglas's work on purity practices and Gramsci's understanding of the roles of intellectuals, it was shown that the same core CMC beliefs that define the Alt-Right are promoted by numerous well-educated, wealthy and well-connected 'conspiracy entrepreneurs'. Despite being presented as 'refreshingly politically incorrect' statements of unpalatable scientific truth, these ideas sublimate into straightforward claims of cultural purity, internal and external impurity, and the impending necessity of a 'purge'. Far from being 'fringe', these ideas, and their ideological embodiment in extremist 'cultural Marxist' tropes are *in* the mainstream – hence, the term 'mainstremeism'.

The chapter problematised how 'fringe' narratives mask that sexism, patriarchy and racism – and, indeed, alienation – are structurally integrated within and across *all* of society. This is reflected in the operation of the Internet, not caused by it. Cyberspace algorithms likely reproduce racist, sexist skews, but so do newspapers, films and the informal practices of countless institutions. When viewed in terms of beliefs, rather than organisational or technological networks, the broader 'alt' project is intellectually steered and supported by numerous well-educated people.

Their ambitions in social policy are extensive. While their attempted and reactionary retrenchment of white, patriarchal and classist power is often dressed in the language of science-fiction neo-eugenics, particularly in articles published in an evolving 'parallel academy', the roll-out of this 'science' is generally brute reaction, that is, personal sexism and racism, cutting benefits, promoting class-based education systems, and attacking programmes, disciplines and people that redress social inequalities. Discrediting and replacing the formal academy is key to this ambition. The role of 'mainstremeist' discourse is therefore arguably more ideological than practical: a scientisation and cultural edification of the misogyny, racism, patriarchy and inequality that its adherents resent losing the 'right' to enjoy. The roll-out of government policies across a broad range of social policy spheres highlight that this is more than ambition, and more than 'fringe'; it is the extreme in the mainstream.

Notes

¹ We use this latter term solely in relation to dubious or manufactured claims of being wrongly, or immorally, 'no-platformed', victimised, misrepresented or silenced *legally* by institutions, academic journals, courts or other outlets for 'voicing uncomfortable truths' – or simply for being criticised on social media. We do not intend this term to refer to genuine protestation over unlawful harassment or threat.

² The precise same ideas permeate Breitbart news, yet, arguably courtesy of classism, *Quillette* is described by Richard Dawkins (2017) as a 'superb online magazine [that] stands up for the oppressed minority who value clarity, logic and objective truth', while Sam Harris (2018) declares that thinking of Breitbart as a credible source is 'so obscene that it really need not even be criticised'. Breitbart news regularly links supportively to *Quillette* articles.

³ Otherwise, IQ scores can be dismissed as proxies for non-genetic social class advantages.

References

Abbas, T. and Awan, I. (2015) Limits of UK counterterrorism policy and its implications for Islamophobia and Far Right extremism, *International Journal for Crime, Justice and Social Democracy*, 4(3): 16–29.

Adams, J. and Roscigno, V.J. (2005) White supremacists, oppositional culture and the World Wide Web, *Social Forces*, 84(2): 759–78.

Apostolakis, L. (2017) King's lecturer sparks racism row: racist pseudoscientific tweets cause KCLSU complaint, *Felix*, http://felixonline.co.uk/articles/2017-2-2-kings-lecturer-sparks-racism-row/

Arel, D. (2017) New Atheism's move from Islamophobia to white supremacism, *The New Arab*, www.alaraby.co.uk/english/comment/2017/7/12/new-atheisms-move-from-islamophobia-to-white-nationalism

Atkinson, D.C. (2018) Charlottesville and the Alt-Right: a turning point?, *Politics, Groups, and Identities*, 6(2): 309–15.

Barkun, M. (2015) President Trump and the 'fringe', *Terrorism and Political Violence*, 29(3): 437–43.

Bartlett, J. (2018) Alt-Right: from 4chan to the White House review – in search of a rightwing rabble, *The Guardian*, www.theguardian.com/books/2018/apr/23/alt-right-from-4chan-to-white-house-mike-wendling-review

Bennett, W.L. and Livingston, S. (2018) The disinformation order: disruptive communication and the decline of democratic institutions, *European Journal of Communication*, 33(2): 122–39.

Bezio, K.M.S. (2018) Ctrl-Alt-Del: GamerGate as a precursor to the rise of the Alt-Right, *Leadership*, 14(5): 556–66.

Blodgett, B. and Salter, A. (2018) Ghostbusters is for boys: understanding geek masculinity's role in the Alt-Right, *Communication, Culture and Critique*, 11(1): 133–46.

Bousted, M. (2017) The consequences of Gove's ideological reforms are now being felt everywhere, *Times Educational Supplement*, www.tes.com/news/consequences-goves-ideological-reforms-are-now-being-felt-everywhere

Bowles, N. (2018) Jordan Peterson, custodian of the patriarchy, *The New York Times*, 18 May, www.nytimes.com/2018/05/18/style/jordan-peterson-12-rules-for-life.html

Caldwell, C. (2016) What the Alt-Right really means, *The New York Times*, 2 December.

Clarke, N. (2010) The baby machine, *Daily Mail*, www.dailymail.co.uk/news/article-1251070/The-baby-machine-The-tale-mother-14-children-taken-away-her.html

Collins , E. (2016) 9 things you need to know about the Alt-Right movement, *USA Today*, https://eu.usatoday.com/story/news/politics/onpolitics/2016/11/22/alt-right-trump-white-nationalist-clinton-breitbart-spencer/94273282/

Cook, J. (2016) US election: Trump and the rise of the Alt-Right, *BBC News*, www.bbc.co.uk/news/election-us-2016-37899026

Daily Mail (2018) Hungary's Far-Right Prime Minister bans gender studies at university because it is 'an ideology not a science', www.dailymail.co.uk/news/article-6285345/Hungarys-Prime-Minister-Viktor-Orban-bans-gender-studies-university.html

Daniels, J. (2018) The algorithmic rise of the 'Alt-Right', *Contexts*, 17(1): 60–5.

Dawkins, R. (2006) *The selfish gene: 30th anniversary edition*, Oxford: Oxford University Press.

Dawkins, R. (2007) Postmodernism disrobed, *Nature*, 394: 141–3.

Dawkins, R. (2013a) Islam is the …, *Twitter*, https://twitter.com/richarddawkins/status/382169025330962432

Dawkins, R. (2013b) Douglas Murray, *Twitter*, https://twitter.com/richarddawkins/status/382169025330962432?lang=en

Dawkins, R. (2017) Quillette, *Twitter*, https://twitter.com/richarddawkins/status/889819353906110474?lang=en

Douglas, M. (2003) *Purity and danger: An analysis of concepts of pollution and taboo*, London: Routledge.

Ember, S. (2016) News outlets rethink usage of the term 'Alt-Right', *The New York Times*, www.nytimes.com/2016/12/02/opinion/sunday/what-the-alt-right-really-means.html

Evans, G. (2018) The unwelcome revival of 'race science', *The Guardian*, www.theguardian.com/news/2018/mar/02/the-unwelcome-revival-of-race-science

Fazackerley, A. (2017) Universities deplore 'McCarthyism' as MP demands list of tutors lecturing on Brexit, *The Guardian*, www.theguardian.com/education/2017/oct/24/universities-mccarthyism-mp-demands-list-brexit-chris-heaton-harris

Forscher, P. and Kteily, N. (2017) A psychological profile of the Alt-Right, *Psyarxiv Preprints*, https://psyarxiv.com/c9uvw

Garavelli, D. (2018) Free speech 'martyrs' don't need publicity, *The Scotsman*, www.scotsman.com/news/opinion/dani-garavelli-free-speech-martyrs-don-t-need-publicity-1-4782642

Gawrylewski, A. (2016) Richard Dawkins and other prominent scientists react to Trump's win, *Scientific American*, www.scientificamerican.com/article/richard-dawkins-and-other-prominent-scientists-react-to-trump-rsquo-s-win/

Gorard, S. and Siddiqui, N. (2018) Grammar schools in England: a new analysis of social segregation and academic outcomes, *British Journal of Sociology and Education*, 39(7): 909–24.

Gove, M. (2013) I refuse to surrender to the Marxist teachers hell-bent on destroying our schools, *Mail Online*, www.dailymail.co.uk/debate/article-2298146/I-refuse-surrender-Marxist-teachers-hell-bent-destroying-schools-Education-Secretary-berates-new-enemies-promise-opposing-plans.html

Gramsci, A. and Forgacs, D. (1988) *An Antonio Gramsci reader: Selected writings, 1916–1935*, London: Lawrence and Wishart.

Gray, J. (2018) *Seven types of atheism*, London: Penguin Books.

Gray, P.W. (2017) 'The fire rises': identity, the Alt-Right and intersectionality, *Journal of Political Ideologies*, 23(2): 141–56.

Green, A. (2016) Was Mass Immigration a Conspiracy?, *Migration Watch*, www.migrationwatchuk.org/press-article/83

Hajek, K. and Opratko, B. (2015) Crisis management by subjectivation: toward a feminist neo-Gramscian framework for the analysis of Europe's multiple crisis, *Globalizations*, 13(2): 217–31.

Harris, J., Davidson, C., Fletcher, B. and Harris, P. (2017) Trump and American fascism, *International Critical Thought*, 7(4): 476–92.

Harris, S. (2015) The limits of discourse, https://samharris.org/the-limits-of-discourse/

Harris, S. (2018) Sam Harris discusses Donald Trump's rewriting of reality and how social media drives us insane, *ABC NEWS*, www.abc.net.au/news/2018-06-01/sam-harris-discusses-truth-and-lies-in-the-donald-trump-era/9819290

Hartzell, S.L. (2018) Alt-White: conceptualizing the 'Alt-Right' as a rhetorical bridge between white nationalism and mainstream public discourse, *Journal of Contemporary Rhetoric*, 8(1/2): 6–25.

Hasan, M. (2013) Douglas Murray, the EDL, dodgy videos and me, *The Huffington Post*, www.huffingtonpost.co.uk/mehdi-hasan/douglas-murray-edl-dodgy-videos-me_b_3675193.html?guccounter=1&guce_referrer_us=aHR0cHM6Ly93d3cuZ29 vZ2xlLmNvbS8&guce_referrer_cs=aiGQNEGNkjoaiJL44V3OQg

Hawley, G. (2017) *Making sense of the Alt-Right*, New York, NY: Columbia University Press.

Heikkilä, N. (2017) Online antagonism of the Alt-Right in the 2016 election, *European Journal of American Studies*, 12(2): 1–22.

Hernstein, R.J. and Murray, C. (1994) *The bell curve: Intelligence and class structure in American life*, London: Free Press.

Heterodox Academy (2018) The problem, https://heterodoxacademy.org/the-problem/

Hicks, S. (2004) *Explaining postmodernism*, New Berlin and Milwaukee: Scholarly Books.

Hitchens, C. (2005) Transgressing the boundaries, *New York Times*, www.nytimes.com/2005/05/22/books/review/transgressing-the-boundaries.html

Hitchens, P. (2017) The Marxist revolution is alive and well – in your child's school, *Mail Online*, http://hitchensblog.mailonsunday.co.uk/2017/05/peter-hitchens-the-marxist-revolution-is-alive-and-well-in-your-childs-school-.html

Hitchens, P. (2018) Marxism didn't die. It's alive and well and living among us, *The Spectator*, www.spectator.co.uk/2018/06/marxism-didnt-die-its-alive-and-well-and-living-among-us/

Jay, M. (2011) Dialectic of counter-enlightenment: the Frankfurt School as scapegoat of the lunatic fringe, *Salmagundi Magazine*, 22 November.

Jones, O. (2013) Not in our name: Dawkins dresses up bigotry as non-belief – he cannot be left to represent atheists, *The Independent*, www.independent.co.uk/voices/comment/not-in-our-name-dawkins-dresses-up-bigotry-as-non-belief-he-cannot-be-left-to-represent-atheists-8754183.html

Jussim, L. (2012) *Social perception and social reality: Why accuracy dominates bias and self-fulfilling prophecy*, New York: Oxford University Press.

Jussim, L. (2018a) Like most, *Twitter*, https://twitter.com/psychrabble/status/1047524365737361410

Jussim, L. (2018b) I have been ..., *Twitter*, https://twitter.com/PsychRabble/status/976267277413834752

Karamessini, M. and Rubery, J. (eds) (2013) *Women and austerity: The economic crisis and the future for gender equality*, London and New York, NY: Routledge.

Kelly, A. (2017) The Alt-Right: reactionary rehabilitation for white masculinity, *Soundings*, 66(66): 68–78.

Kelly, A. (2018) The housewives of white supremacy, *The New York Times*, 1 July.

Love, N.S. (2017) Back to the future: trendy fascism, the Trump effect, and the Alt-Right, *New Political Science*, 39(2): 263–8.

Lyons, M.N. (2017) CTRL-ALT-DELETE: the origins and ideology of the Alternative Right, www.politicalresearch.org/2017/01/20/ctrl-alt-delete-report-on-the-alternative-right/

MacBain, H. (2017) Are these the faces of London's young 'Alt-Right'?, *Evening Standard*, www.standard.co.uk/lifestyle/esmagazine/these-are-the-faces-of-londons-young-altright-a3477731.html

Marwick, A. and Lewis, B. (2017) The online radicalization we're not talking about, *Intelligencer*, http://nymag.com/intelligencer/2017/05/the-online-radicalization-were-not-talking-about.html

Massanari, A.L. and Chess, S. (2018) Attack of the 50-foot social justice warrior: the discursive construction of SJW memes as the monstrous feminine, *Feminist Media Studies*, 18(4): 525–42.

Mayer, A.W. (2016) 'Islamic Jihad, Cultural Marxism, and the Transformation of the West' blurb, www.amazon.co.uk/Islamic-Jihad-Cultural-Marxism-Transformation/dp/0692771948

Michael, G. (2017) The rise of the Alt-Right and the politics of polarisation in America, *Skeptic*, 22(2): 9–17.

Minkenberg, M. (2017) The Radical Right in public office: agenda-setting and policy effect, in C. Mudde (ed) *The populist Radical Right: A reader*, New York, NY: Routledge.

Mondon, A. and Winter, A. (2018) Understanding the mainstreaming of the Far Right, *Open Democracy*, www.opendemocracy.net/can-europe-make-it/aurelien-mondon-aaron-winter/understanding-mainstreaming-of-far-right

Mudde, C. (ed) (2017) *The populist Radical Right: A reader*, New York, NY: Routledge.

Murray, D. (2017a) *The strange death of Europe: Immigration, identity, Islam*, London: Bloomsbury.

Murray, D. (2017b) Geert Wilders doesn't threaten Dutch liberalism: he's defending it, *The Spectator*, www.spectator.co.uk/2017/01/geert-wilders-doesnt-threaten-dutch-liberalism-hes-defending-it/

Murray, D. (2018) Tommy Robinson drew attention to 'grooming gangs.' Britain has persecuted him, *National Review*, www.nationalreview.com/2018/05/tommy-robinson-grooming-gangs-britain-persecutes-journalist/

Nagle, A. (2017) *Kill all normies: Online culture wars from 4chan and Tumblr to Trump and the Alt-Right*, Alresford: Zero Books.

Neiwert, D. (2017) *Alt-America: The rise of the Radical Right in the age of Trump*, London and New York, NY: Verso.

Nunn, A. and Tepe-Belfrage, D. (2017) Disciplinary social policy and the failing promise of the new middle classes: the Troubled Families programme, *Social Policy and Society*, 16(1): 119–29.

O'Donnell, A. (2015) Securitisation, counterterrorism and the silencing of dissent: the educational implications of *Prevent*, *British Journal of Education Studies*, 64(1): 53–76.

Ohlheiser, A. and Dewey, C. (2016) Hillary Clinton's Alt-Right speech, annotated, *The Washington Post*, www.washingtonpost.com/news/the-fix/wp/2016/08/25/hillary-clintons-alt-right-speech-annotated/?noredirect=on&utm_term=.5c9f2710a802

Penny, E. (2018) The martyrdom of Tommy Robinson: free speech and the Far-Right, *Verso Blogs*, www.versobooks.com/blogs/3969-the-martyrdom-of-tommy-robinson-free-speech-and-the-far-right

Perkins, A. (2016) *The welfare trait: How state benefits affect personality*, Basingstoke: Palgrave Macmillan.

Perkins, A. (2018) 'It Has Come to My Attention …' How institutional complaints procedures are being weaponized, *Quilette*, https://quillette.com/author/adam-perkins/

Peterson, J. (2017) Jordan Peterson: Proven differences in men and women & other subjects, *YouTube*, www.youtube.com/watch?v=D8LJs9bbKVc

Peterson, J. (2018) I'll say it, *Twitter*, https://twitter.com/jordanbpeterson/status/1048273783335706624?lang=en

Pettigrew, N. (2018) Good job Toby Young is a free speech advocate, as no one should have to pay for these terrible opinions, *New Statesman*, www.newstatesman.com/2018/01/good-job-toby-young-free-speech-advocate-no-one-should-have-pay-these-terrible-opinions

Phillipp, J. (2017) Jordan Peterson exposes the postmodernist agenda, *The Epoch Times*, www.theepochtimes.com/jordan-peterson-explains-how-communism-came-under-the-guise-of-identity-politics_2259668.html

Pinker, S. (2003) *The blank slate: The modern denial of human nature*, London: Penguin Publishers.

Pinker, S. (2018) *Enlightenment now: The case for reason, progress, science, humanism, and progress*, New York, NY: Viking.

Rafferty, A. (2014) Gender equality and the impact of recession and austerity in the UK, *Revue de l'OFCE*, 133(2): 335–61.

Reid, S.E. and Valasik, M. (2018) Ctrl+ALT-RIGHT: reinterpreting our knowledge of white supremacy groups through the lens of street gangs, *Journal of Youth Studies*, 2(2): 1–21.

Robbins, M. (2013) Richard Dawkins, 'Islamophobia' and the atheist movement, *The Guardian*, www.theguardian.com/science/the-lay-scientist/2013/may/03/atheism-dawkins

RockingMrE. (2015) Universities are Marxist Churches, *Youtube*, www.youtube.com/watch?v=CxQGsLchD8Q

Salazar, P.-J. (2018) The Alt-Right as a community of discourse, *Javnost – The Public*, 25(1/2): 135–43.

Salter, M. (2017) From geek masculinity to Gamergate: the technological rationality of online abuse, *Crime, Media, Culture: An International Journal*, 14(2): 247–64.

Saunders, P. (1995) Might Britain be a meritocracy?, *Sociology*, 29(1): 23–41.

Synnott, A. (2010) Why some people have issues with men: Misandry, *Psychology Today*, www.psychologytoday.com/gb/blog/rethinking-men/201010/why-some-people-have-issues-men-misandry

Virdee, S. and McGeever, B. (2017) Racism, crisis, Brexit, *Ethnic and Racial Studies*, 41(10): 1802–19.

Wax, A. and Alexander, L. (2017) Paying the price for breakdown of the country's bourgeois culture, *The Inquirer*, www.philly.com/philly/opinion/commentary/paying-the-price-for-breakdown-of-the-countrys-bourgeois-culture-20170809.html

Weigel, D. (2016) Steve Bannon's rise points to aggressive, anti-'globalist' Trump media strategy, *The Washington Post*, www.washingtonpost.com/news/post-politics/wp/2016/11/14/steve-bannons-rise-points-to-aggressive-anti-globalist-trump-media-strategy/?utm_term=.f8dddd8033ac

Wendling, M. (2018) *Alt-Right: From 4chan to the White House*, London: Pluto Press.

Wilkinson, A. (2016) We need to talk about the online radicalisation of young, white men, *The Guardian*, www.theguardian.com/commentisfree/2016/nov/15/alt-right-manosphere-mainstream-politics-breitbart

Young, T. (2015) The fall of the meritocracy, *Quadrant*, https://quadrant.org.au/magazine/2015/09/fall-meritocracy/#_ftn2

Young, T. (2018) Who will stop them brainwashing our children?, *Mail Online*, www.dailymail.co.uk/debate/article-6223205/TOBY-YOUNG-stop-teachers-brainwashing-children.html

Zagoria-Moffet, A. (2014) The myth of a Judeo-Christian tradition, *State of Formation*, www.stateofformation.org/2014/04/the-myth-of-a-judeo-christian-tradition/

Zubatov, A. (2018) The importance of cultural nationalism in an era of distrust, *Quillette*, https://quillette.com/2018/05/21/importance-cultural-nationalism-era-distrust/

8

The moving frontier and beyond: the third sector and social policy

Rob Macmillan and Jeremy Kendall

Introduction

Asked to identify the most influential books and articles in social policy, the lists of many social policy scholars would probably include Esping-Andersen's (1990) *The three worlds of welfare capitalism*. The elaboration of three ideal-typical 'welfare regimes' (liberal, conservative-corporatist and social democratic) has transformed the way we think about social policy and welfare states (Powell, 2016: 660). Yet, its theoretical architecture is built upon a curious omission. Remarkably, it says very little about the role of the third sector in social policy and welfare provision. *The three worlds of welfare capitalism* has no indexed references at all to the third sector or allied terms. The follow-up study, *Social foundations of postindustrial economies* (Esping-Andersen, 1999), is bereft of such concepts, with one exception. Here, a welfare regime is defined as 'the combined, interdependent way in which welfare is produced and allocated between state, market, and family' (Esping-Andersen, 1999: 35–6). The accompanying footnote (Esping-Andersen, 1999: 35, n 2) advises: 'To this triad we should rightfully add the "third sector" or voluntary, or non-profit, welfare delivery. In some countries, the voluntary sector (often run by the Church) does play a meaningful, even significant, role in the administration and delivery of services'. It is noted that cross-national comparison of the third sector is rare, but Salamon and Anheier's (1998) analysis is cited – and that is it. On this basis, it would seem that the third sector in social policy is relegated to a footnote.

Further, Richard Titmuss is rightly regarded as one of the intellectual forces behind the development and expansion of social policy. He writes powerfully about altruism in *The gift relationship* (Titmuss, 1970), but, overall, he says very little about charitable or voluntary action. Reisman notes a comment made by Titmuss in a letter to a colleague in 1959: 'The modern state needs, in addition to collective public services, a variety and diffusion of genuine voluntary agencies' (Reisman, 2001: 64). However, that is pretty much it. Titmuss 'admired voluntarism but had a preference for the State' (Reisman, 2001: 66).

Contemporary writing in mainstream social policy appears only slightly less prone to this general neglect. For example, Beresford's (2016) magisterial *All our welfare* contains only a brief and familiar critical description of charity as paternalist and stigmatising, in the context of disabled people's movements. An edited collection of writings on aspects of *The Coalition government and social policy* (Bochel and Powell, 2016) has remarkably little reflection on the role of the third sector, and little consideration of relevant policy developments of the time, such as 'the Big Society'. Pete Alcock's (2016) *Why we need welfare: Collective action for the common good* perhaps stands out as the exception that proves the rule. Alcock highlights the important role played by non-state actors in the historical provision of welfare, notes that the mixed economy of welfare has and always will be with us, and discusses how its character has changed as societies' needs have evolved.

So, it is reasonable to claim that social policy as a whole has tended to underplay the significance of the third sector. We take this argument as the point of departure for this chapter. In the discussion that follows, we consider the possibility that the third sector has been marginalised in social policy, in part, because of entrenched assumptions about 'sectors', in which the state, and latterly the market, are privileged in social policy thinking. As well as ignoring the 'loose and baggy monster', the heterogeneity of organisational forms and approaches (Kendall and Knapp, 1995), and the complex intertwined array of hybrid relationships across sectors, the 'third sector' itself becomes typically defined as a residual (non-bureaucratic, non-profit) category, understood only in terms of its broad relationship to the state and the market. The sector is seen as occupying a space on 'the other side' of a 'moving frontier' with the state (Beveridge, 1949; Finlayson, 1994). We suggest that third sector scholarship has been implicated in reinforcing some of these assumptions in its efforts to identify and define a distinctive and valuable realm of activities for enquiry in social policy.

To pursue this line of argument, we first review and assess, in the next section, the relevance of earlier attempts to promote and prioritise voluntary and community action. The chapter then considers how we might move beyond these perennial debates to develop a more nuanced account of third sector contributions to social policy. The aim here is to challenge the notion of a single 'moving frontier' between state and third sector. In outlining a preliminary map of new thinking in the contemporary political and economic context, we suggest some promising conceptual directions at two levels. A key reference point is the notion that meso-level field dynamics are crucial in shaping institutional relationships, wherein boundaries evolve differently in distinctive areas of policy (so that the 'frontier' in social care can and should be differentiated from the 'frontier' in, eg, health care or social housing). Another is the re-conceptualisation of the macro-environment as a domain for isomorphic pressures, ideologies and governmentalities. These phenomena shape the third sector in complex ways, and may even threaten sectoral identities, although by drawing on more recent new institutionalist formulations and analyses of 'hybridisation', we will see that the associated processes can be fluid, co-evolve with other sectors and should not be understood in a narrowly deterministic way.

Beyond the state: the welfare mix

Following the lead set by Titmuss, post-war social policy often sought to examine and explain the policy objectives, principles of administrative arrangement and distributional outcomes for citizens of the new welfare state. In doing so, it was explicitly critical, albeit within a narrow frame of reference, seeking to discover and repair any gaps in the safety net, to explore unmet needs and to extend welfare rights and provisions. Yet, the assumptions of state-led and -provided welfare services remained. There were some critical voices against this grain within the field itself. Robert Pinker's sophisticated pluralism is perhaps the key example. A multiple array of services organised within and across sectors would, he suggested, mitigate the risk of dependency associated with any one form of provision (Pinker, 1979). However, otherwise, for the three post-war decades, the state remained the primary focus for most scholars.

From the mid-1970s onwards, however, greater space was being given to more critical approaches, from a range of ideological standpoints, to the role of the state in welfare. In various ways, these became part of a resurgence of interest in the role of voluntary action in what increasingly became referred to as the 'welfare mix'. We consider three developments here: welfare pluralism, associative democracy and social capital.

Welfare pluralism – related to, but seeking to move beyond, Pinker's accounts – came to prominence in the late 1970s and early 1980s as one kind of social policy response to a wider set of economic, political and ideological crises undermining the Keynesian social-democratic welfare state. Indeed, from the standpoint of 1983, it was suggested that welfare-pluralist ideas, alongside privatisation, were the most important and influential in welfare at the time (Beresford and Croft, 1983: 21). Explorations of fiscal and legitimation crises on the Left (O'Connor, 1973; Gough, 1979) accompanied critical concerns with political 'overload' and 'ungovernability' on the Right (King, 1975; Birch, 1984), but under a common assumption that capitalism and the welfare state had become locked in an unholy alliance (cf Offe, 1984).

The Right's resurgence in the 1980s led to the first sustained attempts at welfare state retrenchment, based on the idea that market and individualist forms of welfare provision were always preferable to the failures of collective state provision. At the same time, welfare pluralists were accepting a notion of 'state failure', but they envisaged instead a *non-state* version of collective welfare provision in which the voluntary sector would play an enhanced 'radical' role (Gladstone, 1979; Hadley and Hatch, 1981). This was a more ambitious account of non-state welfare provision than that offered by the earlier Wolfenden Committee on the Future of Voluntary Organisations (Wolfenden, 1978), which seemed to offer some recognition of the different existing roles of voluntary organisations, but little more than a modest suite of proposals for supporting these. Hadley and Hatch's (1981) *Social welfare and the failure of the state* ruffled a lot of social policy feathers when it was published in 1981, in part, because it seemed to accept half of the New Right's critique of a bureaucratic welfare state, and was thus thought to have offered revisionist succour to an attack on social-democratic principles, just at the point at which they were most in need of a sturdy defence (Beresford and Croft, 1983). It was heavily criticised for making naive assumptions about the power and potential of voluntary action, and overlooking problems such as inconsistency, patchiness, duplication and lack of accountability to users (Beresford and Croft, 1983: 22; see also Brenton, 1985; Johnson, 1987).

Arguably, however, the debate in social policy quickly moved on and welfare pluralism was eclipsed by largely defensive efforts among analysts to chart the consequences of market- and quasi-market-inspired welfare restructuring in the mid- to late 1980s and early 1990s (Le Grand and Bartlett, 1993), as well as by efforts to open up new dimensions of social policy analysis, particularly around gender and race (Williams, 1989). Some researchers tried to keep a critical and perhaps less evangelical analysis of the mixed economy of welfare alive by looking at the contemporary 'crisis' (Johnson, 1987) or drawing attention to previously underplayed historical third sector roles (Prochaska, 1988; Finlayson, 1994). Overall, the welfare-pluralist project faltered in the early 1990s, even if a semblance of a pluralist welfare system, in the sense of multiple providers and approaches, began to emerge in practice (Deakin, 1987: 177).

However, thinking about welfare beyond the state gained a further boost from outside the social policy mainstream in two significant interventions from political scientists promoting the notions, respectively, of 'associative welfare' and 'social capital'. The late Paul Hirst's (1994) *Associative democracy* was published in 1994 as a work of normative political theory focusing on an enhanced role for associations in governance and welfare. Drawing on a legacy from Harold Laski and G.D.H. Cole, Hirst's aim was simultaneously to renew representative democracy and overcome the problems of centralised state bureaucracy. The central claim was 'that individual liberty and human welfare are both best served when as many of the affairs of society as possible are managed by voluntary and democratically self-governing associations' (Hirst, 1994: 19). Hirst followed familiar pluralist themes in arguments around welfare provision by criticising large-scale hierarchical systems as obstacles to participation. A multiplicity of self-governing associations would instead offer a means both for the expression and pursuit of different ways of meeting needs, and provide both voice and choice for citizens. In Hirst's vision, the state's role changes fundamentally: freed from the overextended burden of providing services to fulfil a public oversight and regulatory role, ensuring the appropriate governance of associations while funding many of them to ensure universal services of guaranteed quality.

Hirst's associational model was a more visionary and ambitious version of welfare pluralism. It draws strength from the same welfare-pluralist lines of argument, for example, doubts about the capacity and quality of centralised state provision, but it has a stronger theoretical and normative underpinning. In some ways, it responds to a recognised weakness in welfare pluralism: that a radical new approach to welfare services was being promoted on only the basis of existing, small-scale empirical examples of neighbourhood and self-help initiatives (Beresford and Croft, 1983: 22–3). In contrast, Hirst proposes nothing less than a complete overhaul of economic and social arrangements, albeit established rather gradually and organically. Subsequently, commentators have sought to apply the framework to existing institutional arrangements and to explore its political and emancipatory value. It has been recognised as possessing some real potential but, in practice, highly constrained in terms of its ability to ensure heightened democratic accountability (see, in particular, Smith, 2011).

Perhaps a more fundamental criticism of the whole associational project would focus on the challenge of pursuing pluralism organically in a society marked by significant inequalities of power, status and resources – whether this can really be overcome by 'the healing powers of non-state networks of association' (Amin, 1996: 309). In the absence of firm state regulation, coordination and intervention, formal rights to join and leave such associations may end up mirroring or even amplifying wider social divisions (see Jordan, 1996).

Associationalism was also at the heart of Robert Putnam's empirical studies of 'social capital' in Italy and the US (Putnam et al, 1993; Putnam, 2000). Echoing De Tocqueville's *Democracy in America*, Putnam's project highlights the importance of non-state civic associational networks, for example, in sports clubs and cultural societies, for generating trust, pro-social norms and cooperation. Social capital is defined as 'those features of social organisation, such as trust, norms and networks that can improve the efficiency of society by facilitating coordinated actions' (Putnam et al, 1993: 167). In later work (Putnam, 2000), different types of social capital were articulated: 'bridging' social capital involves network ties among people with different socio-economic characteristics; 'bonding' social capital refers to the links between people with similar characteristics; and 'linking' social capital attends to the connections between people with more and less power, influence and authority.

During the late 1990s and through the 2000s, social capital became a highly influential concept for academics and policymakers, achieving political resonance with the communitarian strand of New Labour's 'Third Way' narrative (Taylor, 2000; Johnston and Percy-Smith, 2003; Kendall, 2003; Halpern, 2005; Field, 2017). However, just as the extent of attention to social capital grew, so did the level and range of criticism. Doubts were expressed about whether the argument could be generalised across different political and institutional contexts (Hall, 1999). Further, Putnam's social capital tended to be viewed as a relatively benign and productive resource, focusing on trust, reciprocity and cooperation. As such, it downplays or neglects issues of power. Other, more realistic and sociologically nuanced, conceptualisations of social capital were deployed in contesting these debates, emphasising the unevenly distributed power of networks and connections, and their use in everyday struggles for other forms of capital, such as material resources and symbolic status (Grenfell, 2012).

For the argument pursued in this chapter, however, the main concern relates to the framework's pluralist foundations. Putnam's social capital is resolutely society-focused – indicative, perhaps, of its American origins, being ambivalent about the state as potentially 'crowding out' civic action (Hall, 1999; Szreter, 2002). Yet, these arguments have come under significant challenge, especially outside the US, with both quantitative research (see, eg, van Oorschot and Arts, 2005) and with local qualitative work. Regarding the latter, Maloney et al (2000) provide an example of a UK study emphasising the dense interpenetration of state and civil society in ways that have a direct bearing on the latter's role in generating and sustaining social capital.

Getting to grips with the third sector: a growing research field

Research relating to the third sector and its social policy contributions has not been limited to those informed by the particular theoretical lenses discussed so far; a more general field of knowledge was also evolving, gaining momentum from the 1980s onwards. At this time, the UK voluntary sector research agenda focused on five broad questions (Halfpenny and Reid, 2002): (1) 'What organisations comprise the sector?'; (2) 'How is the sector resourced?'; (3) 'Why do voluntary organisations exist?'; (4) 'How do voluntary organisations differ from other organisations?'; and (5) 'What is the voluntary sector's relationship with other sectors?'. Arguably, most attention has been paid to the first, second and fourth of these themes, although the fifth grew as a concern during the closer 'partnership' relationship between the voluntary sector and the state under the 1997–2010 Labour governments (Lewis, 2005).

Questions of organisational composition and resources have been the focus of conceptual and definitional work, linked to efforts to map and measure the scale and scope of the voluntary sector. In the mid-1990s, the UK was part of the Johns Hopkins Comparative Nonprofit Sector project, a major cross-national research effort to quantify and compare the scale and scope of the voluntary sector and civil society across the world, which was then renewed and extended in later work (Kendall and Knapp, 1996; Kendall, 2003). Using a 'structural-operational definition', not only was this the first significant attempt to outline and measure the scope of the sector, but it also provided the empirical foundations of the 'social origins of civil society' model, a welfare regime-related theory that suggests the existence of a small range of distinct civil society regimes (Salamon and Anheier, 1998; Salamon et al, 2017). This theory argues that the voluntary sector is deeply embedded in specific and enduring national welfare contexts, and its size and role is, fundamentally, the product of the balance of power between social groups over time. Drawing on historical as well as contemporary materials, Salamon and Anheier (1998: 241, based on Kendall and Knapp, 1996) characterised the UK as expressing a liberal regime, while also embodying some significant social-democratic features.

More generally, efforts to understand the scale, organisational composition and resources of the sector have traditionally been hampered by limitations in the scope and quality of data (Tarling, 2000). Yet, the situation has improved over the past two decades, and from work building on the Johns Hopkins study, we have gained a better and more consistent picture of the voluntary sector in the UK over time, even if the applied definition has tended to be narrower than many would like, focusing primarily on 'general charities', a subcategory of all charitable bodies (itself a subset of what Kendall and Knapp referred to as the 'broad' voluntary sector). For example, we have learnt of its aggregate income growth since the early 2000s, albeit with a more turbulent pattern during the Coalition government, and of how 'earned income' has become more important over this timescale. Conversely, aggregate income from government grew strongly under New Labour, but this faltered under the Coalition and Conservative administrations, initially against the backdrop of a 'Big Society' ideology correlating politically with hostility towards statutory support.

More recently, we have learnt a great deal more about the differentiated experiences between the largest voluntary organisations (eg those typically with annual incomes of £1 million and above) and other, small and medium-sized agencies. The former amount to only 3 per cent of charities but account for the bulk of the economic weight of the sector, together representing 80 per cent of the sector's aggregate annual income, and they have been faring better financially in recent years. Indeed, income growth in the last couple of years has been confined to the largest organisations (Crees et al, 2016; Benard et al, 2017), adding grist to the mill of those who tend to see the voluntary or third 'sector' not as a single coherent definitional category, policy object or political project, but rather as a fracturing space of different interests and fortunes (Macmillan, 2013; Rochester, 2013).

Allied work using national survey data and carefully constructed large-scale data sets of charity accounts over time has also enabled a clearer picture to emerge through comparing and contrasting a range of different geographical situations, with more details on different sources of income over time in different domains, and analyses conducted on how these situations relate to the climate of austerity prevailing in the aftermath of the economic crisis (Clifford et al, 2013; Clifford and Mohan, 2016; Clifford, 2017; Kendall et al, 2018). These findings are suggestive of diverse experiences and divergent fortunes across the third sector, challenging the idea of a single coherent sector, and implying feasibility limits to any aspirations to achieve 'strategic unity' in relation to the public policy agenda (Alcock, 2010).

A further theme – how voluntary organisations are different to other kinds of organisation – has arguably been more fundamental in defining this area as a field of study. Researchers have been interested in identifying, exploring and responding to the distinctive features, practices, contributions and challenges of running voluntary organisations (Billis and Harris, 1996). Traditional organisation and management theory, derived primarily from work with private firms, is somewhat ill-suited, it is said, to the special characteristics of voluntary organisations and the values and motivations of those involved in them. Theoretically, sources of distinctiveness might involve the trustworthiness that arises from the fact that voluntary organisations are not, on the face of it, in it for the money – they do not distribute surpluses or profits to shareholders (Hansmann, 1980) – or from the comparative advantage derived from 'stakeholder ambiguity', where a complex combination of multiple stakeholders is involved in the governance and management of organisations (Billis and Glennerster, 1998). In practice, claims for distinctiveness tend to make reference to, among other factors, organisations' closeness to marginalised communities of interest and place (Billis, 2001), their independence from government and commercial interests (Baring Foundation, 2012), and the use and combination of particular values in voluntary and community organisations (Blake et al, 2006; Jochum and Pratten, 2008). Yet, empirical evidence for distinctive characteristics and practices is rather threadbare. We are left with the possibility that claims for distinctiveness ought to be analysed as much for their strategic intent as their empirical basis, such that being distinctive implies being 'better' and/or worthy of attention (Macmillan, 2013). Notably, this question has typically been framed in terms of *how* the voluntary sector is different, not *whether* it is. There has been an underlying assumption of distinctiveness, and within this, implicitly, an assumption of value. Arguably, these assumptions have driven the push for resources and policy attention on the voluntary sector, or parts of it, by many intermediary, representative and umbrella bodies (see TSRC, 2014).

An unintended by-product of academic specialisation has arguably been the loosening and fraying of connections with core intellectual disciplines. In voluntary sector studies, the institutionalisation of a specialist field, especially when combined with an underlying assumption or argument that the voluntary sector is somehow different and merits special attention, may have had the effect of marginalising its questions and concerns within the wider field of social policy. This matters in so far as it filters through into social policy writing and research. It leads to the possibility that social policy as a discipline continues its overall neglect of the voluntary sector, while voluntary sector-focused academics inadvertently collude in the reproduction of 'separate spheres' between the state- and (quasi-)market-focused world of welfare, on the one hand, and the world of voluntary organisation, on the other.

Promising new directions

One of the consequences of the consolidation of voluntary sector studies as an area of knowledge building, as discussed earlier, is that scholars have become increasingly sensitive to the variety of forms of voluntary action ('internal diversity'), as well as to the complex ways in which the character of such action is intimately bound up with a range of socio-economic and political processes ('external variety'). We will consider each aspect in turn.

Before the 1990s, practitioners and scholars had already acknowledged significant ways in which organisations' size, legal status and geographical positions mattered, in terms of significance, capacities and influence, but tended not to consistently look at variation between substantive areas of work, activity or problem solving. In other words, there had been no analogy to how markets are conventionally differentiated by 'industry', and state responsibilities by public policy field and associated specialisms of expertise. The Johns Hopkins study rectified this with a bespoke classification system designed using inductive methods, establishing the so-called 'International Classification of Nonprofit Organisations' (ICNPO) as a key entry point for understanding the anatomy of the sector (Kendall and Knapp, 1996; Salamon and Anheier, 1997).

Such a fields-based approach has provided a valuable basis for research in three ways to date. First, it has stabilised and rendered systematic aggregate economic mapping exercises, such as the data series of NCVO (National Council for Voluntary Organisations) and the Third Sector Research Centre, through which it has now become institutionalised (Benard et al, 2018). Second, it has also been used to compare and contrast the trajectories of voluntary sector organisation for the purpose of policy analysis. This stream of work shows how these organisations' capacities to contribute and achieve impacts as policy actors are significantly shaped by the proximate institutions they encounter within the specific policy communities they inhabit – whether social care, development and housing, education, or others (see Kendall, 2003; Rees and Mullins, 2016).

Third, the relevant fields have increasingly been understood in a more sociological way, bringing into focus how such policy communities and areas of activity are socially and politically constructed and contested, involving symbolic as well as more material resources and activities. There are a number of 'varieties of field theory' in play in the international literature (Barman, 2016). In the UK, the influence of Bourdieu (see Crossley, 2002) and Fligstein and McAdam (2012) are becoming important reference points (Macmillan, 2013; Macmillan et al, 2013). Each has helped to show how social power is manifested, and social skill expressed, in field-based situations.

With their emphases on the 'meso' level, field-level analysts have been especially concerned with how specialist (often geographically local) policy community relationships shape third sector policy roles and possibilities. A more 'externally' driven and 'macro' entry point for analysis involves keeping issues relating to sectoral identity and status at the forefront in a more overarching and cross-cutting way, orienting the analysis especially to its collective interactions with the web of socio-political institutions within which its development is enmeshed. Here, social policy developments that cut across levels and fields are assumed to be cumulative and mutually reinforcing, involving political and social forces acting in concert in ways that serve to shape the sector as a whole. Implicitly, the scope for relatively autonomous dynamics *within* specialist fields of policy (and hence for voluntary organisations inside those fields) is depicted as contained by powerful macro-level politics and policies, and it is the environment at this level that is key. This strand of work therefore shares with the sociological version of field theory a focus upon social and political construction, but now attention is directed towards processes that are taken to be more macro and potentially encompassing in character.

This work, which is often broadly 'new institutional' in character (Scott, 2014), has developed along three promising lines. First, in studies stressing isomorphism (cf Powell and DiMaggio, 1991), relationships between the state and voluntary organisations are seen as symbiotic but heavily asymmetric in favour of the former, potentially involving a range of dysfunctional pressures for conformity and compliance as more policy attention is focused on the sector. In the face of the concentration of power and resources in the hands of the state, on the one hand, and social policies systematically promoting commodification across relevant policy fields, on the other, these pressures are portrayed as threats to this sector's capacity to function independently and effectively on behalf of its constituents, adequately differentiated from state and market practices (Milbourne and Cushman, 2015; Milbourne and Murray, 2017).[1]

Second, and relatedly, analysts have sought to consider how macro ideologies (variously defined) and governmentalities (in the Foucauldian tradition) relate to and mould the contours of voluntary action, portraying this domain as subject to ubiquitous and intrusive modes of control, diffused at every level, changing the conditions under which the sector develops. Here, both centripetal and centrifugal forces are said to be in play: centripetally, dominant ideational frameworks and institutionally embedded narratives and dispositions associated with neoliberalism, new public management and marketisation can tend to induce convergence; but centrifugally, competing variants of these approaches emerge, evolve and mutate differently according to the character of power relations and the agendas of those involved. The net result can be unstable combinations of both incorporation and overbearing control, on the one hand, but the existence of some room for continued autonomy and innovation, on the other (see, in particular, Carmel and Harlock, 2008; Harlock, 2014).

Third, some scholars have pointed to hybridisation as an emerging pattern associated with the increased intensity and extensity of relationships between sectors, whereby identities are not only potentially pressurised, stretched and reconfigured in the face of isomorphic and ideological currents and counter-currents, but also ultimately dissolved, reconstituted and multiplied. An emerging literature on 'hybridisation' advances this idea through highlighting social and political processes that challenge and undermine the established conceptual boundaries between formal sectors (ie state, market, third) by systematically fusing or conflating institutions and practices that had previously been treated as relatively distinct (Pestoff and Brandsen, 2008; Billis, 2010; Henriksen et al, 2015).

Conclusion

In this chapter, developing scholarship on the voluntary or third sector in the UK, within the context of social policy, has been reviewed. It was argued that the voluntary sector has traditionally been relatively marginalised in social policy thinking, and overlooked in the analysis of welfare policies, institutions and outcomes. Tentatively, it was suggested that there is a somewhat myopic frame of reference in mainstream social policy scholarship (in its long-standing focus on states, and latterly markets and quasi-markets, in welfare provision), combined with the emergence of a specialist – but sometimes balkanised – field of voluntary sector studies. However, there are healthy counter-currents too, and the chapter considered a range of theoretical developments that, in various ways, attempt to offer contextually sensitive accounts of the role of the third sector in social policy in order to help bridge the divide between the two.

The term 'sector' has been used throughout the discussion as a short-hand for describing a wide range of formal and informal activities, structures and relationships occurring through the auspices of organisations ostensibly beyond the state and the market. The contention is that 'sector' thinking underpins so much, and perhaps too much, policy analysis and commentary in social policy, and there is a need for disaggregation. In pursuing this argument, there is cause to question the notion of 'sector' and to suggest that it risks reifying and enclaving activities behind untested assumptions, and solidifying boundaries that are otherwise emergent, contested and always only provisionally accomplished and fragile (Macmillan, 2013).

Speaking in 1949, William Beveridge (1949) referred to a 'perpetually moving frontier' between the state and philanthropic action (a theme later taken up by Finlayson, 1994). The aim was to reserve a place for voluntary action in the newly emerging state-led post-war welfare settlement. The idea of a 'moving frontier' is typically invoked in order to account for historical shifts in the evolving mixed economy of state, market, commercial and informal welfare (Lewis,

1999; Alcock, 2016). However, it is more realistic and fruitful to think of the existence and interplay of multiple moving frontiers. A multi-level analysis is required here, combining, or at least appreciating the interdependence of, the macro and meso levels (as indicated in the discussion), but also adding a micro level of fluid interpersonal relationships, everyday practices and identities across institutionalised but blurred and dynamic professional and 'sector' boundaries. The institutional efforts involved in creating and maintaining named, privileged and credentialised domains of activity in social policy, welfare-related services and academic scholarship are recognised. However, we should make these processes, and their moving frontiers, part of the object of social policy enquiry, rather than let them channel our thinking so that we become oblivious to the full range of social policy phenomena worth exploring.

Note

[1] It is worth noting that Barman (2016), drawing heavily on US literature, suggests that the study of isomorphic developments can be understood as part of the family of meso-level field theories. However, UK-based applications of the approach tend to focus on macro processes that cut across and encompass fields, perhaps reflecting the extent to which British social policies are typically more centrally directed and tightly coupled than their US counterparts.

References

Alcock, P. (2010) A strategic unity: defining the third sector in the UK, *Voluntary Sector Review*, 1(1): 5–24.

Alcock, P. (2016) *Why we need welfare: Collective action for the common good*, Bristol: Policy Press.

Amin, A. (1996) Beyond associative democracy, *New Political Economy*, 1(3): 309–33.

Baring Foundation (2012) *Protecting independence: The voluntary sector in 2012*, London: Baring Foundation, Civil Exchange and DH Communications.

Barman, E. (2016) Varieties of field theory and the sociology of the non-profit sector, *Sociological Compass*, 10(6): 442–58.

Benard, C., Davies, J., Dobbs, J., Hornung, L., Jochum, V., Lawson, M. and McGarvey, A. (2018) *The UK civil society almanac 2018*, London: NCVO.

Benard, C., Lloyd, G., Egan, J., Dobbs, J., Hornung, L., Lawson, M., Ockenden, N. and Jochum, V. (2017) *The UK civil society almanac 2017*, London: NCVO.

Beresford, P. (2016) *All our welfare: Towards participatory social policy*, Bristol: The Policy Press.

Beresford, P. and Croft, S. (1983) Welfare pluralism: the new face of Fabianism, *Critical Social Policy*, 3(9): 19–39.

Beveridge, W. (1949) Voluntary action for social progress, House of Lords, HL Deb, 22 June, vol 163, col 95.

Billis, D. (2001) Tackling social exclusion: the contribution of voluntary organisations, in M. Harris and C. Rochester (eds) *Voluntary organisations and social policy in Britain: Perspectives on change and choice*, Basingstoke: Palgrave Macmillan, pp 37–48.

Billis, D. (ed) (2010) *Hybrid organizations and the third sector: Challenges for practice, theory and policy*, Basingstoke: Palgrave Macmillan.

Billis, D. and Glennerster, H. (1998) Human services and the voluntary sector: towards a theory of comparative advantage, *Journal of Social Policy*, 27(1): 79–98.

Billis, D. and Harris, M. (1996) Introduction: enduring challenges of research and practice, in D. Billis and M. Harris (eds) *Voluntary agencies: Challenges of organisation and management*, Basingstoke: Macmillan, pp 1–12.

Birch, A.H. (1984) Overload, ungovernability and delegitimation: the theories and the British case, *British Journal of Political Science*, 14(2): 135–60.

Blake, G., Robinson, D. and Smerdon, M. (2006) *Living values: A report encouraging boldness in third sector organisations*, London: Community Links.

Bochel, H. and Powell, M. (eds) (2016) *The Coalition government and social policy: Restructuring the welfare state*, Bristol: Policy Press.

Brenton, M. (1985) *The voluntary sector in British social services*, Harlow: Longman.

Carmel, E. and Harlock, J. (2008) Instituting the third sector as a governable terrain: partnership, procurement and performance in the UK, *Policy & Politics*, 36(2): 155–71.

Clifford, D. (2017) Charitable organisations, the Great Recession and the age of austerity: longitudinal evidence for England and Wales, *Journal of Social Policy*, 46(1): 1–30.

Clifford, D. and Mohan, J. (2016) The sources of income of English and Welsh charities: an organisation-level perspective, *Voluntas*, 27(1): 487–508.

Clifford, D., Geyne-Rahme, F. and Mohan, J. (2013) Variations between organisations and localities in government funding of third-sector activity: evidence from the national survey of third-sector organisations in England, *Urban Studies*, 50(5): 959–76.

Crees, J., Davies, N., Jochum, V. and Kane, D. (2016) *Navigating change: An analysis of financial trends for small and medium-sized charities*, London: NCVO and Lloyds Bank Foundation for England and Wales.

Crossley, N. (2002) *Making sense of social movements*, Buckingham: Open University Press.

Deakin, N. (1987) *The politics of welfare*, London: Methuen.

Esping-Andersen, G. (1990) *The three worlds of welfare capitalism*, Cambridge: Polity Press.

Esping-Andersen, G. (1999) *Social foundations of postindustrial economies*, Oxford: Oxford University Press.

Field, J. (2017) *Social capital* (3rd edn), London: Routledge.

Finlayson, G. (1994) *Citizen, state and social welfare in Britain, 1830–1990*, Oxford: Clarendon.

Fligstein, N. and McAdam, D. (2012) *A theory of fields*, Oxford: Oxford University Press.

Gladstone, F. (1979) *Voluntary action in a changing world*, London: Bedford Square Press.

Gough, I. (1979) *The political economy of the welfare state*, Basingstoke: Macmillan.

Grenfell, M. (ed) (2012) *Pierre Bourdieu: Key concepts* (2nd edn), Abingdon: Routledge.

Hadley, R. and Hatch, R. (1981) *Social welfare and the failure of the state*, London: Allen & Unwin.

Halfpenny, P. and Reid, M. (1992) Research on the voluntary sector: an overview, *Policy & Politics*, 30(4): 533–50.

Hall, P.A. (1999) Social capital in Britain, *British Journal of Political Science*, 29(3): 417–61.

Halpern, D. (2005) *Social capital*, Cambridge: Polity Press.

Hansmann, H. (1980) The role of non-profit enterprise, *Yale Law Journal*, 89(5): 835–901.

Harlock, J. (2014) Diversity and ambiguity in the English third sector, in T. Brandsen, W. Trommel and B. Verschuere (eds) *Manufacturing civil society: Principles, practices and effects*, Basingstoke: Palgrave Macmillan, pp 34–53.

Henriksen, L.S., Smith, S.R. and Zimmer, A. (2015) Welfare mix and hybridity: flexible adjustments to changed environments: introduction to the special issue, *Voluntas*, 26(5): 1591–600.

Hirst, P. (1994) *Associative democracy: New forms of economic and social governance*, Cambridge: Polity Press.

Jochum, V. and Pratten, B. (2008) *Values into action: How organisations translate their values into practice*, London: NCVO.

Johnson, N. (1987) *The welfare state in transition: The theory and practice of welfare pluralism*, Brighton: Wheatsheaf.

Johnston, G. and Percy-Smith, J. (2003) In search of social capital, *Policy & Politics*, 31(3): 321–34.

Jordan, B. (1996) *A theory of poverty and social exclusion*, Cambridge: Polity Press.

Kendall, J. (2003) *The voluntary sector: Comparative perspectives in the UK*, London: Routledge.

Kendall, J. and Knapp, M. (1995) A loose and baggy monster: boundaries, definitions and typologies, in J. Davis Smith, C. Rochester and R. Hedley (eds) *An introduction to the voluntary sector*, London: Routledge, pp 66–95.

Kendall, J. and Knapp, M. (1996) *The voluntary sector in the UK*, Manchester: Manchester University Press.

Kendall, J., Mohan, J., Brookes, N. and Yoon, Y. (2018) The English voluntary sector: how volunteering and policy climate perceptions matter, *Journal of Social Policy*, 47(4): 759–82.

King, A. (1975) Overload: problems of governing in the 1970s, *Political Studies*, 23(2/3): 284–96.

Le Grand, J. and Bartlett, W. (eds) (1993) *Quasi-markets and social policy*, Basingstoke: Macmillan.

Lewis, J. (1999) Voluntary and informal welfare, in R.M. Page and R. Silburn (eds) *British social welfare in the twentieth century*, Basingstoke: Macmillan, pp 249–70.

Lewis, J. (2005) New Labour's approach to the voluntary sector: independence and the meaning of partnership, *Social Policy and Society*, 4(2): 121–31.

Macmillan, R. (2013) 'Distinction' in the third sector, *Voluntary Sector Review*, 4(1): 39–54.

Macmillan, R., Taylor, R., Arvidson, M., Soteri-Proctor, A. and Teasdale, S. (2013) *The third sector in unsettled times: a field guide*, TSRC Working Paper 109, Birmingham: Third Sector Research Centre.

Maloney, W., Smith, G. and Stoker, G. (2000) Social capital and urban governance: adding a more contextualised 'top-down' perspective, *Political Studies*, 48(4): 802–20.

Milbourne, L. and Cushman, M. (2015) Complying, transforming or resisting the new austerity? Realigning social welfare and independent action among English voluntary sector organisations, *Journal of Social Policy*, 44(3): 463–85.

Milbourne, L. and Murray, U. (2017) *Civil society organisations in turbulent times: A gilded web*, London: Trentham Books and UCL-IOE Press.

O'Connor, J. (1973) *The fiscal crisis of the state*, New York, NY: St. Martin's Press.

Offe, C. (1984) *Contradictions of the welfare state*, London: Hutchinson.

Pestoff, V. and Brandsen, T. (eds) (2008) *Co-production: The third sector and the delivery of public services*, London: Routledge.

Pinker, R.A. (1979) *The idea of welfare*, London: Heinemann.

Powell, M. (2016) Citation classics in social policy journals, *Social Policy & Administration*, 50(6): 648–72.

Powell, W.W. and DiMaggio, P. (eds) (1991) *The new institutionalism in organizational analysis*, Chicago, IL: University of Chicago Press.

Prochaska, F. (1988) *The voluntary impulse: Philanthropy in modern Britain*, London: Faber & Faber.

Putnam, R.D. (2000) *Bowling alone: The collapse and revival of American community*, New York, NY: Simon & Schuster.

Putnam, R.D., Leonardi, R. and Nanetti, R.Y. (1993) *Making democracy work: Civic traditions in modern Italy*, Princeton, NJ: Princeton University Press.

Rees, J. and Mullins, D. (eds) (2016) *The third sector delivering public services: Developments, innovations and challenges*, Bristol: Policy Press.

Reisman, D.A. (2001) *Richard Titmuss: Welfare and society* (2nd edn), London: Palgrave.

Rochester, C. (2013) *Rediscovering voluntary action: The beat of a different drum*, Basingstoke: Palgrave Macmillan.

Salamon, L.M. and Anheier, H.K. (1997) *Defining the nonprofit sector: A cross-national analysis*, Manchester: Manchester University Press.

Salamon, L.M. and Anheier, H.K. (1998) Social origins of civil society: explaining the nonprofit sector cross-nationally, *Voluntas*, 9(3): 213–48.

Salamon, L.M., Sokolowski, S.W. and Haddock, M.A. (2017) *Explaining civil society development: A social origins approach*, Baltimore, MD: Johns Hopkins University Press.

Scott, W.R. (2014) *Institutions and organizations: Ideas, interests and identities* (4th edn), London: Sage.

Smith, G. (2011) Putting democracy into welfare provision, in A. Westall (ed) *Revisiting associative democracy: How to get more co-operation, co-ordination and collaboration into our economy, our democracy, our public services, and our lives*, London: Lawrence and Wishart, pp 54–8.

Szreter, S. (2002) The state of social capital: bringing back in power, politics and history, *Theory and Society*, 31(5): 573–621.

Tarling, R. (2000) Editorial: statistics on the voluntary sector in the UK, *Journal of the Royal Statistical Society A*, 163(3): 255–61.

Taylor, M. (2000) Communities in the lead: power, organisational capacity and social capital, *Urban Studies*, 37(5/6): 1019–35.

Titmuss, R.M. (1970) *The gift relationship: From human blood to social policy*, London: Allen & Unwin.

TSRC (Third Sector Research Centre) (2014) *Understanding the UK third sector: The work of the Third Sector Research Centre 2008–2013*, Birmingham: Third Sector Research Centre.

van Oorschot, W. and Arts, W. (2005) The social capital of European welfare states: the crowding out hypothesis revisited, *Journal of European Social Policy*, 15(1): 5–26.

Williams, F. (1989) *Social policy: A critical introduction*, Cambridge: Polity Press.

Wolfenden, Lord (1978) *The future of voluntary organisations: Report of the Committee on the Future of Voluntary Organisations*, London: Croom Helm.

9

Local variations in implementing energy-efficiency policy: how third sector organisations influenced cities' responses to the Green Deal

Rebecca Ince

Introduction

Between 2011 and 2016, the UK Coalition government engaged in a significant effort to encourage owner-occupied households to retrofit their properties in order to improve their energy efficiency and contribute to the UK's targets for reducing carbon emissions, improving energy security and boosting economic development. The 'Green Deal' – a finance mechanism and accreditation scheme for suppliers and installers – and the Energy Companies Obligation (ECO) – a legal obligation on energy companies to fund energy-efficiency measures – were the dominant policies of the time, alongside a growing localism agenda. During this time, responsibility for implementing Green Deal policy was passed to local coalitions of actors, including local authorities, third sector organisations (TSOs) and private companies. These coalitions were encouraged to test the many facets of Green Deal-related policy at various local levels through localised experimentation. One of the key roles that the government perceived for TSOs in the delivery of the Green Deal was in engaging householders with energy efficiency through promotions, demonstrations of energy-efficient homes and advice (DECC, 2011).

This chapter reflects on three contrasting Green Deal schemes in Bristol, Birmingham and Manchester in which despite the same national policy context, coalitions of actors produced dramatically different responses. It explores the particular contribution that TSOs made in each place, illuminating the influences that third sector actors such as cooperatives, charities, social enterprises and voluntary groups had on producing context-specific responses to national policy. TSOs often did occupy expected roles in promoting and advising on retrofit, but they also had more influential roles in providing services, shaping the scale and nature of the responses, and representing multiple local interests. These reflections are relevant not only for energy-efficiency policy, but also for wider energy policy and other social policy fields engaging in the local delivery of policy through local multi-stakeholder networks, with differing and sometimes contested interests and priorities.

The impetus for domestic retrofit

There are approximately 22 million households in England, of which 83 per cent are in urban areas (DCLG, 2014). Around 90 per cent that stand now were built more than 20 years ago (DCLG, 2014), at times when housing was generally not constructed with energy efficiency as a priority. However, a combination of global political pressures, including climate change, fears over resource security and economic crisis, has created a triad of priorities around energy use of carbon regulation, economic resilience and energy security, particularly for urban authorities (Hodson and Marvin, 2010). As a result, the energy efficiency of our domestic dwellings has come under increasingly close scrutiny (Mallaburn and Eyre, 2013), creating an impetus for UK policy to devise new ways to address it. Retrofit was regarded as the 'fix' to deal with poor energy efficiency (Theobald and Shaw, 2014) and upscaling retrofit was touted to achieve multiple grand aims: reducing carbon emissions; decreasing dependency on and vulnerability to energy supply and pricing issues at both the household and national scale; protecting people against fuel poverty and thus ill health and hardship; and creating a new industry that would boost employment and economic growth (Kelly, 2009; Guertler, 2012; Williams et al, 2013; Kerr et al, 2017). The government response to these growing pressures was to create a set of policy instruments and programmes that gave local authorities funds through which they tested various ways of boosting domestic retrofit activity.

Domestic retrofit means making structural or technological alterations to an existing domestic property for the specific purpose of improving that property's energy efficiency. This can involve alterations to either the building fabric or systems (Swan, 2013). Retrofitting the building fabric includes altering the structural elements of the property to reduce heat loss, such as insulating walls, lofts and floors, replacing or improving areas of glazing, and draught-proofing or improving air-tightness. Retrofitting the building's systems includes modifying mechanical and electrical systems such as heating and air conditioning, lighting, power and hot water. Modifications to these systems include upgrading or replacing heating systems (eg boilers), altering the fuel source (eg from gas/electricity to biomass), installing microgeneration technologies such as photovoltaic (solar) panels or heat pumps that can provide power, heating or hot water, and replacing light fittings with more efficient technologies such as LEDs.

Key policies in the Green Deal era

The Green Deal was, in part, a financial mechanism that enabled householders to access loan finance to pay for retrofit measures such as insulation, boilers and double- or triple-glazed windows, and then pay back the cost through energy savings, on a loan attached to their energy bill rather than themselves as an individual. It was intended to overcome the high upfront cost of retrofit (particularly for solid wall insulation), which was perceived as a significant barrier to uptake, and to open up finance options to people who may otherwise not be able to access them, for example, those who have poor credit ratings. In addition to this, the Green Deal provided a framework for supporting and upskilling a supply chain for retrofit, intended to establish a standardised retrofit service provided by professionals such as assessors, finance providers, installers and coordinating 'Green Deal Providers', who were all accredited to an industry standard (PAS 2030 for installers) in order to create trust and confidence in them and avoid the inclusion of 'cowboys' in the industry. The process for accessing the Green Deal is outlined in Figure 9.1.

In contrast, the ECO is a three-part legal obligation on energy companies to provide funding for energy-efficiency measures. They must provide funding for specific households that are vulnerable to fuel poverty (Home Heating Cost Reduction Obligation), funding for specific areas that are considered deprived and in need of energy-efficiency upgrades across an area (Carbon Saving Communities Obligation), and funding for specific household types that are considered 'hard to treat' – those requiring difficult cavity wall insulation, those on off-grid locations or, most commonly, solid-walled homes that require internal or external wall insulation that is a costly and difficult measure to install (Carbon Emissions Reduction Obligation). For private sector homes, which are the focus of the

Figure 9.1: The Green Deal process

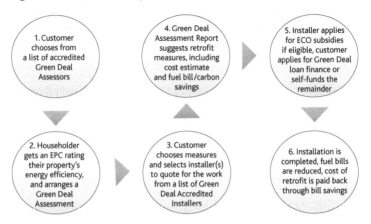

experiments explored in the following case studies, it is the Carbon Emissions Reduction Obligation component of the ECO that was involved.

Encouraging local variation and experimentation

These two quite different policies were interwoven with an increasingly prominent localism agenda embodied in the Localism Act 2011. Local authorities were encouraged to define their own approaches to social and economic issues, including energy efficiency. The then Department for Energy and Climate Change (DECC) created a number of short-term retrofit programmes between 2011 and 2015, offering funding for retrofit 'experiments' in different local authority areas, particularly Green Deal Go Early in 2011–12, which was connected to the City Deals emerging from the Localism Act, and later Green Deal Communities in 2013. These had explicit geographically targeted and experimental priorities, designed to: (1) 'kick-start the market' for retrofit by offering subsidies, particularly for external wall insulation, which would socially 'normalise' retrofit and therefore increase uptake; (2) 'create partnerships' or different local models for delivering retrofit (eg collaborations between local authorities and large contractors, energy companies or multiple delivery partners); and (3) 'test the "street-by-street" approach', in which households of varying tenures and circumstances could be offered a retrofit service of some kind (DECC, 2012).

These programmes were the product of a deal between DECC and the Department for Communities and Local Government, and were expected to produce not uniform results, but a variety, depending on decision-making and capacity within the cities' governance networks: "What we would expect to see is that some cities will have particular strengths or interests when it comes to energy efficiency, and others will have less, and it's up to them how much they commit to this" (Cities Policy Unit representative, interview, 2014).

This particular policy context created space and possibility for localised experimentation, and an expectation of variation between places. It necessitated the involvement of networks of actors crossing multiple scales and with various areas of expertise in responding to different parts of the domestic retrofit problem.

What role for the third sector in localised experimentation with retrofit policy?

The purpose of this chapter is to better understand the roles and influences that TSOs had on delivering domestic retrofit policy through localised experimentation. In designing the Green Deal, policymakers valued TSOs for their strengths in engaging householders (DECC, 2011), but the following case studies show that their roles were much more varied. This section outlines some debates that help to understand the potential importance and influence of TSOs on decision-making and policy implementation.

A significant aspect of policy implementation is the ways in which state and non-state actors make decisions in the process of delivering policy (Conteh, 2011; Nilsen, 2015). Hill and Hupe (2002) and Barrett (2004), among others, have highlighted the ways in which policy implementation is heavily affected by the various actors, interests and decision-making processes at play in the specific places and organisations who enact it, particularly in the context of a move from direct government to the more fluid 'governance' of policy issues (Spicker, 2014). There is a need to better understand these dynamics in the context of trends towards decentralised delivery and the devolution of responsibilities to local partnerships, with different roles and levels of responsibility for different stakeholders in service delivery (Kettl, 2000; O'Toole, 2000; Pal, 2006). In relation to the third sector generally, Rees and Mullins (2016) highlighted how in a government context of the privatisation and marketisation of public services, TSOs – such as large national charitable businesses, small charities and voluntary groups, social enterprises, and cooperatives – have become increasingly involved in the delivery of public services over the last 20 years. Their activities span sectors from employment to housing, and from criminal justice to health and social care, and their involvement ranges from the provision of voluntary capacity to contracted services and infrastructure bodies.

The influence and roles of TSOs are of particular interest for understanding policy implementation because TSOs are often courted for partnerships with actors in other sectors because of certain 'comparative advantages' – or characteristics that are seen as distinctive – such as their organisational values, closeness to communities and ability to engage directly and sensitively with members of the public (Billis and Glennerster, 1998; see also, more recently, Macmillan, 2013). Despite the sector, in fact, being very heterogeneous in terms of organisational types, approaches and values (Macmillan, 2013; Salamon and Sokolowski, 2016), these perceptions of distinctiveness can bolster TSOs' reputation in existing fields of service provision, and may explain why state and private sector organisations such as DECC, energy companies and local authorities would want to involve them in delivering the Green Deal. However, the ability of TSOs to act in any context is conditioned by the state at both national and local levels, through landscape changes such as marketisation (Macmillan, 2015), contracting and commissioning arrangements (Rees, 2014), and attitudes of state institutions towards the third sector. Arvidson et al (2018), for example, recently explored the ways in which municipal authorities create different localised 'civil society regimes' that shape TSOs' involvement in service delivery; therefore, for this exploration of TSOs' involvement in retrofit, it is necessary to acknowledge the impact of relationships between TSOs and local state or private sector actors in each place as being as important as the characteristics of the TSOs themselves.

Little is known, though, about the particular role of TSOs in implementing retrofit policy. However, there is a need to understand these processes in the field of energy and climate change policy because although it is governed at multiple levels, from the international (the Kyoto Agreement), to the supranational (directives from the European Union [EU]) and through national policy (Bulkeley and Betsill, 2005; Meadowcroft, 2009), many responses to energy issues are carried out through local projects acting on specific parts of the problem (Durant et al, 2017), embodying the mantra 'think global, act local'. It has therefore been posited that climate change and sustainability are now 'governed by experiment' (Hoffman, 2011; Bulkeley and Castan Broto, 2013; Evans and Karvonen, 2014; Evans, 2016; Caprotti and Cowley, 2017), that is, the nature of the problem requires innovative technical solutions, which must be shown to work in social contexts. In relation to local energy and sustainability projects, van der Schoor and Scholtens (2015) discuss the strength of community organisations in assisting transitions to decentralised, sustainable energy, as well as their role in creating a shared vision across a local area, while Parag et al (2013) highlight central and peripheral community actors in local energy governance and the importance of TSOs in facilitating the flow of information between actors. Furthermore, Seyfang and Haxeltine (2012) view community-based, grass-roots innovations and experiments as part of a civil society and 'action-oriented' form of change, drawing attention to the importance of tacit social knowledge alongside technical knowledge.

Three examples of localised domestic retrofit experiments: Bristol, Manchester and Birmingham

The following cases were selected on the basis of having active responses to the Green Deal in operation at the time, which were different in orientation and locally focused. Representatives from the key organisations and actors involved in each scheme were interviewed, and observations taken at internal meetings and public events, as well as a thematic analysis of organisational documents, was carried out. Each case study presented in the following will provide a brief outline of the scheme's background and its key actors, then an exploration of the influence and role of the various TSOs involved.

The Green Deal was axed in 2015 with no replacement scheme, and since then, there has been no policy framework specifically addressing domestic energy efficiency in the owner-occupied housing sector. However, the recent 2017 Clean Growth Strategy (BES, 2018) has begun to explore elements of energy efficiency again, with energy policy now largely governed by the department for Business, Energy and Industrial Strategy. There are also legal obligations in the Energy Efficiency Directive 2015 to improve the energy efficiency of the worst-performing privately rented properties. The role of the third sector and other stakeholders in this scheme remains undefined, but the following case studies will explore some of the ways in which TSOs were involved in delivering previous domestic retrofit policy and were able to influence its implementation. It is hoped that this exploration will encourage reflections about what may constitute productive contributions from TSOs in collaboration with the public and private sector in future retrofit schemes.

Bristol: the Bristol Home Energy Upgrade

The Bristol Home Energy Upgrade (BHEU) was a local authority-led pilot programme of solid wall insulation and boiler/heating system upgrades offered to owner-occupiers across the Bristol City area as part of the Go Early programme associated with the Green Deal. Funding of £2 million was awarded to Bristol City Council (BCC) from DECC, connected to the Core Cities' City Deals, and Scottish and Southern Energy (SSE) then offered a further £800,000 from its ECO budget. The programme ran between December 2012 and May 2013, and was delivered through a partnership between BCC and the Centre for Sustainable Energy (CSE), a national sustainability charity. BCC were responsible for defining the scheme offer in terms of the measures available, which were internal *or* external insulation, *or* a heating system upgrade (new boilers and controls). They also managed the budget and the grants, reported to DECC, sought out capable installers, and marketed the scheme. BHEU completed 157 installations: 23 for solid wall insulation and 134 heating system retrofits. BHEU was a straight policy experiment, testing the process of delivering the Green Deal and ECO in combination, from recruiting householders and using reporting software, to blending finance sources and finding accredited installers.

Centre for Sustainable Energy: policy knowledge, staff capacity and protecting householders

The Centre for Sustainable Energy (CSE) is a national charity focused on policy research and community projects relating to energy, including advising householders and community groups about energy efficiency. CSE assisted BCC with the original bid to DECC, and were awarded the contract on the basis of their existing expertise in the policy area. CSE was responsible for 'scheme delivery', which consisted mainly of dealing with customers:

> 'If someone was interested, they'd phone up CSE and somebody would have a chat with them for about 20 minutes ... finding out whether [the scheme] was right

for them. If the people then said "Yeah, this sounds good", they would get sent an information pack and be invited to get a Green Deal Assessment. Then, they get an EPC [Energy Performance Certificate], so we can calculate the level of grant and loans. They then communicate that back to the customer who can then decide whether to proceed with the installation if they want to. We, as CSE, are facilitators not managers – we give the householders a list of people who can do installs, the customer then chooses who does the install.' (CSE project officer)

CSE provided considerable staff resources, and were the first point of contact and source of advice to interested householders. CSE's capacity and existing knowledge enabled the policy response in Bristol to operate at a much wider scale than those in Birmingham or Manchester. However, as the scheme progressed, they also began to occupy a protective role, primarily for householders but also for installers, because of complications with reporting data: "we said we'd give the customers a certain grant, and we could only claim less of a grant from SSE because of the difference between how we scored it and how the signed-off scoring was. So, we had to supplement that gap with our own project finance" (CSE project coordinator).

CSE took a decision to protect the householders from these discrepancies, paying grants to the householders in order for them to pay the installers, while they waited for grant sign-off from the Office of Gas and Electricity Markets (OFGEM), thereby acting as a financial buffer for the householder and the installer. Unlike Carbon Co-op, where there was a continuous dialogue with householders about the changing levels of subsidy, CSE project officers were determined that the complications with the ECO and Green Deal happening behind the scenes would not impact on the householders.

Wessex Home Loans: finance providers

BCC had an existing relationship with Wessex Home Loans, a not-for-profit finance provider operating across the South-West, providing low-cost subsidised loans to people whose privately owned and rented homes were in a poor condition but who could not afford to upgrade them. This meant that BCC was able to use this existing provision to circumvent broader issues with the cost of loan finance from the Green Deal Finance Company: "We were very lucky to have that company and that mechanism already working locally" (BCC project coordinator).

Regen SouthWest: installer accreditation

Regen SouthWest was a regional charity working on general sustainability projects, including renewables, education and campaigning, and policy analysis. At the time of the BHEU, Regen SouthWest was assisting small works contractors in gaining PAS 2030 accreditation to become Green Deal installers. BCC's existing relationship with Regen SouthWest meant that upon realising that there were only two accredited Green Deal installers in Bristol – which meant that demand for solid wall insulation was greater than the scheme could provide for – they began to address this gap in the system:

> 'It showed us that there was a serious lack of solid wall insulation installers in the area and what we've now done is to go along to events that Regen SouthWest or the Local Economic Partnership are doing and telling them what we're up to – what's coming up in terms of other programmes, and really highlighting the demand for their services.' (Technical project manager, BCC)

Bristol Energy Network and its members: marketing and householder engagement

The Bristol Energy Network is a Community Interest Company (CIC) that acts as an umbrella organisation for charities and voluntary groups, small businesses, and individuals working on energy-related projects in and around Bristol. Members included Bristol Green Doors, an open-home retrofit demonstration network, Transition Montpelier, who conducted energy performance certificates in their community, and Bedminster Energy Group, who provided energy-efficiency advice and outreach. Bristol Energy Network's main influence on BHEU was seen less in terms of affecting the nature of its implementation and more in terms of creating a high level of political will around sustainability and retrofit:

> 'One of the biggest strengths of Bristol is the community energy network. We have got quite a lot of grass-roots

organisations here pushing the agenda, or even what are now large organisations that came up from grass roots. There's definitely something about Bristol that has this kind of alternative, counterculture ambience to it.' (BCC retrofit officer)

Bristol Energy Network's monthly, face-to-face meetings of multiple community groups, as well as the existing tools of their newsletter and email list, provided CSE and BCC with ready-made channels of communication into communities that were engaged with and interested in energy and retrofit-related issues. This generated 55 applications to and 11 installations under the scheme.

Manchester: Carbon Co-op and Green Deal Go Early

Carbon Co-op is a householder cooperative operating across Greater Manchester. Its primary activities through 2012–14 were conducting detailed whole-house surveys and project-managing 12 whole-house retrofits, working with the Greater Manchester Combined Authority (GMCA) as part of one of the core cities' 'Go Early' pilot projects for the Green Deal – like BHEU. GMCA were awarded £2 million of funding from DECC in early 2012, and GMCA awarded Carbon Co-op £200,000 of the £2 million to retrofit owner-occupied homes. Carbon Co-op managed the 12 'deep' retrofits with technical input from URBED Architectural Solutions, a design cooperative, aiming for very high (80 per cent) carbon reductions in each house through a suite of measures. These included loft, internal and external solid wall insulation, new boilers and controls, ventilation systems, microgeneration technologies, underfloor insulation, and triple-glazed windows and doors. By the end of the Go Early pilot, Carbon Co-op had completed 60 whole-house surveys with long-term recommendations, and completed eight of the 12 full whole-house retrofits, resulting in considerable visual and material changes to the properties, dramatically reduced energy use and renewable energy generation.

Carbon Co-op: environmental values and personal relationships

The organisation's membership is comprised mainly of householders in the Greater Manchester area, many of whom had professional jobs related to sustainability and/or had been involved in environmental activism and other cooperatives. This created a high level of personal commitment and voluntary capacity, as well as personal connections, which were mobilised as part of the Carbon Co-op's work. Members of Carbon Co-op provided peer support to each other through information sharing and advice about their experiences of retrofit, both online and in neighbourhoods, and Carbon Co-op also organised regular tours of each other's retrofitted homes. The project manager's own personal relationships were also significant in maintaining the momentum of the Go Early project. He commented on this in relation to householders experiencing issues around accessing funding, disruptive works and accurate pricing: "A lot of people told me that, basically, they were doing it for me. It was such a nightmare that they would have pulled out if we hadn't had that connection. I don't think I realised how important that was" (board member 2/project manager).

These personal local relationships built over time were also seen to generate partnerships at other levels, such as with council officers. Existing relationships with URBED and GMCA enabled Carbon Co-op to procure a contractor for the retrofit installations when their previous arrangement fell through, and being part of the GMCA procurement framework mobilised an ECO contribution from building contractor Keepmoat for some of the measures in Carbon Co-op's Go Early installations. DECC Green Deal funding from GMCA also enabled Carbon Co-op to offer 0 per cent interest loans to householders for their retrofits, which cost around £40,000 on average. As a partner from Salford University described: "it's a complex, personally driven series of relationships. People having pints with each other, and those people actually get on".

However, the voluntary nature and personal commitment of Carbon Co-op's membership also created a tension between a desire to have a greater impact on carbon emissions through retrofitting more houses, and concern about its ability to manage more retrofits. Delivering the Green Deal had widened Carbon Co-op's scope and scale from the grass roots to the city-regional, but limited the scale and number of retrofits that it could carry out. A board member stated:

> 'With the funding we have and the partners we have at the moment, we can do about ten a year [retrofits], if we want to do say 30 or 40 a year, we will need extra capacity and we will have to grow. But there's a big debate about whether or not we want to grow and do more, or should we just stick with the ten a year.'
> (Board member 3/Stockport)

URBED: *technical expertise*

The involvement of URBED as a technical advisor to Carbon Co-op shaped the Go Early project into a much more technically focused experiment than the BHEU or the Energy Saving Co-operative. Previous URBED projects on whole-house retrofits provided technical expertise and learning, and their detailed knowledge of survey techniques contributed to the development of Carbon Co-op's unique whole-house assessment method, which incorporates a much higher level of individual property-specific detail than the Green Deal-approved method.

Sustainable Living in the Heatons, Groundwork and Cooler CIC: networking and householder engagement

Carbon Co-op had a clear strategy of utilising existing networks and focusing its efforts on householders who were already engaged with the environmental movement:

> 'We have always been very clear that we are starting with pioneers – people who already want to do it for reasons that are more connected to the environment. But to go to people who are motivated by money, we have needed these pioneers to test this process – at financial risk – because that is not their primary motive. But they can show the savings, like "I used to spend £600 on gas and now I spend £300".'
> (Board member 4/Sustainable Living in the Heatons)

Connections with local voluntary sustainability groups and projects, such as Sustainable Living in the Heatons, the Carbon Literacy Project (CLP) delivered by social enterprise Cooler CIC across Manchester and Groundwork's existing fuel poverty project in Stockport, resulted in an increase in whole-house assessments and membership for Carbon Co-op, creating a network of community champions. Due to the locations of these groups and projects, though, the increased interest was concentrated in particular areas of South Manchester.

Birmingham: the Energy Saving Co-operative

The Energy Saving Co-operative (ESC) was a multi-stakeholder cooperative launched in April 2012, providing retrofit services nationally but with a particular focus on Birmingham. ESC offered two interdependent services. First, they vetted local retrofit installers/tradespeople against ethical and quality standards to become supplier members, and local community group members – usually small charities – were paid referral fees for recruiting interested householders. Second, ESC offered project management for the householder, including a detailed home energy survey and coordination of a bespoke package of retrofit measures from the installer members, who would quote for and carry out the installation under a contract with the ESC. During its short life, ESC attracted over £500,000 of investment, mostly from other cooperatives, and employed around 20 staff. It attracted 100 individual investor members and 13 stakeholder members (both community groups and installers), and facilitated new relationships between community organisations and retrofit installers in the Birmingham area. The number of homes retrofitted in the Birmingham part of the business, however, was only 20: in South Birmingham, West Bromwich, Walsall and Lichfield. Due to poor sales and too few installations, the ESC was forced into insolvency in December 2013.

ESC: organisational structure and cooperative values

ESC's organisational form meant that through representation on ESC's board of executives, funders, community partners and suppliers from the Birmingham area (as well as other areas) were able to actively negotiate their own particular interests into the organisation's characteristics and the nature of the response, as shown later. Its approach was based on a shared view within the organisation that the financial crisis would create a market for them because people and organisations would cease to trust private sector, commercial entities for services, instead flocking to more ethical forms of business: "People like co-ops at the moment. You know, with all the banking crisis, I think the Co-op Bank membership has increased tremendously" (ESC sales director).

Other organisations became involved with the ESC because they felt that their organisations and the ESC had shared values in the commitment to developing local supply chains and avoiding working with large commercial entities, such as the big six energy companies: "We hold a strong belief in integrated local supply chains instead of these big companies screwing the little guy all the time and Energy Saving Co-op really get that" (installer member). The ESC's relationship with the wider cooperative movement also provided funding, advice and administrative resources, such as templates for cooperative rules, defining the roles and responsibilities of board members, and structuring the ESC's share offer.

Midlands Co-op and Phone Co-op: funders

As the ESC's main funders, Midlands Co-op had a significant impact. First, their offices were near Birmingham, and they expressed a preference for the business to focus its efforts on the West Midlands in return for their funding contribution. As the largest funders, the Midlands Co-op and Phone Co-op board members also took the lead in holding the management team to account, quizzing the ESC chief executive officer (CEO) and chair on profit and sales targets. This prompted a strategic shift within the ESC in prioritising sales activity and the recruitment of sales staff. However, as the ESC struggled to meet its sales targets, the Midlands Co-op lost faith in it as an investment. Their decision to withdraw funding from the ESC ultimately contributed to its ceasing of trading and demise.

Northfield Ecocentre and South Staffordshire Community Energy: householder engagement, assessments and advice

Northfield Ecocentre is an environmental community organisation promoting and encouraging sustainable living in and around South Birmingham. It employs two domestic energy assessors, and prior to working with the ESC, it was already engaged in outreach to households providing home energy assessments and linking households to previous government retrofit schemes. ESC contracted Northfield Ecocentre to promote and market its services during a pilot phase between January and April 2012, in which it offered a competition for two demonstration retrofits. Similarly, South Staffordshire Community Energy (SSCE) was an existing voluntary group located in Lichfield who had previous experience of creating share offers and raising funds for renewable energy installations in the local community. It was instrumental in recruiting, advising and locating a group of homes for retrofit on an estate in Lichfield, which received external wall insulation as well as upgraded heating systems and draught-proofing. Working through these organisations shaped the scale and spaces in which ESC was working: "Where we work depends on who our partners are. So, with Northfield, it's generally South Birmingham, or a large part of South Birmingham" (CEO). Both Northfield Ecocentre and SSCE's close links to householders also brought feedback from customers to the ESC board and increased attention on the 'customer experience', influencing ESC's strategy to create a smoother, quicker handover from the sales team to the installation team (management team meeting observations, 2013).

New World Solar and Jericho Construction social enterprises: installation capacity

Retrofit installers had been operating for some time in the Birmingham area, including photovoltaic and insulation installers such as New World Solar, and highly regarded small works contractor Jericho Construction, both social enterprises and both accredited Green Deal installers. The presence of skilled, accredited installers was seen as another reason to focus ESC efforts on Birmingham. These organisations also got involved to represent training and unemployment as an issue of importance and make sure that this was at the forefront of ESC strategy:

> 'One of the main reasons that I'm there is to wave the banner for trade and employment in industry. Jericho's core mission is about employment and training, and providing opportunities to people who have been disadvantaged in the labour market. So, I'm there to make sure there's a strong focus on employment and training in the business as it develops.' (Jericho Construction representative)

Observations from board meetings ranging from February 2013 to July 2013 show that this progressed from a fringe issue of the business to becoming a more prominent part of the ESC agenda, resulting in a proposal to the board that upskilling and job creation in the supply chain be explicitly included in the ESC's mission statement.

How did TSOs influence the local delivery of Green Deal policy?

In all three cases, TSOs were involved in providing some element of retrofit services to householders. For Carbon Co-op, URBED and ESC, this consisted of surveys and project management; for URBED, this consisted of design and monitoring. Wessex Home

Loans crucially provided loan finance for the BHEU, and for CSE, their project-management role consisted of advice and information as well. Significantly, there was also a key role occupied by social enterprises in providing physical installations and materials – in the cases of New World Solar and Jericho, as well as the accreditation for installers provided by Regen SouthWest. However, the ways in which these services were provided were very different in the three cases, in part, due to the varying influence of TSOs in shaping and negotiating crucial features of the schemes. These include representing the interests of multiple stakeholders, the ways in which householders were engaged and related to the schemes, and the spaces and scales at which each case operated.

Representing and negotiating multiple stakeholders' interests

The two cooperative organisations outlined earlier were deliberately established as cooperatives because of the perceived trustworthiness and democracy of that particular organisational form. The structure of a cooperative, with strict rules and processes involving the members in decision-making and regular board meetings, meant that discussion of a range of interests and approaches were inherent in its governance.

ESC engaged with local issues around unemployment through the inclusion of Jericho and New World Solar in their membership; this was not because of a desire of ESC founders to act on this specific issue, but a negotiated condition of attempting to utilise their strengths as established suppliers in the city-region. BHEU – with its more narrowly constituted network and vision – made effective use of local TSOs' capacity and reputation in lobbying and community energy-related activity, but apart from CSE, these organisations were less active in the design of the policy response and more active in enabling a predefined approach.

Carbon Co-op, on the other hand, despite a strong relationship with the local authority, prioritised deeper retrofits based on its commitment to grass-roots action on climate change, and the strong presence of URBED meant that technical excellence and detail were a prominent feature of their activities in both surveying and installing retrofit measures. Its own capacity as a voluntary organisation, combined with the complexity of whole-house retrofits rather than the single measures installed in BHEU, for example, meant that the scale of Carbon Co-op's Go Early programme was dramatically different.

Shaping and brokering relationships between policy and households

One of the reasons that TSOs are often seen as valuable partners in delivering policy is because of their closeness to communities and to people. Across the three responses, the existence of voluntary or grass-roots organisations enabled the message of retrofit to get out to interested and engaged people. Carbon Co-op's organisational form as a householder cooperative meant that they already had a strong relationship with householders, and their existing relationships with other community groups and schemes meant that they had a communication network available for further engagement. Similarly, in Bristol – despite BHEU having no marketing or community engagement budget – the existing Bristol Energy Network offered routes to communicate their promotional message, and in Birmingham, the presence of Northfield Ecocentre and SSCE presented promotion opportunities for ESC.

There were, however, inherent differences in the dynamics of those communication channels that shaped householders' role and position in each of the responses. As Carbon Co-op's board and membership consisted mostly of householders with retrofitting experience and high levels of technical and financial understanding, householders took an active role in governing the organisation and there was continuous and open discussion about problems with the Go Early project, such as issues with ECO funding and difficulties with contractors. On the other hand, because of CSE's protective attitude, BHEU took the opposite approach to Carbon Co-op in relation to communicating difficulties with ECO and pricing, with CSE accepting considerable risk by acting as a buffer against these financial issues in an effort *not* to pass them on to the householder.

Both organisations viewed their role as a protective or supportive measure – for CSE, this meant financial protection, and for Carbon Co-op, this meant both emotional and technical protection through peer support, information and advice, and intense support and detailed monitoring of the retrofit projects. For ESC, while its partners in Northfield Ecocentre, SSCE, Jericho and New World Solar were already established and well known in the area, ESC itself had no existing relationship with householders. Hence, it relied on the reputations of its third sector partners to promote the cooperative 'brand' and ESC retrofit offer. These different approaches to engaging householders reflect the different positions of householders in shaping the schemes. In the case of Carbon Co-op, householders were active participants in both the definition and execution of the experiment and in its links to other householders, whereas in BHEU and ESC, householders were more passive recipients of predefined services – viewed more as a 'market'.

Shaping the scales and spaces of policy delivery

CSE's staffing capacity and financial coffers enabled large-scale delivery and a high number of installations as a product of fielding a high number of enquiries and being able to screen effectively for eligibility, which would not have been possible if they had been a smaller organisation without the ability to staff an advice line. Although the location of Bristol's Green Deal activity was already decided by the nature of the project being led by BCC, CSE enabled BHEU to offer retrofits across the whole city of Bristol. Carbon Co-op being a largely voluntary organisation, on the other hand, in combination with its technical priorities of deep retrofits and high energy savings, meant much smaller-scale activities with only 12 homes, and a concentration of membership in areas where their community partners were active. Similarly for ESC, the TSOs' influence on the scale and territory of the scheme was considerable: Midland Co-op determined the focus of the business initially in the West Midlands; the presence of installer capacity led ESC to Birmingham; and Northfield Ecocentre and SSCE resulted in installations in their local and familiar turfs of South Birmingham and Lichfield.

Conclusion: make no assumptions – the multifaceted roles and influences of TSOs in delivering retrofit policy

The range of TSOs involved in the three retrofit initiatives very much reflected the heterogeneous nature of the third sector described by both Macmillan (2013) and Salamon and Sokolowski (2016). The range of actors included:

- large charities such as CSE and Groundwork;
- small charities and voluntary groups such as Sustainable Living in the Heatons, Northfield Ecocentre, Bristol Green Doors, Bedminster Energy Group and SSCE;
- social enterprises and not-for-profit organisations such as Bristol Energy Network itself, Wessex Home Loans, Jericho Construction and New World Solar; and

- cooperatives of various sizes and forms such as Carbon Co-op, URBED, ESC, Phone Co-op and Midlands Co-op.

Between them, these actors offered capacity, skills and knowledge across all parts of retrofit policy implementation, and although many did adopt what policymakers assumed would be roles in householder engagement or advice, many other roles extended far beyond this into providing services and resources, such as funding, finance, surveys, installations and project management, again reflecting the range of roles that the third sector has in delivering public services more broadly (Rees and Mullins, 2016).

The range of roles for TSOs could be grouped into three: providing, protecting and promoting. Roles focused on providing retrofit services generally involved organisations with some form of specialist skill or resource in surveying, designing, installing or funding and finance. Roles focused on promoting retrofit were largely passive in that organisations simply passed on a message that a programme was happening, except for Carbon Co-op, in which the relationship with householders was much more iterative. Finally, there were significant roles for TSOs in protecting householders – largely from problems created by the Green Deal policy context or from the strain of the retrofit experience – which involved advice (eg Northfield Ecocentre, CSE) and peer support and demonstrations (Carbon Co-op, Bristol Green Doors), and was taken to another level by CSE, who also provided financial protection to householders.

What the preceding case studies also tell us is that the third sector can, indeed, have significant influences on decisions made about designing and implementing policy at the local level, including the way in which the public (in this case, householders) relate to the policy in question, the scale and spaces of its operation, and the interests and priorities embedded in the response. Despite a complex and problematic policy context, the variety of TSOs in retrofit had a huge impact on the shape and nature of the responses in each place. In part, this was because the Green Deal was set up to encourage local variation, but how this variation might manifest was not evident until after these responses emerged.

Reflecting on what might be expected from TSOs in delivering retrofit policy, it is certainly true that many TSOs were utilising their perceived distinctive characteristics (Billis and Glennerster, 1998; Macmillan, 2013) of closeness to communities and being trusted by householders in order to promote retrofit on behalf of the Green Deal. However, for cooperatives such as Carbon Co-op and ESC, their values-based and trustworthy identity was not just a marketing tool, but an organisational structure that allowed multiple local interests and priorities to be represented and negotiated, and unique approaches and relationships with other stakeholders to be developed (whether or not they were ultimately successful). Even in the case of BHEU, which gave little opportunity to TSOs to represent their interests, the presence of CSE and the community networks in Bristol enabled widespread community buy-in, as did the interorganisational relationships around Carbon Co-op in Manchester. In this sense, the roles of TSOs in retrofit certainly reflect the strengths of community organisations in local energy and sustainability projects identified by van der Schoor and Scholtens (2015), Parag et al (2013) and Seyfang and Haxeltine (2012), who highlighted their action-oriented approach and ways of facilitating communication and building relationships.

This chapter has provided a brief, descriptive overview of the roles and influences that TSOs had in implementing a particular policy around energy efficiency. Two parts of this picture are, however, still underexplored. The first is the influence that local government, private sector and national government collaborators had on the ability of TSOs to perform those roles, and how these relationships enabled and constrained their influence, relating to the 'civil society contexts' referred to by Arvidsson et al (2018). The second is the tensions that emerge by TSOs occupying multiple roles, particularly those in the most influential roles, such as CSE, ESC and Carbon Co-op, who were all simultaneously providers, protectors and promoters with varying effects. The internal dynamics of TSOs occupying multiple positions and retaining the trust and values seen as distinctive about the third sector are worthy of more detailed examination.

For readers both inside energy and environmental policy and in social policy more widely, this chapter should have broadened the view of TSOs' roles in delivering policy-related services. Assumptions about TSOs' homogeneity, relationship to people and communities, and provision of voluntary capacity should be avoided as these are heavily context-specific and do not make the best use of the wide variety of skills and contributions that the third sector can potentially offer.

References

Arvidson, M., Johansson, H., Johansson, S. and Nordfeldt, M. (2018) Local civil society regimes: liberal, corporatist and social democratic civil society regimes in Swedish metropolitan cities, *Voluntary Sector Review*, 9(1): 3–20.

Barrett, S.M. (2004) Implementation studies: time for a revival? Personal reflections on 20 years of implementation studies, *Public Administration*, 82: 249–62.

BEIS (Department for Business, Energy and Industrial Strategy) (2018) Clean growth strategy: executive summary, www.gov.uk/government/publications/clean-growth-strategy/clean-growth-strategy-executive-summary

Billis, D. and Glennerster, H. (1998) Human services and the voluntary sector: towards a theory of comparative advantage, *Journal of Social policy*, 27(1): 79–98.

Bulkeley, H. and Betsill, M. (2005) Rethinking sustainable cities: Multilevel governance and the 'urban' politics of climate change, *Environmental Politics*, 14(1): 42–63.

Bulkeley, H. and Castán Broto, V. (2013) Government by experiment? Global cities and the governing of climate change, *Transactions of the Institute of British Geographers*, 38(3): 361–75.

Caprotti, F. and Cowley, R. (2017) Interrogating urban experiments, Urban Geography, 38(9): 1441–50.

Conteh, C. (2011) Policy implementation in multilevel environments: economic development in Northern Ontario, *Canadian Public Administration*, 54: 121–42.

DCLG (Department for Communities and Local Government) (2014) English housing survey 2012: energy efficiency of English housing report, www.gov.uk/government/statistics/english-housing-survey-2012-energy-efficiency-of-english-housing-report

DECC (2011) Local authorities and the Green Deal: information note, https://assets.publishing.service.gov.uk/government/uploads/system/uploads/attachment_data/file/120715/3491-local-authorities-and-the-green-deal-information-.pdf

DECC (2012) DECC local authority funds: DECC local authority competition 2012–2013, www.gov.uk/government/uploads/system/uploads/attachment_data/file/65570/6712-local-authority-competition-fund-application-pack.pdf

Durant, R.F., Fiorino, D.J. and O'Leary, R. (2017) *Environmental governance reconsidered: challenges, choices, and opportunities*, London: MIT Press.

Evans, J. (2016) Trials and tribulations: problematizing the city through/ as urban experimentation, *Geography Compass*, 10(10): 429–43.

Evans, J. and Karvonen, A. (2014) 'Give me a laboratory and I will lower your carbon footprint!' Urban laboratories and the governance of low-carbon futures, *International Journal of Urban and Regional Research*, 38(2): 413–30.

Gooding, L. and Gul, M.S. (2017) Achieving growth within the UK's domestic energy efficiency retrofitting services sector: practitioner experiences and strategies moving forward, *Energy Policy*, 105: 173–82.

Guertler, P. (2012) Can the Green Deal be fair too? Exploring new possibilities for alleviating fuel poverty, *Energy Policy*, 49: 91–7.

Hill, M.J. and Hupe, P.L. (2002) *Implementing public policy: Governance in theory and practice*, Thousand Oaks, CA: Sage Publications.

Hodson, M. and Marvin, S. (2010) *World cities and climate change: Producing urban ecological security*, Maidenhead: McGraw-Hill Education.

Hoffman, M.J. (2011) *Climate governance at the crossroads: Experimenting with a global response*, New York, NY: Oxford University Press.

Kelly, M.J. (2009) Retrofitting the existing UK building stock, *Building Research & Information*, 37(2): 196–200.

Kerr, N., Gouldson, A. and Barrett, J. (2017) The rationale for energy efficiency policy: assessing the recognition of the multiple benefits of energy efficiency retrofit policy, *Energy Policy*, 106: 212–21.

Kettl, D.F. (2000) Public administration at the millennium: the state of the field, *Journal of Public Administration Research and Theory*, 10(1): 7–34.

Macmillan, R. (2013) 'Distinction' in the third sector, *Voluntary Sector Review*, 4(1): 39–54.

Macmillan, R. (2015) Starting from elsewhere: reimagining the third sector, the state and the market, *People, Place and Policy*, 9(2): 103–9.

Mallaburn, P.S. and Eyre, N. (2014) Lessons from energy efficiency policy and programmes in the UK from 1973 to 2013, *Energy Efficiency*, 7(1): 23–41.

Meadowcroft, J. (2009) What about the politics? Sustainable development, transition management, and long term energy transitions, *Policy Sciences*, 42(4): 323–40.

Nilsen, P. (2015) Making sense of implementation theories, models and frameworks, *Implementation Science*, 10(53): 1–13, doi: 10.1186/s13012-015-0242-0

O'Toole, L., Jr (2000) Research on policy implementation: assessment and prospects, *Journal of Public Administration Research and Theory*, 10(2): 263.

Pal, L.A. (2006) *Beyond policy analysis: Public issue management in turbulent times*, Scarborough, Ontario: ITP Nelson.

Parag, Y., Hamilton, J., White, V. and Hogan, B. (2013) Network approach for local and community governance of energy: The case of Oxfordshire, *Energy Policy*, 62: 1064–77.

Ravetz, J. (2008) State of the stock – what do we know about existing buildings and their future prospects?, *Energy Policy*, 36(12): 4462–70.

Rees, J. (2014) Public sector commissioning and the third sector: old wine in new bottles?, *Public Policy and Administration*, 29(1): 45–63.

Rees, J. and Mullins, D. (eds) (2016) *The third sector delivering public services: Developments, innovations and challenges*, Bristol: Policy Press.

Salamon, L.M. and Sokolowski, S.W. (2016) Beyond nonprofits: re-conceptualizing the third sector, *Voluntas*, 27: 1515.

Seyfang, G. and Haxeltine, A. (2012) Growing grassroots innovations: exploring the role of community-based initiatives in governing sustainable energy transitions, *Environment and Planning-Part C*, 30(3): 381.

Spicker, P. (2014) *Social policy: Theory and practice*, 3rd edn, Bristol: Policy Press, p 1.

Swan, W. (2013) Retrofit innovation in the UK social housing sector, in W. Swan and P. Brown (eds) *Retrofitting the built environment*, Oxford: Wiley, pp 36–52.

Theobald, K. and Shaw, K. (2014) Urban governance, planning and retrofit, in T. Dixon, M. Eames, M. Hunt and S. Lannon (eds) *Urban retrofitting for sustainability: Mapping the transition to 2050*, Abingdon: Routledge, p 87.

van Der Schoor, T. and Scholtens, B. (2015) Power to the people: local community initiatives and the transition to sustainable energy, *Renewable and Sustainable Energy Reviews*, 43: 666–75.

Williams, K., Gupta, R., Hopkins, D., Gregg, M., Payne, C., Joynt, J.L. and Bates-Brkljac, N. (2013) Retrofitting England's suburbs to adapt to climate change, *Building Research & Information*, 41(5): 517–31.

10

Is the 'lump of labour' a self-evident fallacy? The case of Great Britain

Jacques Wels and John Macnicol

Introduction

The lump of labour fallacy is nowadays used by policymakers as one of the strongest arguments against early retirement. In essence, the case is that the labour market is not based on a fixed sum of jobs and, consequently, retirement ages can be adjusted without any harm. It may seem logical to argue that increasing the age of retirement may lead to a decrease in youth employment. However, opponents of the lump of labour argue that there is no share of jobs between the young and the old. The dominant literature also tends to support the idea that increasing older workers' employment participation leads to an increase in youth employment; what is good for one is good for all. In other words, the current idea is that the labour market is a dynamic environment where jobs are created and destroyed at the same time (Cahuc and Zylberberg, 2015), integrating the population whatever its size and composition. In summary, supporting the lump of labour fallacy leads one to think that an increase in retirement ages is good for the economy – as it reduces pensions expenditure, raises overall employment and increases tax revenue – and good, consequently, for all workers.

This chapter looks at the evolution of the concept of the lump of labour fallacy over time. The first part looks at its origins, its policy implications and recent works dedicated to it, focusing particularly on retirement ages. It is shown that the lump of labour fallacy is used as a theoretical background for much of the recent empirical work but that its background has never been deeply investigated. Using recent British data provided by the Office for National Statistics (ONS), the second section of this chapter analyses the association between youth unemployment and inactivity and the employment participation of the other age groups. Comparing results obtained in the empirical part with the theoretical background presented in the first section, the conclusion raises further issues that deserve to be investigated in depth in more detailed research.

Theoretical background

The origins of the notion of a lump of labour are difficult to determine with precision. Usually, the literature refers to the famous book by Henry Mayhew (1864) entitled *London labour and the London poor*. In this descriptive monograph dedicated to poverty in London during the Victorian era, Mayhew particularly stressed the need to reduce working time in order to improve the work participation of poor non-employed people. The notion of 'lump work' is used but it refers to a form of labour subcontracting that was common in the docks and the building trades. Some two decades before Mayhew, John Mills's (1843) novel *The stage coach; or, the road of life* uses the exact term 'lump o'labour', referring to a given expenditure of effort, relating it to the expectation of a proportionate reward for that effort: 'and we ought to be well satisfied when we get moderate profits to a lump o'labour or pain. However, Jack, get on my back, and I'll carry ye home' (Mills, 1843: 174). In its first usages, therefore, the concept of a lump of labour was not properly defined, referring to several aspects of work, including its arduousness.

The notion of a lump of labour considered as a fallacy appeared shortly afterwards (Walker, 2000, 2007). In 1891, an article by the economist D.F. Schloss (1891), entitled 'Why working-men dislike piece-work', underlined the idea that labour market dynamics are not based on a *lump sum of work*. Looking at the potential negative effects of piecework (ie jobs paid a fixed piece rate for each unit produced), Schloss highlights the belief, 'so firmly entertained by a large section of our working-classes', that pieceworkers are taking the work of the other categories of workers (Schloss, 1891: 324). In this view, workers may think that there is a fixed sum of work and that it would be necessary to reduce their productivity in order to keep their jobs, when, in reality, labour market dynamics are not based on a fixed sum of work. According to Schloss, this thinking can be considered as a fallacy – named 'the theory of the Lump of Labour' – insofar as statistical measurements do not confirm this belief.

More than a century later, the notion is still often mentioned in order to counter arguments supporting the view that reducing the retirement age – or, at least, not increasing it – would produce a negative effect on youth employment. For instance, Tom Walker has shown that from 1993 to 2005, the influential *Economist* magazine published 17 articles about the lump of labour fallacy (Walker, 2007: 280). Arguing against the lump of labour in an opinion piece published in the *New York Times* in 2003, the economist Paul Krugman qualified the idea of job sharing as a 'fallacy of the economically naïve left', and particularly underlined two consequences flowing from this fallacy: on the one hand, that it encourages fatalism as people supporting it believe that new jobs cannot be created; and, on the other, that it feeds protectionism (Krugman, 2003).

The lump of labour in the UK

'Industry cannot be compared to a cab rank, on which, as the first cab moves off the rank, the bottom one moves up' – so declared a government spokesman in the House of Commons in 1934 when opposing a Labour Party scheme for a new higher state pension, to be paid at age 60 and carrying a retirement condition in order to encourage older workers to leave industry and make room for the young unemployed (Macnicol, 1998: 257). There has been a long debate over the whole question of whether in a time of high unemployment, older workers should retire a little earlier in order to redistribute jobs to the young (who, by and large, have far greater family responsibilities and concomitant household expenditure). It might seem obvious that one new 'young' job would be made available for every 'old' one vacated, and that was the belief that motivated the leading trades unionist Ernest Bevin, the research organisation Political and Economic Planning and many others as mass unemployment created such hardship and hopelessness for younger workers in the 1920s and 1930s. It was also the logic behind the Job Release Scheme (JRS) of 1977–88 (Banks et al, 2010), which was introduced as a way of redistributing available jobs to the unemployed. Indeed, the 1980s saw much political and public support for the idea that early retirement was a means of massaging the unemployment statistics through an age-based redistribution of jobs. Over the last 80 years, therefore, there have been pendulum-like swings in policy towards older workers: the 1930s and 1980s were times of economic restructuring, necessitating the existence of a large reserve army of labour, and therefore the emphasis was on early exit; by contrast, the 1950s and the period since the early 1990s have been times of economic growth, albeit sporadic, and accordingly the emphasis has been on retention and an expansion of labour supply.

However, there have always been several problems inherent in such job-redistribution schemes. The labour market may not be like a cab rank, but it certainly resembles a patchwork quilt of considerable complexity, characterised by mismatches of skill, status, location, age, gender, remuneration and so on. It has always been the case that unemployment in the UK has been regionally concentrated in 'black spots', while other areas have done well. Hence, in recent years, Merthyr Tydfil has had roughly 30 job-seekers chasing every vacancy, whereas in the City of London, there have been approximately seven vacancies per job-seeker. Labour shortages can therefore exist at a time of mass unemployment. Workers who retire may be replaced by technology rather than humans; a factory may close in one area and reopen with a smaller (or bigger) workforce in another area (or in another country); full-time jobs may be replaced by part-time ones, or vice-versa. In short, a modern labour market is dynamic, not static: old workers with long experience are constantly departing and young ones are joining. The processes of change are exceedingly complex.

Governments in the interwar years raised many practical objections to all job-redistribution schemes designed to lower unemployment. They offered seemingly sensible criticisms (such as the length of time it would take to train the unemployed up to the right skill levels, or the spatial mismatches between job-seekers and vacancies), but, at heart, their objections were based upon the cardinal principle of neoclassical economics that nothing should be done to interfere with market forces and the 'natural' evolution of the UK economy. Related to this was the view that expanding the supply of labour would automatically create a demand for it – providing that inflation was kept under control and wage levels (ie employment costs) remained low (then, as now, this was to be assisted by holding down the value of welfare benefits to unemployed people). Nearly all suggestions for state interference in the labour market to create jobs (eg via public works schemes) were accordingly rejected. The first point to note, therefore, is that the debate has been highly political: those on the Right have favoured an expansion of labour supply, with more job-seekers competing for every available job, which has the effect of holding down wages and weakening the bargaining power of organised labour; conversely, those on the Left have tended to favour a tightening up of the labour market, with precisely the opposite effect. Virtual full employment in the 1950s and 1960s appeared to have vindicated the view that if the correct monetary, fiscal and pricing policies were implemented by a government, then recessions could be avoided (Samuelson, 1958: 551–2).

Neoclassical economics is back with us – indeed, it has been for several decades, even if it has, at times, masqueraded in different guises (as it did under New Labour). Since the 1970s' oil price shock and the consequent 1980s' recession, it has been a long-running macroeconomic strategy to stimulate economic growth by expanding labour supply, thereby holding down wages. The industrial restructuring of the 1980s was assisted by mass unemployment as a means of deflating the economy and breaking trade union power. Unemployment then fell, rising briefly in 1989–92. However, from the early 1990s, the employment rates of nearly all social groups began to rise, albeit slowly (the exceptions were those on disability benefits). In response to this, governments decided to take credit for the inevitable and place an expansion of labour supply at the heart of economic policy. Indeed, for New Labour, such a strategy became absolutely central, figuring strongly in the arguments of theorists like Richard Layard (1997) and Anthony Giddens (2000), and advocates of labour market activation like Nigel Campbell (1999). Labour market activation to push people off benefits and into work via greater conditionality would not only reduce the welfare bill, but also boost demand in the economy (since more spending power would be created) and increase income tax revenue. In this way, a seemingly perfect virtuous circle would be set up. In addition, the expansion of the labour supply would be anti-inflationary since more job-seekers looking for jobs would hold down wages. As the government publication *Winning the generation game* (Performance and Innovation Unit, 2000: 39) put it: 'increasing the number of people effectively competing for jobs actually *increases* the number of jobs in the economy.... More people competing for jobs means that people are less keen to demand wage increases'.

It was an intriguing combination of neoclassical supply-side approaches and Keynesian demand management, and it has had an interesting effect on the old age and social policy agenda, motivating governments to encourage longer working lives and a concomitant raising of state pension ages. The justification is that people are living longer, and that pensions are therefore ultimately unsustainable. Interestingly, age discrimination in employment was 'discovered' exactly at this time – the Equality Act 2010, translating European Union (EU) regulation into British law, makes it unlawful to discriminate against employees, job-seekers and trainees on grounds of age – as a major legitimating principle behind the labour market activation of older people. It is against this background that the phrase 'there is no such thing as a lump of labour' has emerged as possessing canonical significance. In terms of public policies, this belief influenced the 2007 and 2011 Pension Acts, which raised the state pension age to 66 and abolished the mandatory retirement age, respectively (Lain, 2017).

The lump of labour in the scientific literature

Justification of the lump of labour fallacy is also provided by a large amount of scientific publications. The recent scientific literature focusing on the impact of early retirement schemes on youth employment may be divided into two waves. A first wave, published at the end of the 1970s, underlined the complexity of labour market dynamics, taking into consideration differences across sectors of activity and professions. In 1979, D. Hamermesh and J. Grant published a critical synthesis of the growing literature on work sharing among the labour force, focusing specifically on the relationship between young and older workers. After a short review of the literature, they concluded that 'the degree to which [young workers] are substitutes for older workers is unclear' (Hamermesh and Grant, 1979: 518). One of the main reasons mentioned for explaining this lack of clarity is the difference in substitution depending on the sector of activity. Indeed, according to Weiss (1977: 769), analysing substitution dynamics requires a 'high degree of disaggregation of industries and labour types'. The heterogeneity of what is observed depending on the sector of activity is a key point of this first wave of research and the notion of the lump of labour is not mentioned as a fallacy.

Twenty years later, a second wave of research, fed by both cross-national databases and time-series data sets, underlined the negative impact of early retirement schemes on youth employment. In an article published in 2000, Esping-Andersen puts the accent on the positive correlation between youth and elderly employment. Using data from the Organisation for Economic Co-operation and Development (OECD), he stresses that early retirement rates do not impact on youth unemployment outflow, and points out the potential negative impact of early retirement on youth employment. In other words, rather than increasing youth participation, early retirement schemes produce the opposite effect: increasing youth unemployment (Esping-Anderson, 2000). More recently, using American data from the

Current Population Survey (CPS), Gruber and Milligan have pointed out that a substitution phenomenon between old and young workers might have occurred during the period 1962–2008. Even though their findings suggest a possible substitution effect between generations, the authors remain nevertheless prudent about it as the period is also characterised by increasing female labour market participation and the results observed may be affected by this trend (Gruber and Milligan, 2008). At the same time, many papers underlined the zero impact (or even, sometimes, the positive correlation) of early retirement schemes (or older workers' employment rates) on youth employment (or youth unemployment) in countries such as the UK (Banks et al, 2010), Germany (Börsch-Supan and Schnabel, 2010), Italy (Brugiavini and Peracchi, 2010), the US (Munnell and Wu, 2012a, 2012b) and China (Zhang and Zhao, 2014). Confirming what has been found country by country, Kalwij, Kapteyn and Vos use panel data for 22 OECD countries over the period 1960–2004. Their findings do 'not support the hypothesis that employment of the young and old are substitutes and finds some minor complementarities of employment in the different age groups' (Kalwij et al, 2009: 9). Unlike previous works underlying the complexity of labour market dynamics depending on the sector of activity or the types of labour market, recent analysis – performed at an aggregated level – points out that job sharing is not really efficient. As a consequence, public policies dedicated to job sharing would be inappropriate as they are based on the idea that the labour market operates in a vacuum – based on a fixed number of workers – while this is not the case in reality: higher employment rates may increase the size of the economy and thus create more jobs and demands for other categories of workers. The fact that there would not be a fixed amount of work is assumed as a cause explaining why a decrease in older workers' employment participation does not positively affect youth employment. Association is rather assumed as null or even, in certain cases, as having a positive value.

Despite a relative consensus observed in the literature over the last two decades, a few recent papers have shown contradictory results, being affected by the recent 'Great Recession' of 2007–08 or the economic slump caused by the dot-com bubble in 1999–2001, together with an increasing number of reforms of pension systems. This is the case in Italy, which has been subject to many reforms following the Great Recession (Fornero, 2013). In an article published in 2016, Boeri, Garibaldi and Moen (2016) show that, before and after the reform, firms that were more exposed to the increase in employment duration of senior workers significantly reduced youth hirings. More precisely, using administrative data, the authors estimate that a lock-in of five workers for one year reduces youth hiring of approximately one full-time equivalent worker. The impact of the economic downturn, together with the recently implemented pension reforms, produced a sharp decrease in youth employment. A similar observation has been made in Norway. Using an administrative data set covering the full Norwegian population for the period 1994–2004, Vestad estimates that for every additional early-retirement pensioner, there is room for one new labour market entrant (Vestad, 2013). Looking at the Belgian administrative database from 2005 to 2011 (Wels, 2014b), Wels has shown that substitution varies depending on the type of arrangement used for leaving the labour market (early retirement, part-time early retirement or invalidity) and underlines that job-sharing dynamics vary depending on the sector of activity. They are also affected by collective bargaining.

Nevertheless, studies emphasising the positive role played by early retirement on youth employment are still few in number; they show that, over a more recent period, results observed at the country level may be different from what has been observed previously. The impact of the Great Recession, together with the increasing number of pension reforms, explain this potential trend. According to these new findings, the lump of labour fallacy cannot be considered as a universal law anymore as it is deeply affected by contextual backgrounds.

Empirical perspective: is the lump of labour fallacy so evident?

Although the lump of labour fallacy is a widespread belief, no recent empirical analysis has been performed on British data. The last study focusing on this matter was published in 2010 and covered data from 1968 to 2005 (Banks et al, 2010). Nothing has been done so far looking at the recent period, characterised by a sharp increase in the employment rate of older workers. Looking at the average effective age of retirement (AEAR) provided by the OECD (for a definition of this indicator, see Keese, no date; for a critical approach, see Wels, 2016), the female AEAR was estimated at 60.7 in 1995 and 62.4 in 2014, and the male AEAR was 62.0 in 1995 and 64.1 in 2014. In other words, the actual retirement age has increased by about 1.7 years for women and 2.1 years for men in about 20 years. Looking at the total number of workers by age group, Figure 10.1 clearly shows the ongoing trend.

Figure 10.1: Total employment participation (in thousands) by age group, from 1992 (second quarter) to 2016 (third quarter)

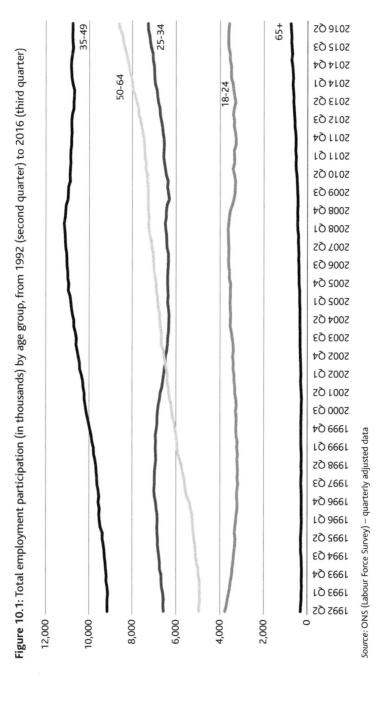

Source: ONS (Labour Force Survey) – quarterly adjusted data

From 1992 to 2016, the employment participation of people aged 18–24 has been reduced by 6 per cent. The 18–24 age group is the only one that has been affected by a decrease in its employment participation. Over the same period, the gross employment participation of people aged 25–34, 35–49, 50–64 and 65+ has increased by 10 per cent, 17 per cent, 73 per cent and 150 per cent, respectively. These figures bear no comparison with demographic changes as, over the same period, the 18–24 and 25–34 age groups have lost less than 1 per cent of their population while the increase in people aged 35–49, 50–64 and 65+ has been 12 per cent, 65 per cent and 30 per cent, respectively. The aim of this second part of the chapter is to assess whether there is an association between the variations in youth employment and the variations of the employment participation of the other age categories once the education attendance rate and economic variations are controlled for.

Methodology

The methodological framework used in this chapter rests on four assumptions. First, we assume that, conversely to what has been done in a large part of the previous research dedicated to this matter, the lump of labour cannot be analysed using variables based on percentages (eg the [un]employment rate) as they tend to give the same weight to each age category while, in reality, the demographic factor plays a key role and the number of jobs varies from one period to another. It is quite paradoxical that previous research using the lump of labour fallacy as a main argument has performed analyses using percentages and rates rather than gross values. Second, we assume that youth employment participation is too broad an indicator as the definition of what is considered as work in the Labour Force Survey is based on the International Labour Organisation's (ILO's) definition, which considers a person working at least one hour a week as a worker (Wels, 2016). Furthermore, employment participation tends to be affected by variations in school and higher-education attendance. Using unemployment and inactivity rates seems a more accurate way to assess the association between youth employment and other age groups. Third, to determine whether increasing the employment participation of older workers has an impact on youth employment, it is necessary to take into consideration the full age structure of the labour market. That is the reason why the association between youth employment and other age groups (not only older workers) needs to be taken into consideration. Fourth, as early retirement schemes do not play a key role in reducing older workers' employment participation anymore, what is relevant is looking at older workers' employment participation as such, rather than looking at their withdrawal, as was done previously when the JRS was implemented (Banks et al, 2010). Finally, this issue requires carefully analysing time-series data and paying attention to the quality of the statistical modelling in order to avoid potential spurious associations.[1]

The statistical models presented in the following aim at assessing whether and to what extent youth unemployment and inactivity is affected by older workers' employment participation, once changes in the demographic structure and the economic context are controlled for. For that purpose, quarterly adjusted data provided by the ONS covering the period 1992–2016 have been used. Two main dependent variables (ie the variable that the model wants to explain) were used: the total number of people aged 18–24 Not in Employment, Education or Training (NEET), that is, the number of young people both inactive (but not attending higher education) and unemployed, on the one hand; and the unemployment rate of people aged 18–24, on the other. The change in both NEET and unemployment rates is explained using several independent variables: the employment participation of the 25–34, 35–49, 50–64 and 65+ age group; Gross Domestic Product (GDP) at constant prices (2004) provided by the OECD; and a demographic ratio (the ratio between the total population aged 18–24 and the population aged 25+). Three statistical models were performed. The first model is an Ordinary Least Square (OLS) regression using gross variables (the total number of people). The second type is an OLS regression based on a moving average calculation for each variable (the mean of each variable over a period of four quarters). Finally, the third model is an OLS regression in which the difference between the value of the variable at time t and the value of the variable at time $t − 1$ is calculated (lag). These three models are consistent with methods used in previous studies dedicated to this topic. Additionally, these models are tested with no delay on the dependent variable, one quarter delay and two quarters delay.[2] Two indicators are provided for estimating the quality of the models: the adjusted R-square and the Durbin–Watson Statistic (Berndt, 1976).[3]

Results

The OLS regression performed using the total number of unemployed and inactive people (NEET) aged 18–24 as a dependent variable (see Table 10.1) provides unclear results about the association between the non-employment of people aged 18–24 and the employment participation of the other age groups. According to this model, one observes a negative association when looking at the 25–34 and 50–64 age groups. This means that an increase in employment participation for people aged 25–34 and 55–64 tends to reduce youth unemployment and inactivity. This is also true when a one quarter or two quarters delay is introduced for the dependent variable. Conversely, one observes the opposite phenomenon when looking at the 35–49 and 65+ age groups. However, the model seems affected by autocorrelations as the R^2 is unreasonably high (close to 1).

Similar results may be observed when introducing a moving average. Again, the association between the employment participation of people aged 25–34 and 50–64 and the NEETs is negative, while the association with the 35–49 and 65+ age groups shows positive results. The value of the R^2 is very high (0.92), which means that the variables introduced in the equation explained 92 per cent of the independent variable's variance. This is typically what can be observed when there is a spurious regression using time-series data. Hence, models 1 and 2 are not relevant in explaining why youth unemployment and inactivity vary over time. The Durbin–Watson Statistic confirms that these models raise a problem of autocorrelation (results obtained using the Durbin–Watson Statistic are very low while they should be close to 2 for confirming that the model is not affected by autocorrelation).

The third model, introducing a lag, is the one that best fits the data. The Durbin–Watson statistic shows a result near 2, which means that there is no autocorrelation problem in the time-series, and the adjusted R^2 is 0.37 (0.12 when a delay of one or two quarters is introduced), which means that 37 per cent of the variance of the dependent variable is explained by the model. The unemployment and inactivity of people aged 18–24 is negatively associated with the employment participation of the 25–64 age group. However, the increase in the employment participation of people aged older than 65 has a positive impact on the number of NEET young people, that is, older workers' employment participation is associated with an increase in inactivity and unemployment for people aged 18–24. This puts into question figures provided by previous research focusing on this matter.

Table 10.1: Time-series regression for NEET

	NEET 18–24			NEET 18–24 Moving average (4)			NEET 18–24 Lag 1		
	No delay	1 – q	2 – q	No delay	1 – q	2 – q	No delay	1 – q	2 – q
Employed 25–34	-0.34**	-0.29*	-0.27*	-0.19	-0.24*	-0.26*	-0.43***	0.03	-0.01
Employed 35–49	1.67***	1.51***	1.28***	2.47***	2.00***	1.59***	-0.19**	-0.07	-0.14
Employed 50–64	-1.09**	-1.16***	-1.33***	-1.04***	-1.21***	-1.42***	-0.19**	-0.13	0.02
Employed 65+	2.35***	2.36***	2.41***	2.62***	2.65**	2.66***	0.16**	-0.03	0.12
Demo ratio	0.24**	0.27***	0.27***	0.25***	0.23**	0.21**	0.17**	0.33***	0.36***
GDP	-2.33***	-2.13***	-1.8***	-3.31***	-2.77***	-2.19***	-0.15*	-0.14	-0.15
Adjusted R^2	0.86	0.86	0.86	0.92	0.92	0.92	0.37	0.12	0.12
Durbin–Watson	0.50	0.58	0.52	0.13	0.13	0.14	2.26	2.24	1.98

Note: $*p < 0.1$; $**p < 0.05$; $***p < 0.01$.

233

To ensure the validity of the results observed for the NEETs, Table 10.2 looks particularly at the number of unemployed people aged 18–24, distinguishing four types depending on unemployment duration (up to six months, 6–12 months, over 12 months or over 24 months). Only results for the lag 1 are shown in Table 10.2 as they show satisfactory results for the Durbin–Watson Statistic and reasonable R^2.

What can be observed by looking at the different unemployment categories is that none of the cases shows a significant negative association between youth unemployment and the employment participation of the 65+ age group, conversely to what can be observed for other age categories. In other words, one cannot assume that an increase in older workers' employment participation is associated with a decrease in youth unemployment. Results are particularly clear when looking at the unemployment durations of 6–12 months and over 24 months. In both cases, one observes a strong and significant positive association between youth unemployment and 65+ employment participation. Put another way, the increase in older

Table 10.2: Time-series regression for unemployment duration (lag 1 only)

	No delay	1 – q	2 – q	No delay	1 – q	2 – q
	Unemployment up to 6 months 18–24			Unemployment 6–12 months 18–24		
Employed 25–34	–0.22**	–0.16	0.01	–0.22**	–0.01	–0.17
Employed 35–49	–0.13	–0.03	–0.16	0.04	–0.1	–0.06
Employed 50–64	–0.06	0.07	–0.06	0.023	–0.04	–0.01
Employed 65+	0.03	–0.07	–0.08	–0.083	–0.15	0.28***
Demo ratio	0.06	0.00	0.18*	0.085	0.19*	0.04
GDP	–0.21**	–0.34***	–0.17	–0.322***	–0.07	–0.13
Adjusted R^2	0.10	0.10	0.59	0.15	0.03	0.06
Durbin–Watson	2.37	2.43	2.27	2.24	2.10	1.92
	Unemployment over 12 months 18–24			Unemployment over 24 months 18–24		
Employed 25–34	–0.26**	0.24**	0.03	–0.14	0.18	0.07
Employed 35–49	–0.34***	–0.10	–0.16	–0.19*	–0.16	–0.17
Employed 50–64	–0.13	–0.30***	–0.12	–0.27***	–0.08	–0.29
Employed 65+	0.12	0.06	0.16	0.21**	–0.07	0.10
Demo ratio	0.06	0.37***	0.16	0.03	0.20*	0.04
GDP	0.04	–0.04	–0.03	0.04	0.01	0.04
Adjusted R^2	0.20	0.25	0.09	0.10	0.02	0.06
Durbin–Watson	2.20	2.10	2.10	1.66	1.59	1.58

Note: $*p < 0.1$; $**p < 0.05$; $***p < 0.01$.

workers' employment participation is associated with an increase in youth unemployment. Results are not significant when looking at unemployment under six months and over 12 months.

What these results show is that the impact of employment participation on youth unemployment and inactivity might vary depending on the age group that is considered. The results clearly show that the employment participation of people age 50–64 and 65+ does not have the same effect on youth unemployment and inactivity. Even though it can be assumed that the employment participation of people aged 50–64 tends to reduce unemployment and inactivity for the age group 18–24, the opposite effect is observed when looking at the employment participation of people aged 65 and over. It is a particularly relevant result as the share of the population aged 65+ in employment has increased by 150 per cent over the last two decades.

The method used in this chapter is similar to what was used in previous studies looking at this issue, but significantly different results are observed. Nevertheless, there are some limitations to this method (eg controlling for gross GDP does not fully control for labour market conditions and the demographic ratio does not account for population growth over the selected period). More fundamentally, there would be a need to use more accurate methods in further research (eg latent growth modelling) or life-course data that contain longitudinal information about workers' trajectories.

Conclusion

The lump of labour is currently a major theoretical argument used against policies aimed at reducing retirement ages. The debate on whether there is a lump of labour has a very long history, going back to at least Henry Mayhew and David F. Schloss in the late 19th century. Yet, the dynamics underlying the quantity of jobs and their distribution among the population are still insufficiently discussed. As Tom Walker (2000: 23) argued regarding working-time reduction policies, 'the claim of a lump-of-labour fallacy is an unwarranted rationalization that obstructs serious discussion of the benefits of shortening work time'. Furthermore, recent empirical evidence does not support this assertion. A small number of studies have recently been published showing that increasing older workers' employment participation has had a negative impact on youth employment. It has to be said that rarely is any empirical *evidence* offered. Instead, supporters of the 'fallacy' view tend to offer *a priori*, dogmatic assertions, to the effect that expanding labour supply will increase aggregate purchasing power and therefore lead to economic growth and more jobs. Such was the line taken by Ros Altman (2015) in her recent government report, 'A new vision for older workers', where she claimed that the idea of a 'lump of labour' has been 'roundly discredited by academic studies but still colours people's views'. Yet she cited only three sources in support (very briefly), discussing this complex and crucial question in only a few lines and offering the argument that 'as the number of workers aged 55 and over increases, overall employment rises and unemployment falls' (Altman, 2015: 21–2).

The empirical part of this chapter confirms for Britain what has been recently found for Italy and Norway. Over a period characterised by an increase in the actual retirement age leading to a sharp increase in employment participation over age 65, youth employment participation has fallen, not only because the higher education attendance rate has increased, but also because the number of NEETs has substantially increased as well. These findings put into question the lump of labour fallacy and open the way to new research looking in depth at what the dynamics underlying job redistribution are.

As matter of fact, a more complex investigation of long-run changes in labour force composition by sector, age, gender, skill level, region and so on is needed. Three main aspects should be analysed in depth in order to confirm whether or not there is a lump of labour. First, one needs to look at the association between working time and employment participation. A quick analysis of changes in the UK labour force since the Second World War produces evidence that supports the 'lump of labour' idea, for several reasons. In the first place, the growth of part-time employment since the Second World War has been remarkable and little considered – indeed, this is the form in which virtually all employment growth has occurred. Since 1951, part-time jobs have grown tenfold. When governments tell us that there are more jobs than ever – some 32,248,000 – they overlook this vital fact. An instructive experiment in necessary scepticism is to give each part-time job a 50 per cent full-time equivalent. This is somewhat flawed, of course, because the hours of part-time jobs vary so greatly, even applying to only one hour a week. Nevertheless, it is an interesting exercise because it demonstrates that, since 1951, there has been virtually no employment growth at the aggregate level relative to population size: the cake may now be sliced more thinly, but it is a similar size of cake. The evidence is as follows: in 1951, there were 22,600,000 employees, employers or self-employed in the UK labour force. Of these, 831,000 were part time and 475,000 were out of work through sickness or unemployment. Deducting those out of work from the total therefore reduces it to 22,125,000, and giving each part-time job a 50 per cent full-time equivalent (415,500) further reduces it to about 21,710,000 full-time equivalents in 1951. By 2018, the labour market (excluding the unemployed) consisted of 23,715,000 people working full time and a massive 8,533,000 working part time. Giving each part-time job a 50 per cent full-time equivalent reduces that latter figure to 4,266,000, producing a grand total for 2018 of 27,981,000 full-time equivalents. The increase in full-time equivalent jobs between 1951 and 2018 is therefore 6,271,000, or 29 per cent. The increase in total population between 1951 (50,300,000) and 2018 (65,518,000) has been 15,218,000, or just over 30 per cent. Therefore, in terms of full-time equivalents, the labour market is, on the face of it, almost exactly the same as it was in 1951. In other words, there *is* a lump of labour. This corresponds with what has been contended by the experienced economic historian Roger Middleton (2000: 33): 'at the aggregate level … there has been almost no employment growth in the British economy for nearly forty years'. Up to now, the contribution of working time in employment participation has not been evaluated in depth (with few exceptions, eg Blundell et al, 2011, 2013; Merkl and Wesselbaum, 2011) and the nature of the relationship between working time and employment participation is not well known.

Another cautionary aspect relates to the overall strategy of pushing more older people into work in order to improve the UK's economic performance. In fact, workforce numbers probably have much less of a beneficial effect compared with factors like technology, the price of raw materials, skill levels, the demand for goods and services, and so on. Hence, the UK had a higher overall employment rate (with more older men still working) in 1931 (a time of economic recession and mass unemployment) than in 1951 (a time of full employment and prosperity). The employment rate of all women hardly changed between 1931 and 1951, at 34.2 per cent and 34.9 per cent, respectively, though that stability included a fall in the employment rate of women aged 60 and over. The employment rate of all men fell over the same period, from 90.5 per cent to 87.5 per cent, with the sharpest fall among men aged 65 and over. In other words, the improved economic performance in 1951 was accompanied by fewer older people working.

A final aspect to consider is whether it is the right strategy for an advanced economy like the UK's to expand via the creation of a large, casualised low-wage sector. Such a strategy may have dysfunctional consequences in the long term, such as encouraging employers to adopt labour-intensive solutions rather than investing in technological innovations that will eventually produce greater economic growth and improve per worker productivity (currently a source of concern in the UK economy). It is also highly political in that it minimises questions of redistribution by the state in favour of the philosophy that all must support themselves via waged labour. We also need to remember that many economists today are predicting a dystopian future in which technological developments cause the UK to achieve much greater economic growth with a smaller workforce. There has recently been much discussion of the massive job losses that may well accompany a 'fourth industrial revolution' based upon new developments in artificial intelligence, robotics, nanotechnology and the like (Schwab, 2016; Ahmed, 2018). Indeed, the whole history of economic growth has been the story of increasing productivity being achieved with progressively smaller workforces, thanks to technology. Hence, the American workforce is twice as large as it was in 1945, yet total productivity has grown eight times; on average, productivity per worker has quadrupled. It is curious that most commentators, especially those at the cutting edge of the new economic strategies, strenuously deny that a lump of labour can possibly exist even when their denial involves ignoring the fact that, by and large, labour market expansion is constrained by total population expansion; thus, the proportion actually in work remains roughly constant.

Notes

[1]   Time-series regressions are likely to be affected by trends and/ or seasonal variations that artificially increase the coefficient of determination (R^2), that is, the proportion of the variance in the dependent variable that is predictable from the independent variable(s). One of the ways of assessing whether there is a spurious association is to look at the *autocorrelation* of the time-series, that is, the correlation between the values of the process at different times. Despite the fact that this risk of spurious regression is well known in the scientific literature (see, eg, Yule, 1921; Granger and Newbold, 1974), it is unfortunate that most research on this matter does not provide accurate indicators for evaluating the quality of the models.

[2]   That is, the models assess the impact of the independent variables on the value of the dependent variable at time t, at time $t + 1$ and at time $t + 2$, respectively.

[3]   The Durbin–Watson Statistic is calculated as follows:

$$d = \frac{\sum_{t=2}^{N}(e_t - e_{t-1})^2}{\sum_{t=1}^{N}e_t^2},$$

where N is the number of observations and e_t is the residual associated with the observation at time t. The Durbin–Watson statistic aims at assessing whether time-series are autocorrelated as, in order to avoid a spurious regression, one needs to avoid autocorrelation in the time-series. For more information, see Durbin and Watson (1971).

References

Ahmed, K. (2018) Bank of England chief economist warns on AI jobs threat, *BBC News*, 20 August, www.bbc.co.uk/news/business

Altman, R. (2015) A new vision for older workers: retain, retrain, recruit, London, www.gov.uk/government/uploads/system/uploads/attachment_data/file/411420/a-new-vision-for-older-workers.pdf

Banks, J., Blundell, R., Bozio, A. and Emmerson, C. (2010) Releasing jobs for the young? Early retirement and youth unemployment in the United Kingdom, in J. Gruber and D.A. Wise (eds) *Social security programs and retirement around the world: The relationship to youth employment*, Chicago, IL: University of Chicago Press, pp 319–44, www.nber.org/chapters/c8261.pdf

Berndt, E.R. (1976) Reconciling alternative estimates of the elasticity of substitution, *The Review of Economics and Statistics*, 58(1): 59–68, https://doi.org/10.2307/1936009

Blundell, R., Bozio, A. and Laroque, G. (2011) Labour supply responses and the extensive margin: the US, UK and France, *Labour*, January: 28, www.homepages.ucl.ac.uk/~uctp39a/AEA-30-12-10.pdf

Blundell, R., Bozio, A. and Laroque, G. (2013) Extensive and intensive margins of labour supply: work and working hours in the US, the UK and France, *Fiscal Studies*, 34(1): 1–29, https://doi.org/10.1111/j.1475-5890.2013.00175.x

Boeri, G., Garibaldi, P. and Moen, E.R. (2016) A clash of generations? Increase in retirement age and labor demand for youth, CEPR Discussion Paper, No. DP11422, https://papers.ssrn.com/sol3/papers.cfm?abstract_id=2820077

Börsch-Supan, A. and Schnabel, R. (2010) Early retirement and employment of the young in Germany, in J. Gruber and D.A. Wise (eds) *Social security programs and retirement around the world: The relationship to youth employment*, Chicago, IL: University of Chicago Press, pp 147–166, www.nber.org/chapters/c8255.pdf

Brugiavini, A. and Peracchi, F. (2010) Youth unemployment and retirement of the elderly: the case of Italy, in J. Gruber and D.A. Wise (eds) *Social security programs and retirement around the world: The relationship to youth employment*, Chicago, IL: University of Chicago Press, pp 167–215, www.nber.org/chapters/c8256.pdf

Cahuc, P. and Zylberberg, A. (2015) *Les ennemis de l'emploi. Le chômage, fatalité ou nécessité?*, Paris: Flammarion.

Campbell, N. (1999) The decline of employment among older people in Britain, CASE Paper 19, January, http://papers.ssrn.com/sol3/papers.cfm?abstract_id=1158910

Durbin, J. and Watson, G.S. (1971) Biometrika Trust testing for serial correlation in least squares regression, *Biometrika*, 38(1): 159–77, www.jstor.org/stable/2332325

Esping-Andersen, G. (2000) Regulation and context: reconsidering the correlates of unemployment, in G. Esping-Andersen and M. Regini (eds) *Why deregulate labour markets*, Oxford: Oxford University Press, pp 99–112.

Fornero, E. (2013) Reforming labor markets: reflections of an economist who (unexpectedly) became the Italian Minister of Labor, *IZA Journal of European Labor Studies*, 2(20), https://doi.org/10.1186/2193-9012-2-20

Giddens, A. (2000) *The Third Way and its critics*, Cambridge: Polity Press.

Granger, C. and Newbold, P. (1974) Spurious regressions in econometrics, *Journal of Econometrics*, 2(2): 111–20, https://doi.org/10.1016/0304-4076(74)90034-7

Gruber, J. and Milligan, K. (2008) Do elderly workers substitute for younger workers in the United States?, in J. Gruber and D.A. Wise (eds) *Social security programs and retirement around the world: The relationship to youth employment*, Chicago, IL: The University of Chicago Press, pp 345–60, www.nber.org/chapters/c8262.pdf

Hamermesh, D.S. and Grant, J. (1979) Econometric studies of labor–labor substitution and their implications for policy, *The Journal of Human Resources*, 14(4): 518–42.

Kalwij, A., Kapteyn, A. and De Vos, K. (2009) Early retirement and employment of the young, RAND Working Paper Series, WR-679, http://papers.ssrn.com/sol3/papers.cfm?abstract_id=1371889

Keese, M. (no date) A method for calculating the average effective age of retirement, Paris: OECD, www.oecd.org/els/emp/39371923.pdf

Krugman, P. (2003) Lumps of labor, *The New York Times*, 7 October.

Lain, D. (2017) *Reconstructing retirement. Work and welfare in the UK and USA*, Bristol: Policy Press.

Layard, R. (1997) *What labour can do*, London: Warner Books, http://eprints.lse.ac.uk/5976/

Macnicol, J. (1998) *The politics of retirement in Britain, 1878–1948*, Cambridge: Cambridge University Press.

Mayhew, H. (1864) *London labour and the London poor: The condition and earnings of those that will work, cannot work and will not work*, London: Charles Griffen and Company.

Merkl, C. and Wesselbaum, D. (2011) Extensive versus intensive margin in Germany and the United States: any differences?, *Applied Economics Letters*, 18(9): 805–8, https://doi.org/10.1080/13504851.2010.507170

Middleton, R. (2000) *The British economy since 1945: Engaging with the debate*, London: Palgrave Macmillan.

Mills, J. (1843) *The stage coach; or, the road of life*, London: Henry Colburn.

Munnell, A.H. and Wu, A.Y. (2012a) Will delayed retirement by the baby boomers lead to higher unemployment among younger workers?, Center for Retirement Research at Boston College, October, p 22.

Munnell, A.H. and Wu, A.Y. (2012b) Are aging baby boomers squeezing young workers out of jobs?, Center for Retirement Research at Boston College, October, pp 12–18.

Performance and Innovation Unit (2000) *Winning the generation game. Improving opportunities for people aged 50–65 in work and community activity*, London: HMSO.

Samuelson, P. (1958) *Economics. An introductory analysis*, New York, NY: McGraw-Hill.

Schloss, D.F. (1891) Why working-men dislike piece-work, *Economic Review*, 1(3): 311–26.

Schwab, K. (2016) The fourth industrial revolution: what it means, how to respond, World Economic Forum Annual Meeting 2016, www.weforum.org/agenda/2016/01/the-fourth-industrial-revolution-what-it-means-and-how-to-respond

Vestad, O.L. (2013) Early retirement and youth employment in Norway, IZA Conference, April (31), http://conference.iza.org/conference_files/older_workers_2013/vestad_o7177.pdf

Walker, T. (2000) The 'lump-of-labor' case against work-sharing: populist fallacy or marginalist throwback?, in L. Golden and D. Figart (eds) *Working time: International trends, theory and policy perspectives*, London: Routledge, http://hussonet.free.fr/lumplab.pdf

Walker, T. (2007) Why economists dislike a lump of labor, *Review of Social Economy*, 65(3): 279–91, https://doi.org/10.1080/00346760701635809

Weiss, R.D. (1977) Elasticities of substitution among capital and occupations in U.S. manufacturing, *Journal of the American Statistical Association*, 72(360): 764–71.

Wels, J. (2014a) La politique des fins de carrière. Vers un modèle européen convergent?, *Sociologie*, 5(3): 233–53.

Wels, J. (2014b) Le partage d'emploi entre générations. Analyse des effets régulateurs et redistributifs de la réduction du temps de travail en fin de carrière sur l'emploi des jeunes, *Recherches Sociologiques et Anthropologiques*, 45(2): 157–74.

Wels, J. (2016) The statistical analysis of end of working life: methodological and sociological issues raised by the average effective age of retirement, *Social Indicators Research*, 129(1): 291–315, https://doi.org/10.1007/s11205-015-1103-6

Yule, G.U. (1921) On the time-correlation problem, with especial reference to the variate-difference correlation method, *Journal of the Royal Statistical Society*, 84(4): 497–537.

Zhang, C. and Zhao, Y. (2014) Will postponing retirement crowd out youth employment?, Munich Personal RePEc Archive, MPRA Paper No. 52931.

11

Family as a socio-economic actor in the political economy of welfare

Theodoros Papadopoulos and Antonios Roumpakis

Introduction

Decades of market-driven welfare reforms have resulted in 'the reconstitution of the nature of social welfare', marked by 'a shift towards more market-based, privatised and individualised forms of social reproduction' (Roberts, 2014: 235). This is increasingly manifested in what Smith and Rochovská (2007: 1175) described as the 'domestication of neo-liberalism', a process in which households 'do not necessarily resist neo-liberalism (although they may under certain circumstances) but [make] attempts – sometimes unsuccessful ones – to find ways to make material life more tolerable'. The process of domesticating neoliberalism coincides with the extensive neoliberal restructuring of the welfare state itself that, especially after the 2008 financial crisis, has led to the institutionalisation of austerity in nearly all advanced welfare-capitalist states (Streeck 2013; Hermann, 2014; Farnsworth and Irving, 2015; Kennett, 2017; Dukelow and Kennett, 2018; Papadopoulos and Roumpakis, 2018). Under conditions of continuing welfare cuts, reductions in benefit entitlements, the curtailment of socio-economic rights, stagnating wages (Vaughan-Whitehead et al, 2016), increasing inequalities (Milanovich, 2016) and ballooning household debt (eg Papadopoulos and Roumpakis, 2013, 2015, 2017a; Hiilamo, 2018), the vast majority of households and families are now expected to act even more strategically as collective socio-economic actors to absorb the ever-increasing social risks and costs associated with their social reproduction in the era of financialised capitalism (Dixon, 2014).

For at least two decades, the majority of comparative social policy literature had focused on the role that the family plays as a provider of care, its politics and its implications for gender relations and especially women (eg Lewis, 1992; Saraceno, 2004; Millar, 2016; Chau et al, 2017; Daly and Ferragina, 2018). However, with few exceptions (see Wheelock and Baines, 1998; Wheelock et al, 2003), less attention has been paid to the institutional conditions that enable families as *collectivities* to generate socio-economic security and independence for its members vis-a-vis both the market and the state. In this chapter we argue that, given the scale of change under the neoliberal reconstitution of social welfare, it is imperative to expand our theoretical understanding of families as socio-economic actors to encompass strategies and practices that extend beyond care provision. Like Donati (2008: 266), we view the centrality of the state in (re)producing 'the family' as being 'at the same time necessary and problematic': necessary due to 'the practicability of laws and welfare entitlements' and 'problematic because of the fluid feature of relations it refers to'. Indeed, the very boundaries of what is considered 'private' and 'public' in terms of family rights and obligations are in constant flux, produced by – and via – the state and its gender regime (Walby, 2015), and always contingent upon the politics of what is a family and the policies affecting families, directly or indirectly. This is especially the case in the contemporary political economy of welfare, characterised by institutionalisation of austerity and the marketisation of politico-economic governance (Berndt, 2015). Against this background, the theoretical challenge to articulate the family as a socio-economic collective actor leads us to rethink 'the family' as a 'supra-personal subjectivity' that is more than the sum of its members (Donati, 2008: 286), as a historically (re)constituted subjectivity that involves a relationship between spouses/partners (comprising different or the same genders) and between generations (parents and children), regulated by the state but also conditioned by its interactions with both the state and the market.

The chapter comprises three main parts. First, we critically review existing approaches that address the dynamic between the family and the (welfare) state, mainly in the comparative social policy literature. We review the existing analytical approaches focusing on 'familisation' and 'defamilisation' used in comparisons of family policies across welfare states. We also borrow from the work of radical feminists who contextualise the importance of the family as a site for the social reproduction of (welfare) capitalism to highlight how employers and the state offset or offload the costs and risks of social reproduction onto the family. We argue that most of the existing approaches tend to narrowly focus on how policies affect the family as a care provider and neglect how the role of the family is (re-)institutionalised as a collective socio-economic actor in welfare capitalism, especially under conditions of permanent austerity, extensive recommodification and expanding refamilisation.

In the second part, we revisit Karl Polanyi's work on the economy as an instituted process. We particularly engage with his distinction between substantivist and formalist understandings of 'the economic' in order to demonstrate the limited value of utility-maximising individualism in understanding economic action, especially within households. Following Polanyi's identification of different types of economic practices (autarchy, reciprocity, redistribution, market exchange), we elaborate on the key role of the household as a strategic coordinator of such practices in the political economy of welfare.

In the third part, we review contributions from relational sociology advancing a theorisation of the family as a relational subject, one that comprises 'infungible' and irreplaceable properties in nurturing trustful, reciprocal and responsible social relations (Donati, 2016), even when it engages in market-oriented economic exchanges. The epistemological argument here highlights the importance of treating the terrain of family's agency as a separate level of analysis. Based on a critical review of the selected literature, we agree with Donati (2016) insofar as family represents an agent that comprises more than the sum of its individual members and that is more than a unit of production and consumption. However, we radicalise Donati's notion of the family as a relational subject by approaching it as a collective actor, the character of which, while pre-dating capitalism, is nevertheless (re)defined and fundamentally affected by its interactions with both the state and the market in capitalism, especially as the latter evolves under the pressures of financialisation.

Effectively, the aim in this chapter is to elevate 'the family' as an analytical concept in social policy research to an analogous position of that of 'the firm' in management research, without resurrecting traditionalist or essentialist conceptualisations of (patriarchal) 'family values'. We aspire to open a wider debate on the role of the family as a socio-economic actor in the social reproduction of welfare capitalism. Especially, in light of successive waves of austerity and pro-market reforms that, while promoting the refamilisation of social risks and costs, are undermining the family's capacities to protect its members from both state and market failures.

Family and social policy: de/familisation and social reproduction in capitalism

Reflecting on the role of the family – and of women *in* the family – many social policy scholars writing from a feminist/gender-politics perspective have accurately highlighted the gender-blindness and implicit androcentrism in traditional mainstream comparative welfare state literature. For example, Esping-Andersen's (1990) focus on decommodification was heavily criticised on the grounds that it did not acknowledge women's unpaid caring work at home; work that allowed, in the first place, men to gain access to the labour market and, thereafter, to social protection and welfare rights (Pascall and Lewis, 2004). Unpaid work was not recognised as waged work and women were therefore not able to be independently 'decommodified' (O'Connor, 1998; see also Orloff, 1993). In addition, as an analytical term, 'decommodification' did not capture the implications of the 'gendered division of labour' for the social reproduction of welfare capitalism (Sainsbury, 1999). Instead, Mclaughlin and Glendinning (1994: 65) proposed the concept of *defamilisation* as an analytical term to capture the extent to 'which people engage in families and the extent to which they can uphold an acceptable standard of living independently of "family" participation'. In this context, defamilisation can be achieved by transferring care responsibilities to the state (eg public childcare) and the market (eg private childcare) whereas (re)familisation is achieved by transferring care responsibilities away from the state and back to families (see also Saxonberg, 2013). Leitner and Lessenich (2007) use the terms 'economic' and 'social' defamilisation to distinguish between financial and care dependencies, respectively, in order to highlight that the relationship between caregiver and care-receiver could involve a recognition on behalf of the state to absorb financial costs (defamilisation) but also provide the opportunity for the carer (mainly women) to receive income for offering care within the family (familisation).[1] Furthermore, numerous studies attempted to measure the diversity of family and gender support policies comparatively and internationally (eg Yu et al, 2015; Lohmann and Zagel, 2016; Chau et al, 2017; Daly and Ferragina, 2018), with some analysing the differential strength of both familisation and defamilisation measures as indicative of the existence of different patterns and 'varieties of familialism' (Leitner, 2003; Keck and Saraceno, 2010; Saraceno 2016).

Papadopoulos and Roumpakis (2017b) argued that there are key limitations with such conceptualisations of de/familisation. To begin with, in these accounts, the family is approached primarily as the micro-terrain where the responsibility for care is negotiated between genders in a power dynamic affected by state policies and cultural norms. The family's agency as a collective socio-economic actor is usually either underplayed or perceived as a remnant of pre-modernity; the family is seen as an institution that fills the 'welfare gap', especially in residual welfare regimes. Further, the substantial increases in women's labour market participation rates over recent decades has not been accompanied with similar trends of men absorbing caring responsibilities. Thus, care provision towards dependent members like children or the elderly, as well as domestic work, continued to be gendered. It has remained largely feminised, provided by other women, either close relatives (eg grandmothers) or women outside the family who are often migrants (on migration and domestic care arrangements, see Degavre and Merla, 2016).[2] In short, the gender bias against women in care provision does not seem to have changed substantially despite the increases in women's participation in formal labour markets. Rather, it seems that it has been either 'externalised' to the extended family or commodified, especially during the era of post-crisis austerity, when most welfare states made substantial cuts in – or gave low priority to – the supply of care services, like public childcare or social care.

In this context, for those dual-earner family households that can afford it, care services are being bought from the market, mainly provided by low-paid women who are often migrants. For those families who cannot afford private childcare or elderly care, the solution is the familisation of associated costs, resulting in, among other things, higher cohabitation rates with older parents and familial 'in-house' childcare arrangements. The burdens of these are usually borne by women whose income from paid employment is now a necessity for the family's welfare (Wheelock et al, 2003; Simonazzi and Villa, 2010; Sung and Pascall, 2014; Zhong and Li, 2017; Croucher et al, 2018).

Against this background, the political pursuit of defamilisation, while the neoliberal restructuring of welfare state was underway, had perverse effects. Originally, defamilisation was advocated as a socio-politically progressive process whereby women could unburden their care responsibilities in order to be able to independently access the labour market and, similar to men, raise independent market income and accumulate socio-economic rights. Still, some of the arguments – made especially by liberal scholars of second-wave feminism – also involved a critique against the 'family wage' of the so-called 'male breadwinner' model. As feminist political philosophers like Fraser (2013) pointed out, neoliberal socio-economic policies were inadvertently sanctioned by such a critique: women may have been granted 'recognition' through the market but claims for 'redistribution' through the (welfare) state were silenced within a narrative that effectively legitimised neoliberal assaults on wages, employment rights and welfare security for both men and women. According to Fraser (2013: 220–1, 223):

> Neoliberal capitalism's … indispensable workers are disproportionately women, not only young single women, but also married women and women with children; not only racialized women, but women of virtually all nationalities and ethnicities. As such women have poured into labor markets around the globe, the effect has been to undercut once and for all state-organized capitalism's ideal of the family wage.… [T]he reality that underlies the new ideal [the two-earner family] is depressed wage levels, decreased job security, declining living standards, a steep rise in the number of hours worked for wages per household, exacerbation of the double shift – now often a triple or quadruple shift – and a rise in female-headed households.… Disturbing as it may sound, I am suggesting that second-wave feminism has unwittingly provided a key ingredient of the new spirit of neoliberalism.… After all, this capitalism would much prefer to confront claims for recognition over claims for redistribution, as it builds a new regime of accumulation on the cornerstone of women's waged labor and seeks to disembed markets from democratic political regulation in order to operate all the more freely on a global scale.

Supported by neoliberal states, the new world of the post-industrial, post-Westphalian political economy of 'flexible' capitalism relies heavily on the low-waged labour and low job security of both women and men. At the same time, under the pretext of encouraging individual 'choice' and 'flexibility' while privatising decisions over the so-called 'work–family balance', neoliberal states, employers and businesses managed to unburden themselves from any serious socio-economic responsibilities towards supporting families as collectivities. Under conditions where secure jobs are diminishing and wages are stagnant, with private debt rising and welfare rights being curtailed, young people find it very difficult to start new families while parents (couples and lone parents) find themselves under ever-increasing pressure to secure sustainable livelihoods for their families' members (see also Wheelock et al, 2003; Fine, 2014).

Against this background, the new political economy of 'flexible' (welfare) capitalism not only imposes more demands on working-age family members, but also offloads substantial costs and risks upon families as collectivities while undermining their capacity to act as socio-economic actors to secure their social reproduction, as well as society's at large. Here, we borrow from the scholarship of feminist political economy the concept of 'social reproduction in capitalism', an expanded concept of social reproduction that is not confined to the idea of the 'care economy', but includes wider questions of power and production relations that are directly related to the conditions that shape capital accumulation. As Bakker and Silvey (2008: 3, emphasis added) put it: 'the family and the state become important sites where the needs of social reproduction are linked to the need of accumulation and where the state intervenes to *offset* or *offload* the high costs of social reproduction *onto* or *away* from the family at different moments in different locales'.

Consequently, we argue that it has become imperative to move beyond the rather narrow conceptualisations of the family assumed in the de/familisation debate and engage with a broader conceptualisation of the family as a collective socio-economic agent embedded in the deep structures and politico-economic processes driving the contemporary political economy of welfare (LeBaron, 2010; Douglass, 2012, Dixon, 2014). Such an approach allows us to extend our understanding of the family beyond care and gender relations to incorporate how the family's collective agency is conditioned and affected by both the (neoliberal) state and the market, enabling it to consolidate and mobilise the necessary resources (financial, emotional, symbolic) to protect its members.

In the next section, we demonstrate how the work of economic anthropologist Karl Polanyi can offer fruitful analytical insights for conceptualising the family's economic agency in the political economy of welfare.

Theorising the family as an economic actor

In his essay 'The economy as instituted process', Polanyi (1957a) drew a sharp distinction between two irreconcilable perspectives in approaching the character of 'the economic': the *formal* and the *substantive*. The formalist approach universalises the 'logic of economising' for all economic exchanges – that is, the utility-maximising rationale under conditions of scarcity – across time and space. It is an axiomatic, rather than empirically based, approach that, with respect to the family, begins from the axiom that the family and family members are individuals who will behave in a rational and self-interested manner, even when they are engaged in seemingly cooperative or altruistic behaviour (see, especially, Becker, 1981). Ermisch (2016: 2), for example, emphatically argued that 'when putting a social institution like the family under analytical scrutiny, it is helpful to assume that individuals understand their environment and act rationally to maximize their own welfare'.

According to such approaches, usually advanced by neoclassical economists, decisions regarding marriage, financial transfers to children, home production or investments in children's education can be explained through models of individual behaviour/preferences and the different comparative advantages of men and women (Becker, 1981; for a critique, see Woolley, 1996). In short, economic formalism deconstructs internal family ties and approaches the family as a mere sum of its individual members motivated by self-interest. Actions internal to the family can be explained by reference to utility-maximising behaviours, where each individual is assumed to sustain the same capacity to assess needs and provide care (Tronto, 2013; see also Wrenn and Waller, 2018). With regards to actions external to the family, formalist accounts privilege the market-oriented 'rationale' over all other 'rationales' (eg reciprocity, redistribution, autarchy) in the family's economic practices vis-a-vis the extended family network,[3] other families and households, its local community, and even the economy as a whole (see Waller and Jennings, 1991; Laamanen et al, 2018; Melhuus, 2018). Finally, when it comes to evaluating welfare state policies, formalist arguments adopt the well-known narratives of public choice theory that view socio-economic rights as posing restrictions to the exercise of individual choice in the market and as being responsible for welfare dependencies and labour market disincentives (Becker, 1981; Ermisch, 2016).

The substantivist approach rejects the 'economistic fallacy' (Polanyi, 1977: ch 1) that all forms of economic action are driven by the individual's utility-maximising motive assumed in the formalist understanding of economic behaviour. Instead of starting from unproven axioms, the substantivist approach begins by empirically grounding its analysis both in the present and, especially, in the history of how humans sustain their livelihoods and their associated practices. The 'economy' is not separated from its political and social dimensions, but instead approached as the *instituted* process of interaction between men and women and their environment in order to produce the material means that facilitate their social reproduction. Polanyi (2001 [1957]) eloquently argued that there is nothing pre-given or 'natural' in the way the economy is institutionalised (especially the contemporary market economy); instead, it is essentially expressed through acts that represent and shape the 'political and cultural spheres of society at large' (Polanyi, 1977: 35). For Polanyi, the societal effects of individual behaviour depend on the presence of particular institutional conditions and what he named 'forms of integration' (Polanyi, 1977: 250), which, in turn, condition the 'economic' behaviour of individuals and collectivities. Against this background, Polanyi (1977: 250–1) argued that 'the economy acquires unity and stability' through combinations of at least three patterns of integration, as he called them:

- *reciprocity*, which relies on organised patterns of symmetry in the movement of goods, circulating in 'acts of good will' – like gift exchanges – among a 'definite community', commonly present in relations of kinship and friendship (the practice of altruistic blood donation or organ donation are contemporary examples of applying this rationale at the societal level)[4];
- *redistribution*, which relies on organising patterns of centricity and is characterised by the 'movement of goods and money towards the centre and out of it again' (welfare policies and progressive taxation are contemporary examples of applying this rationale at the societal level)[5]; and
- *market exchange*, which relies on an organised system of price-making markets and is defined as the 'mutual appropriative movement of goods between hands at set or bargained rates'.

In his earlier work, Polanyi (1957a, 1966) also included a fourth pattern of integration:

- *householding*, which relies on organising patterns of economic *autarchy* (aka self-sufficiency, that is, producing for one's own use and consuming in a symmetrically reciprocal fashion), which archetypically is exemplified in the economic practices of extended pre-capitalist families and households (Polanyi refers to the Greek

251

oikos, the Roman *familia* and the English *manor* as empirical examples).

Polanyi argued that given this plurality of forms of economic integration and practices, the economistic postulate behind the formalistic approach (which grants market exchange the status of the only form of 'economic' action) not only went contrary to historical and anthropological experience, but constituted, epistemologically and ethically, a political attempt to suppress the substantive meaning of the economic. As Polanyi (1957a: 240) wrote:

> there is no necessary relationship between economizing action and the empirical economy. The institutional structure of the economy need not compel, as with the market system, economizing actions. The implications of such insight for all the social sciences which must deal with the economy could hardly be more far-reaching. Nothing less than a fundamentally different starting point for the analysis of the human economy as a social process is required.

The most elementary societal unit where these economic 'rationales' coexist and combine to serve the purposes of the social well-being of its members is the household, especially the family household. Their differences aside,[6] Polanyi agreed with Weber that the household ('*oikos*') was not a primitive form of economic organisation, but a key unit of socio-economic life that not only pre-dates capitalism, but continues under it. They also both identified householding as being 'the dominant [economic] form in most periods in the past' (Weber, 1978 [1921/22]: 80). Revisiting Aristotle's proposals on economic institutions and economic principles appropriate for a good society, Polanyi (1957b: 81) agreed that '[t]he economy – as the root of the word shows, a matter of the domestic household or *oikos* – concerns directly the relationship of persons who make up the natural institution of the household'.

Still, as Polanyi moved into studying the history and institutions of large, mainly archaic, economies, the concepts of household and householding (with its *autarchic* economic orientation) became marginal to his work (see Gregory, 2009). Indeed, apart from criticising the disastrous effects of disembedded markets in capitalism, Polanyi did not research how householding interrelated with the other forms of economic integration and practices within market societies (Dale, 2010: 141). As Stanfield (1986) notes, this inadequacy has led to interpretations that perceived these forms of economic integration as mainly applicable to archaic societies. Along with a growing literature adopting a substantivist perspective in studying institutional economics (Hann and Hart, 2009; Maucourant and Plociniczak, 2013), and householding in particular (Laamanen et al, 2018), we agree that these aspects of Polanyi's work can and ought to be extended to the investigation of the contemporary political economy of welfare.

In particular, the household, as a collective agent that coordinates and practices different logics of socio-economic action, and its relationship to the moral imperative behind householding are of great significance in our attempt to re-conceptualise the family as a socio-economic actor. Melhus (2018: 83–4) put it succinctly:

> The household, in my usage, is not reserved for non-market economies. It is not a term solely applicable to pre-industrial societies [and cannot] be confined to autarkic, self-sufficient peasant production. Rather ... I view householding as embedded in market relations, straddling both the market and non-market domain.... This will necessarily involve a double focus: on the one hand, on those relations and practices that contribute towards reproducing a particular economy (through relations of labour); and, on the other, on those relations and practices that contribute towards creating a livelihood. These two domains are mutually constitutive, if not overlapping, incorporating at one and the same time the transformative and integrative potentials of social life.

In this context, we link Polanyi's insightful substantivist understanding of the different forms of 'economic' action to the discussions on the conditions of social reproduction in capitalism, and especially on the role of the family as a collective agent in it. This enables us to advance elements of a new research agenda, both conceptually and empirically.

Key issues in this new agenda are to explore how and under what conditions the family is, as '*oikos*', institutionalised in contemporary welfare capitalism and how its capacity to act as a collective agent is facilitated, or hampered, by both the state and the market (Polanyi, 1957a: 50). In this effort, an extra dimension in the family's agency needs to be taken into account. This dimension concerns a deeper and more complex layer of social relations in which the family's economic agency is embedded. We need to theorise the family not merely as an economic actor (deploying different 'rationales'), but as a distinct subjectivity simultaneously combining social *and* economic attributes and practices – as a *socio*-economic actor with unique qualities. Thus, we find it fruitful to engage with contributions from relational sociology, where the family is defined as a 'relational subject' generating 'relational goods'.

Theorising the family as a relational subject

We borrow from relational sociology the concept of *relational subject* (Donati, 2008) to engage, ontologically, with the family as a unique collectivity whose social agency is the emergent property of its particular set of relationships and practices (Donati, 2016: 160). This view sees the family as 'a system of relations exceeding the contingent interactions between individuals' (Donati and Prandini, 2007: 219), 'a supra-personal social and legal subject' (Donati, 2008: 286) that involves 'a *sui generis* nexus between freedom and responsibility' with respect to relationships between spouses/partners and between generations. The crucial difference between the family and other primary relationships (eg friendships) or other relational subjectivities (eg a labour union, a political party, a corporation, a firm or a foundation) is that it is unique in its non-differentiation of human life: 'Empirically, the family relation involves *all* the dimensions of human life. Only in the family the human person is considered and addressed in her *full personality*, and not for a particular quality or function she performs [eg as in the work environment, political life or the market]' (Donati, 2008: 286, emphasis added).

In addition, a key aspect of the family's social agency concerns its capacity to generate *relational goods*. These comprise particular qualities of social relationships 'which stem from the family-relationship and can be generated and enjoyed only by those that share it by acting together' (Donati, 2008: 287). Relational goods are immaterial, intangible, non-aggregative goods that, due to the fact that they comprise qualities of relationships, cannot be generated individually.[7] Instead, in the case of the family, they can be generated in, and enjoyed within, the collective, 'as the sharing [of] the relationships from which derive both individual and community goods' (Donati, 2016: 149).

Against this background, a deeper understanding of the family as a relational subject emerges. Due to its unique set of relationships, the family represents a fundamental generative resource for society, pivotal for society's material, symbolic and relational reproduction (in fact, Donati considers the family not only as a generator of relational goods, but also as a relational good for society itself[8]). In highlighting the need to protect and support the family, Donati (2016) goes as far as arguing for the extension of citizenship rights to families as collectivities. Still, he frames his advocacy in a context where the traditional heterosexual nuclear family is perceived to be the norm. We have reservations with this approach, which, in our view, is predicated on an essentialist view of the family. It is a heavily normative approach, potentially exclusionary of other types of families, and underplays the politics of how the family has been *historico-legally* instituted as a collectivity.

An '*oikos*' perspective: towards a new theoretical synthesis and research agenda

Reservations aside, what is really inspiring within the 'relational' approach is its ontological premise, which we critically adopt. Thus, as a tentative synthesis, we propose a view of the family as the layered reality of a unique socio-economic subjectivity, predicated on a social relation that is exceptional in its non-differentiation of life of the human persons in it. It is a social subjectivity that can generate unique relational goods and, simultaneously, an economic actor that coordinates and deploys different types of economic practices (ie householding, reciprocity, redistribution and market exchange) for the welfare of its members. Seen in all its dimensions, the family is a *historically (re)constituted* socio-economic actor whose legal definition varies through time and between societies. The family acts in a context of intense power relations vis-a-vis both the state and market to secure the well-being of its members while its capacities to exercise agency are directly affected by the governance of social reproduction in the wider political economy of welfare. By exercising its agency, it also 'provides a mechanism for aggregating and redistributing resources among its members' (Allen et al, 2004: 116), with the aim to offer them[9] socio-economic security and relative independence from both the state and the market (see also Moreno, 2006).

In previous empirical work we demonstrated how different welfare regimes institutionalised the conditions for families' role as both welfare providers and economic actors in the regions of Southern Europe and East and South-East Asia (Papadopoulos and Roumpakis 2013, 2017b). In particular, we demonstrated that the centrality of the family in welfare provision in these regimes reflected, among other things, how employers and the state, historically, shifted the responsibility to absorb social costs and risks for social reproduction towards the family. Families not only continued their pre-capitalist role as key agents in social provisioning – with women acting as 'compulsory altruists' (Land and Rose, 1985) – but also resorted to exercising extensive economic agency, as investors in real estate, education and the human capital of their members, and, often, as employers, where reliance on 'family values' went hand-in-hand with the creation and running of family businesses. These experiences are not unique to Southern Europe or East/South-East Asia. For example, Wheelock and Baines's (1998) qualitative work on the importance of non-market social arrangements for the UK's small family businesses has remarkable resonance with the approach outlined here:

> The empirical work ... did uncover values of self-reliance within the small business family, but such values were not driven primarily by the external, market-derived incentives to be expected of an enterprise economy. Self-reliance was apparent as an internally created value, linked closely with family dignity and self-respect. It was a value based upon self-exploitation and dependency within the business family. The extent of self-exploitation and the sacrifices made by some individuals should be considered seriously. Business owners worked punishingly long hours for precarious rewards. Even so, their businesses often were sustainable only because other members of their families also adjusted their daily lives around the unpredictable workload characteristic of very small businesses. (Wheelock and Baines, 1998: 55)

Social policy research needs to explore in much more detail the extent and forms of families' engagement with various markets (ideally, in comparative studies covering the Global North and Global South). In particular, we should examine how market exchanges affect families' capacity to act as socio-economic actors, as well as how their capacity to exercise socio-economic agency intersects with class, racial, gender and generational inequalities. Furthermore, we should examine how families coordinate their multiple engagements with markets: as purchasers of care and welfare-related insurance products; as owners of assets and wealth (see Appleyard and Rowlingson, 2010);

as shareholders in financial markets; as supporters of family migration projects and remittances; and as investors in the human capital and education of their members or through family-run businesses. Although space does not allow us to expand further on the tensions between the '*oikos*' logic and the market logic, suffice it to say that as a collective actor, '*oikos*' embeds market exchanges in its deeper moral fabric of self-reliance, independence and trust (see Booth, 1991). For example, in the case of family businesses, it is worth highlighting that one of the key principles and most characteristic trait of family-run businesses is familial 'trust' in running the business, regardless of whether this refers to running a taverna on a Greek island, a farm in the UK or a 'super-car' empire like the Ferrari family firm (see, again, Wheelock and Baines, 1998; Pichler and Wallace, 2007).

We also argue that we need to explore in much more detail how families practise reciprocity in, for example, forming intergenerational relationships of care among extended families and making intergenerational transfer of resources or goods. Evidence of these reciprocal relationships includes (indicatively) studies like those of informal social capital (Pichler and Wallace, 2007), informal social relations of support (Kolhi et al, 2009), or family income transfers and proximity of residence (Blome et al, 2010). Still, familial practices of reciprocity (eg a parent caring for a young child, or a child caring for an old parent) can be re-institutionalised into acts that promote different economic rationales as state policies can transform them into manifestations of redistribution (eg elderly care leave in Sweden) and even market exchange (eg wages to children that care for parents in Germany; see Keck and Saraceno, 2010; on England, see Pickard et al, 2015). Interesting examples of how the state can mediate and facilitate these intergenerational transfers is the provision of tax-free cash allowances in Japan for grandparents to fund their grandchildren's education (Izuhara, 2016) or the financial incentives for children to buy homes in close proximity to their parents' homes in Singapore. Conversely, an increasing number of grandparents in the US take out student loans to finance their grandchildren's education (CFPB, 2017), a demonstration of how even in the archetypical liberal welfare-capitalist regime, solidarity survives among the extended family. Additionally, there is a growing literature that explores the importance of intergenerational transfers to children and grandchildren (Heath and Calvert, 2013) in the UK,[10] as well as in Europe (Hagestad and Gunhild, 2006; Albertini et al, 2007).

Furthermore, as far as householding practices (producing for own consumption) are concerned, these differ if their institutionalisation pre-dates the institutionalisation of the market (on feudalism, see Bloch, 1961), or if they are established during periods of 'embedded' or 'disembedded' market economies (see Polanyi, 2001 [1957]), or during Soviet-style socialist regimes. Regardless of the variation over time and place, we need to explore in much more detail how householding as a strategy aims to provide family members with autarchy and protection from the uncertainties and insecurities associated with profit-making or production-maximising logics and practices. As mentioned earlier, we are aware that householding may involve undesirable hierarchical and power relations, especially gender inequalities, but similar to Fraser (2013) and Nelson (2016), we argue that this should not prevent us from also seeing positive or even progressive elements in this familial strategy where they exist.

Conclusion

In this chapter, we provided a new conceptualisation of the family as a socio-economic actor. We proposed a new research agenda that treats the terrain of the family's collective agency as a separate level of analysis. This agency is (re)defined and fundamentally affected by its interactions with both the state and the market in capitalism, especially as the latter transforms in the era of financialisation. Our aim was to move beyond narrow conceptualisations of the family as a care provider by elevating the family as an analytical concept in social policy research without resurrecting traditionalist or essentialist conceptualisations of (patriarchal) 'family values'. We argued that the family is a social subjectivity that can generate unique relational goods. It comprises 'infungible' and irreplaceable properties in nurturing trustful, reciprocal and responsible social relations, essential for individual and societal well-being. At the same time, the family is an economic actor that coordinates and deploys different types of economic practices (ie householding, reciprocity, redistribution and market exchange) to secure the well-being of its members. Our approach challenges us to re-imagine the family's socio-economic agency in its intersections of class, racial, gender and generational inequalities within the wider political economy of welfare. This is an urgent task in light of successive waves of austerity and pro-market reforms that, while promoting the refamilisation of social risks and costs, have been undermining families' capacities to generate high-quality relational goods and protect their members vis-a-vis both state and market failures.

Notes

[1] Similar to decommodification, the term '(de/re)familisation' refers to dynamic processes and tendencies and not an absolute condition.

[2] Saxonberg (2013: 33) argues in favour of using the term 'de-genderisation' to better depict 'policies that promote the elimination of gender roles', rather than defamilisation.

[3] One could argue that the debate on 'intergenerational conflict' captures a similar logic. While many scholars often cite this 'conflict' to highlight new social risks or divert attention to issues of welfare sustainability, one cannot miss the underlying assumption of what is, effectively, a narrative of self-interested individuals. However, this is not always verified as there is significant evidence of an economy of intra-household transfers that include both financial and time resources that bridge this division (see Albertini et al, 2007; Blome et al, 2010).

[4] Other economic practices integrated under a reciprocity 'rationale' are easily identifiable at the community level through voluntary contributions in terms of labour, services and goods (eg trade union work, charity and voluntary work, 'soul kitchens', 'food banks', etc), as well as in the practices of the so-called sharing and social economy (for interactions between households and the sharing economy, see Laamanen et al, 2018).

[5] Polanyi cites the taxation system as an example of redistribution in market societies that developed welfare states to describe the movement of goods and money towards the centre – understood as modern governments – and their movement out of the centre again via public redistributive welfare programmes.

[6] Weber drew a sharp distinction between the production of goods for consumption – a practice identified in individual households – and production for gain (profit), a practice that is primarily identified with 'firms' in a capitalist economy. For Weber, householding and profit-making are not mutually exclusive categories, with both economic actions being present at all times (Swedberg, 2001). He argued, however, that households do employ a variety of strategies that allow families to meet their consumption demands, which may include exploiting opportunities for profit-making insofar as to meet these demands. Polanyi (1957a, 1960, 1966) refuted this point and argued that households, even when they were involved

in exchanges, lacked the 'logic of economising' that Weber (1978 [1921/22]) assumed. An empirical verification of this point was offered by Chayanov's (1991 [1927]) study of the Russian peasantry, where households prioritised their own self-sufficiency over profit-making or maximising their production, a logic that contrasted with the key economic aims of both market economy and Soviet-style socialism.

[7]   However, as Donati (2008: 287) rightly points out 'the family can also generate "relational bads", when it does not work properly'.

[8]   'The family is a relational good (i) in itself for its members, given the fact that it can generate what other life styles cannot generate, and (ii) it is a relational good for the society because it develops functions that no other form of life can fulfil' (Donati, 2016: 160).

[9]   In this context, although we agree with Falkingham and Baschieri (2009) that not all members of households share equally their resources or have equal access to welfare and labour market security, we also argue that we need more research on how families pool and consolidate the resources that are later redistributed among its members.

[10] According to a 2017 report by Santander Bank, 'the number of people buying their first home who turn to their grandparents for help with a deposit has soared four-fold during the past five years'. The report stated that 'the move is part of a growing trend for first-time buyers to turn to their family for financial support, with 32% saying they will ask their family for a loan towards their deposit, something just 13% of existing homeowners did' (see: http://www.zoopla.co.uk/discover/property-news/one-in-10-first-time-buyers-rely-on-bank-of-gran-and-grandad/#RdT5O3pqj9V24b3q.99).

References

Albertini, M., Kohli, M. and Vogel, C. (2007) Intergenerational transfers of time and money in European families: common patterns – different regimes?, *Journal of European Social Policy*, 17: 319–34.

Allen, J., Barlow, J., Leal, J., Maloutas, T. and Padovani, L. (2004) *Housing & welfare in Southern Europe*, Oxford: Blackwell.

Appleyard, L. and Rowlingson, K. (2010) *Home ownership and the distribution of personal wealth*, York: Joseph Rowntree Foundation.

Bakker, I. and Silvey, R. (2008) *Beyond states and markets: The challenges of social reproduction*, Abingdon: Routledge.

Becker, G.S. (1981) *A treatise on the family*, Cambridge, MA: Harvard University Press.

Berndt, C. (2015) Ruling markets: the marketization of social and economic policy, *Environment and Planning*, 47(9): 1866–72.

Bloch, M. (1961) *Feudal society*, Chicago, IL: University of Chicago.

Blome, A., Keck, W. and Alber, J. (2010) *Family and the welfare state in Europe: Intergenerational relations in ageing societies*, Cheltenham: Edward Elgar.

Booth, K. (1991) Security and emancipation, *Review of International Studies*, 17: 313–26.

CFPB (Consumer Financial Protection Bureau) (2017) Snapshot of older consumers and student loan debt. Office for Older Americans & Office for Students and Young Consumers.

Chau, R.C.M., Yu, S.W.K., Foster, L. and Lau, M.K.W. (2017) Defamilisation measures and women's labour force participation – a comparative study of twelve countries, *Journal of International and Comparative Social Policy*, 33: 73–86.

Chayanov, A. (1991 [1927]) *The theory of peasant co-operatives*, Columbus, OH: Ohio State University Press.

Croucher, K., Quilgars, D. and Dyke, A. (2018) *Housing and life experiences: Making a home on a low income*, York: Joseph Rowntree Foundation.

Dale, G. (2010) *Karl Polanyi: The limits of the market*, Cambridge: Polity.

Daly, M. and Ferragina, E. (2018) Family policy in high-income countries: five decades of development, *Journal of European Social Policy*, 28: 255–70.

Degavre, F. and Merla, L. (2016) Defamilialization of whom? Re-thinking defamilialization in the light of global care chains and the transnational circulation of care, in M. Kilkey and E. Palenga-Möllenbeck (eds) *Family life in an age of migration and mobility. Migration, diasporas and citizenship*, London: Palgrave Macmillan.

Dixon, A.D. (2014) *The new geography of capitalism: Firms, finance, and society*, Oxford: Oxford University Press.

Donati, P. (2008) The state and family in a subsidiary society, in M. Archer and P. Donati (eds) *Pursuing the common good: How solidarity and subsidiarity can work together*, Acta 14, Vatican City: Pontifical Academy of Social Sciences, www.pass.va/content/dam/scienzesociali/pdf/acta14/acta14-donati.pdf

Donati, P. (2016) The family as a source of relational goods (and evils) for itself and for the community, *Italian Journal of Sociology of Education*, 8(3): 149–68.

Donati, P. and Prandini, R. (2007) The family in the light of a new relational theory of primary, secondary and generalized social capital, *International Review of Sociology*, 17: 209–23.

Douglass, M. (2012) Global householding and social reproduction: migration research, dynamics and public policy in East and Southeast Asia, Working Paper Series No. 188, National University of Singapore.

Dukelow, F. and Kennett, P. (2018) Discipline, debt and coercive commodification: post-crisis neoliberalism and the welfare state in Ireland, the UK and the USA, *Critical Social Policy*, 38: 482–504.

Ermisch, J.F. (2016) *An economic analysis of the family*, Princeton, NJ: Princeton University Press.

Esping-Andersen G. (1990) *The three worlds of welfare capitalism*, Cambridge: Polity Press.

Falkingham, J. and Baschieri, A. (2009) Gender and poverty: how misleading is the unitary model of household resources? An illustration from Tajikistan, *Global Social Policy*, 9: 43–62.

Farnsworth, K. and Irving, Z. (2015) *Social policy in times of austerity: Global economic crisis and the new politics of welfare*, Bristol: Policy Press.

Fine, B. (2014) The continuing enigmas of social policy, Working Paper 2014-10, Geneva: United Nations Research Institute for Social Development (UNRISD).

Fraser, N. (2013) *The fortunes of feminism: From women's liberation to identity politics to anti-capitalism*, London: Verso.

Gregory, C. (2009) Whatever happened to householding?, in C. Hann and K. Hart (eds) *Market and society: The great transformation today*, Cambridge: Cambridge University Press, pp 133–59.

Hagestad, A. and Gunhild, O. (2006) Transfers between grandparents and grandchildren: the importance of taking a three-generation perspective, *Zeitschrift für Familienforschung*, 3: 315–32.

Hann, C. and Hart, K. (eds) (2009) *Market and society: The great transformation today*, Cambridge: Cambridge University Press.

Heath, S. and Calvert, E. (2013) Gifts, loans and intergenerational support for young adults, *Sociology*, 47: 1120–135.

Hermann, C. (2014) Crisis, structural reform and the dismantling of the European social model(s), *Economic and Industrial Democracy*, 38(1): 51–68.

Hiilamo, H. (2018) *Household debt and economic crises: Causes, consequences and remedies*, Cheltenham: Edward Elgar.

Izuhara, M. (2016) Reconsidering the housing asset-based welfare approach: reflection from East Asian experiences, *Social Policy and Society*, 15: 177–88.

Keck, W. and Saraceno, C. (2010) Caring for a parent while working for pay in the German welfare regime, *International Journal of Ageing and Later Life*, 5: 107–28.

Kennett, P. (2017) (Dis)Integration, disjuncture and the multidimensional crisis of the European social project, in P. Kennett and N. Lendvai-Bainton (eds) *Handbook of European social policy*, Cheltenham: Edward Elgar, pp 416–32.

Kohli, M., Hank, K. and Künemund, H. (2009) The social connectedness of older Europeans: patterns, dynamics and contexts, *Journal of European Social Policy*, 19: 327–40.

Laamanen, M., Wahlen, S. and Lorek, S. (2018) A moral householding perspective on the sharing economy, *Journal of Cleaner Production*, 202: 1220–7.

Land, H. and Rose, H. (1985) Compulsory altruism for some or an altruistic society for all?, in P. Bean, J. Ferris and D. Whynes (eds) *In defence of welfare*, London: Tavistock.

LeBaron, G. (2010) The political economy of the household: neoliberal restructuring, enclosures, and daily life, *Review of International Political Economy*, 17: 889–912.

Leitner, S. (2003) Varieties of familialism: the caring function of the family in comparative perspective, *European Societies*, 5: 353–75.

Leitner, S. and Lessenich, S. (2007) (In)Dependence as a dependent variable: conceptualizing and measuring de-familization, in J. Clasen and N. Siegel (eds) *Investigating welfare state change*, Cheltenham: Edward Elgar, pp 244–60.

Lewis, J. (1992) Gender and the development of welfare regimes, *Journal of European Social Policy*, 2(3): 159–73.

Lohmann, H. and Zagel, H. (2016) Family policy in comparative perspective: the concepts and measurement of familization and defamilization, *Journal of European Social Policy*, 26(1): 48–65.

Maucourant, J. and Plociniczak, S. (2013) The institution, the economy and the market: Karl Polanyi's institutional thought for economists, *Review of Political Economy*, 25: 512–31.

McLaughlin, E. and Glendinning, C. (1994) Paying for care in Europe: is there a feminist approach?, in L. Hantrais and C. Glendinning (eds) *Family policy and the welfare of women*, Cross-National Research Papers, Third Series, Loughborough: European Research Centre, pp 52–69.

Melhuus, M. (2018) Recapturing the household: reflections on labour, productive relations, and economic value, *The Journal of the Royal Anthropological Institute*, 24(S1): 75–88.

Milanovic, B. (2016) *Global inequality: A new approach for the age of globalization*, Cambridge, MA: Harvard University Press.

Millar, J. (2016) Family and state obligation: the contribution to family policy studies, in G.B. Eydal and T. Rostgaard (eds) *Handbook of child and family policy*, Cheltenham: Edward Elgar, pp 36–48.

Moreno, L. (2006) The model of social protection in Southern Europe: enduring characteristics?, *Revue francaise des affaires sociales*, 5: 73–95.

Nelson, J.A. (2016) Husbandry: a (feminist) reclamation of masculine responsibility for care, *Cambridge Journal of Economics*, 40: 1–15.

O'Connor, J.S. (1998) Gender, class, and citizenship in the comparative analysis of welfare state regimes: theoretical and methodology issues, in J. O'Connor (ed) *Power resources theory and the welfare state: A critical approach*, Toronto: University of Toronto Press, pp 209–28.

Orloff, A.S. (1993) Gender and the social rights of citizenship: the comparative analysis of gender relations and welfare states, *American Sociological Review*, 58(3): 303–28.

Papadopoulos, T. and Roumpakis, A. (2013) Familistic welfare capitalism in crisis: social reproduction and anti-social policy in Greece, *Journal of International and Comparative Social Policy*, 29: 204–24.

Papadopoulos, T. and Roumpakis, A. (2015) Democracy, austerity and crisis: Southern Europe and the decline of the European social model, in S. Romano and G. Punziano (eds) *The European social model adrift*, Aldershot: Ashgate, pp 189–211.

Papadopoulos, T. and Roumpakis, A. (2017a) The erosion of Southern Europe's middle classes: debt, insecurity and the political economy of austerity, *Sociologia e politiche sociali*, 20: 67–89.

Papadopoulos, T. and Roumpakis, A. (2017b) Family as a socio-economic actor in the political economies of East and South-East Asian welfare capitalisms, *Social Policy & Administration*, 51: 857–75.

Papadopoulos, T. and Roumpakis, A. (2018) Rattling Europe's ordoliberal 'iron cage': the contestation of austerity in Southern Europe, *Critical Social Policy*, 38: 505–26.

Pascall, G. and Lewis, J. (2004) Emerging gender regimes and policies for gender equality in a wider Europe, *Journal of Social Policy*, 33: 373–94.

Pichler, F. and Wallace, C. (2007) Patterns of formal and informal social capital in Europe, *European Sociological Review*, 23: 423–35.

Pickard, L., King, D., Brimblecombe, N. and Knapp, M. (2015) The effectiveness of paid services in supporting unpaid carers' employment in England, *Journal of Social Policy*, 44(3): 567–90.

Polanyi, K. (1957a) The economy as instituted process, in K. Polanyi, C.M. Arensberg and H.W. Pearson (eds) *Trade and markets in the early empires: Economies in history and theory*, Glencoe, IL: Free Press.

Polanyi, K. (1957b) Aristotle discovers the economy, in K. Polanyi, C.M. Arensberg and H.W. Pearson (eds) *Trade and markets in the early empires: Economies in history and theory*, Glencoe, IL: Free Press, pp 64–94.

Polanyi, K. (1960) On the comparative treatment of economic institutions in antiquity and illustrations from Athens, Mycanae, and Alalakh, in C.H. Kraeling and R.M. Adams (eds) *City invincible*, Chicago, IL: University of Chicago Press, pp 329–50.

Polanyi, K. (1966) *Dahomey and the slave trade: An analysis of an archaic economy*, Seattle, WA, and London: University of Washington Press.

Polanyi, K. (1977) *The livelihood of man*, New York, NY, San Francisco, CA, and London: Academic Press.

Polanyi, K. (2001 [1957]) *The great transformation: The political and economical origins of our time*, Boston, MA: Beacon Press.

Roberts, A. (2014) New constitutionalism, disciplinary neoliberalism and the locking-in of indebtedness in America, in S.A. Gill and A.C. Cutler (eds) *New Constitutionalism and world order*, Cambridge: Cambridge University Press, pp 233–46.

Sainsbury, D. (1999) Gender and social democratic welfare states, in D. Sinsbury (ed) *Gender and welfare state regimes*, Oxford: Oxford University Press, pp 75–115.

Saraceno, C. (2004) The Italian family from the 1960s to the present, *Modern Italy*, 9: 47–57.

Saraceno, C. (2016) Varieties of familialism: comparing four Southern European and East Asian welfare regimes, *Journal of European Social Policy*, 26(4): 314–26.

Saxonberg, S. (2013) From defamilialization to degenderization: toward a new welfare typology 1, *Social Policy & Administration*, 47: 26–49.

Simonazzi, A. and Villa, P. (2010) La grande illusion: how Italy's 'American dream' turns sour, in D. Anxo, G. Bosch and J. Rubery (eds) *The welfare state and life transitions*, Cheltenham: Edward Elgar, pp 231–56.

Smith, A. and Rochovská, A. (2007) Domesticating neo-liberalism: everyday lives and the geographies of post-socialist transformations, *Geoforum*, 38: 1163–78.

Stanfield, J.R. (1986) *The economic thought of Karl Polanyi: Lives and livelihood*, New York: St. Martin's Press.

Streeck, W. (2013) *Buying time: The delayed crisis of democratic capitalism*, London and New York, NY: Verso.

Sung, S. and Pascall, G. (2014) *Gender and welfare states in East Asia: Confucianism or gender equality?*, Basingstoke: Palgrave Macmillan UK.

Swedberg, R. (2001) Max Weber's central text in economic sociology, in M. Granovetter and R. Swedberg (eds) *The sociology of economy life*, Boulder, CO: Westview, pp 62–77.

Tronto, J.C. (2013) *Caring democracy: Markets, equality and justice*, New York, NY, and London: New York University Press.

Vaughan-Whitehead, D., Vazquez-Alvarez, R. and Maitre, N. (2016) Is the world of work behind middle-class erosion?, in D. Vaughan-Whitehead (ed) *Europe's disappearing middle class? Evidence from the world of work*, Cheltenham: Edward Elgar, pp 1–48.

Walby, S. (2015) *Crisis*, Cambridge: Polity Press.

Waller, W. and Jennings, A. (1991) A feminist institutionalist reconsideration of Karl Polanyi, *Journal of Economic Issues*, 25(2): 485–97.

Weber, M. (1978 [1921/22]) *Economy and society: An outline of interpretive sociology*, Berkeley, CA: University of California Press.

Wheelock, J. and Baines, S. (1998) Dependency or self-reliance? The contradictory case of work in UK small business families, *Journal of Family and Economic Issues*, 19: 53–73.

Wheelock, J., Oughton, E. and Baines, S. (2003) Getting by with a little help from your family: toward a policy-relevant model of the household, *Feminist Economics*, 9: 19–45.

Woolley, F. (1996) Getting the better of Becker, *Feminist Economics*, 2: 114–20.

Wrenn, M.V. and Waller, W. (2018) The pathology of care, *Œconomia*, 8(2): 157–85.

Yu, S., Chau, C.M. and Lee, K.M. (2015) Using defamilisation typologies to study the Confucian welfare regime, *Journal of International and Comparative Social Policy*, 31: 74–93.

Zhong, X. and Li, B. (2017) New intergenerational contracts in the making? The experience of urban China, *Journal of Asian Public Policy*, 10: 167–82.

Index

Note: page numbers in *italic* type refer to figures; those in **bold** type refer to tables.

P